WORKING MOTHERS
AND THE WELFARE STATE

KIMBERLY J. MORGAN

Working Mothers and the Welfare State

Religion and the Politics of Work-Family
Policies in Western Europe and the
United States

STANFORD UNIVERSITY PRESS

STANFORD, CALIFORNIA 2006

©Stanford University Press
Stanford, California

Printed in the United States of America on acid-free, archival-
quality paper

Library of Congress Cataloging-in-Publication Data

Morgan, Kimberly J., date-
    Working mothers and the welfare state : religion and the politics
of work-family policies in Western Europe and the United States /
Kimberly J. Morgan.
      p. cm.
    Includes bibliographical references and index.
    ISBN 0-8047-5413-6 (cloth : alk. paper)—ISBN 0-8047-5414-4
(pbk. : alk. paper)
      1. Working mothers—Government policy—Cross-cultural
studies.   2. Working mothers—Government policy—History.
3. Mothers—Employment—History.   4. Work and family—
History.   5. Welfare state—Cross-cultural studies.   I. Title.
HQ759.48.M663 2006
362.85—dc22   2006010490

Typeset by G & S Book Services in 10/14 Janson Roman

Contents

Acknowledgments

My first debt is to Sonya Michel, without whom I never would have stumbled onto this topic. Working as her research assistant early in my graduate school career, I became fascinated with child care and other policies for working parents. It was my advisor, Nancy Bermeo, who made me realize that this topic could and should be the subject of my dissertation. I am thankful that she steered me away from the other dreary topics I was considering and encouraged me to follow my own interests rather than the current fads in political science. Sonya and Nancy have been my intellectual mentors and friends ever since.

The essential ingredient of money came from numerous sources: a Chateaubriand scholarship from the French government in 1997–98; the École Normale Supérieure, which provided me a place to live in Paris; research support from various institutions at Princeton University (the Council on Regional Studies, the Center for Domestic and Comparative Policy Studies, and the Woodrow Wilson Society of Fellows); George Washington University's Institute for European, Russian, and Eurasian Studies, which paid for a very able research assistant, Christian Ruehling; and GWU's University Facilitating Fund, which financed some of my research abroad. In 2000–2001, I was supported by a post-doctoral grant at New York University's Institute for French Studies and received valuable reactions to my work from scholars and visiting fellows there, including Herrick Chapman, Erik Fassin, Emmanuelle Saada, and Martin Schain. The Robert Wood Johnson Foundation's Scholars in Health Policy Research program then enabled me to spend two fruitful years at Yale University. Although I mostly worked on health policy during this period, I was able to present fledgling drafts of this manuscript to various groups on campus, including seminars organized by the Children's Research Group and the Council on European Studies, and to discuss my work with Sally Cohen, Jacob Hacker, Frances Rosenbluth, and Edward Zigler.

One of the joys of studying this topic is that people who work in this area are often thrilled to find others who care about it. I cannot thank all of my interviewees personally, but I am particularly indebted to a number of scholars and government officials who were willing to spend hours explaining, and re-explaining, how things work in their country. These include Christina Bergqvist and Irene Wennemo in Sweden; Jacqueline Ancelin, Jeanne Fagnani, Jérôme Minonzio, and Liliane Périer in France; and in the Netherlands, Jet Bussemaker, Serv Vinders, and three people from the Sociaal and Cultureel Planbureau: Wil Portegijs, Mariëlle Cloïn, and Heleen van Luijn. In the United States, I had very long and insightful discussions with Martin La Vor, Martha Phillips, and Richard Warden about past battles over child care policy. Lena, Peter, and Karin Wallensteen were generous and full of great ideas for my research on Sweden, as were Karen Anderson, Barbara Hobson, and Rianne Mahon. Similarly, Johan Hansen, Miranda Jansen, and Vries Kool gave me some good leads for my Dutch research, as did Jane Jenson for my research in France. I also am very grateful to Kees van Kersbergen and the Department of Political Science at the Vrije Universiteit Amsterdam for allowing me some scarce office space.

I wish also to thank those who have generously opened their homes to me each time I invade their country. Many thanks to Malika Al Mansouri and Sebastien Weijer, Marieke Voeten, and Gerrie and Rinus Voeten in the Netherlands, and to my very dear friend, Anne-Marie Menut, in Paris.

I am deeply indebted to the many friends and colleagues who read parts of the manuscript and gave critical comments along the way. Sheri Berman, Jennifer Hochschild, and Ezra Suleiman gave helpful suggestions on various versions of the dissertation while I was at Princeton. At GWU, I have benefited from the warm collegiality of the Department of Political Science, including the willingness of a number of colleagues to read my work. Henry Farrell, Steven Kelts, Gina Lambright, Elliot Posner, Chad Rector, and Melissa Schwartzberg all read parts of the manuscript and offered reactions at a critical stage of writing. On chapters and related conference papers, I received helpful comments and advice from Ann Orloff, Jacob Hacker, Jane

Lewis, Miranda Jansen, Rianne Mahon, Andrei Markovits, Sonya Michel, Rachel Roth, Herman Schwartz, Laurel Weldon, and Charmaine Yoest. I also gained tremendously from a workshop on religion and the welfare state at the Max Planck Institute in Cologne, Germany, organized by Philip Manow and Kees van Kersbergen. The reactions of Thomas Ertman and the other workshop participants to my paper were of great help in advancing my thinking on this topic.

All this work could have been for naught without a publisher. I am very grateful for the efficiency and responsiveness of Amanda Moran and Stanford University Press and for their enthusiasm for this project. Both Sonya Michel and Jonah Levy gave me wonderfully constructive comments that helped me to revise the manuscript for publication. Evan Lieberman and Kathrina Zippel then valiantly read the entire manuscript at a late stage. Their comments were invaluable in highlighting omissions and areas of fuzzy writing and thinking. Kathrina has read and commented on many pieces of the manuscript at various stages of its existence over the past few years, and I am in her debt for the many hours she has spent thoughtfully pondering my work.

My friends and family have been faithful supporters throughout the long and difficult process of writing a book. I cannot express enough my appreciation for my brilliant and inspiring friends—Monica Bhattacharyya, Marion Fourcade-Gourinchas, Cynthia Hooper, Katia Papagianni, Dietlind Stolle, and Kathrina Zippel. My parents, Marilyn and Patrick, as well as my brother and sister, Chris and Kelly, also have lent sympathetic ears to my endless tales of woe. I am lucky they are still willing to pick up the phone.

My greatest thanks go to my husband, Erik, who has read draft after draft, patiently offering advice and ideas and supporting me through some of the more discouraging stages of this project. His love and companionship have made it all worth it. I dedicate this book to him.

Abbreviations

ABC	Act for Better Child Care
AFDC	Aid to Families with Dependent Children
AFEAMA	*Aide à la famille pour l'emploi d'une assistante maternelle agréée*
AGED	*Allocation de garde d'enfant à domicile*
APE	*Allocation parentale d'éducation*
CCDBG	Child Care Development Block Grant
CDA	Christen-Democratisch Appèl
CDA	Child Development Act (United States)
CNAF	Caisse Nationale d'Allocations Familiales
D66	Democraten 66
DCTC	Dependent Care Tax Credit
FIDCR	Federal Interagency Day Care Requirements
FMLA	Family and Medical Leave Act
KD	Kristdemokraterna
KrF	Kristelig Folkeparti
MRP	Mouvement républicain populaire
OECD	Organization for Economic Cooperation and Development
PMI	Protection maternelle et infantile
PvdA	Partij van de Arbeid

SAP   Sveriges socialdemokratiska arbetareparti
UNAF   Union Nationale des Associations Familiales
VVD   Volkspartij voor Vrijheid en Democratie

WORKING MOTHERS
AND THE WELFARE STATE

CHAPTER ONE

The Politics of Mothers' Employment

Across the Western world, societies have been transformed by the rise of mothers' employment. Most countries have experienced a substantial change in mothers' attachment to the world of paid work over the past three to four decades, raising questions about how to assure the care of young children. Policy makers in nearly all Western countries have at some point wrestled with this issue, yet their responses have been quite divergent. Comparing the policy decisions made across these countries, we can see differences in the extent to which societies accept both the idea of mothers working while their children are young and the idea that the state should have a role in shaping gender roles and children's lives.

In Sweden, for example, government policy since the 1970s has fueled the transformation of Swedish society into one of "universal breadwinners" in which all parents participate in paid work. Universal, state-run day care programs, as well as policies to encourage greater male involvement in child rearing, embody an activist state tradition in shaping family arrangements, the care of children, and the equality of women. We can see a similarly activist state in France, reflected in its array of universal subsidies and services for families. Although French governments have not attempted a radical overhaul of gender relations, their approach toward working mothers often has been pragmatic and supportive. In the Netherlands, by contrast, public policy long endorsed and upheld the male-breadwinner model of social relations, encouraging mothers to be home while their children were young. This has been matched by leeriness toward state involvement in the lives of young children and an effort to leave responsibility for the care and education of children to the voluntary sector. The Dutch case resonates with the U.S. one, where there is virtually no tradition of family policy and a well-established pattern of leaving questions of family morality to individuals. Because of Americans' sharply divided views on mothers' employment, American policy has sought to shift this issue from the political to the market sphere, leaving parents to figure out their own child care arrangements with minimal direct support from the state.

This book examines and explains patterns of work-family policies in Sweden, France, the Netherlands, and the United States, giving particular attention to child care policy but also looking at parental leave and flexible work-time arrangements. The analysis focuses on how religion has influenced this dimension of the welfare state. Although much research emphasizes the role of Left parties and powerful unions in driving the welfare state's expansion, policies on child care and mothers' employment are not only about material redistribution and labor markets; they also reflect ideologies about gender relations and the family. More specifically, extending the programs of the welfare state to promote mothers' employment requires accepting that mothers should work while their children are young and that the state should influence family care arrangements. As the succeeding chapters will show, organized religion has played a critical role in shaping political ideologies about gender roles and the appropriate relationship between the state and the family.

Uncovering the roots of these ideologies and the ways in which they have influenced public policy requires a historical perspective. Contemporary welfare states represent over a century of policy decisions, with the politics and policies of one period often influencing decisions later on. Many scholars argue that the programs enacted during the welfare state's "golden

age"—the period of rapid economic growth and public sector expansion between 1945 and 1975—still affect the politics of social policy today, and this
book will offer support for these arguments. These golden-age policies also
did not emerge sui generis but were influenced by the political and policy
legacies of an earlier period. Therefore, I begin my study in the latter part of
the nineteenth century, exploring early public policies that would have great
relevance for mothers' employment. I also investigate the roots of political
forces and ideologies that would predominate in the decades after the
Second World War and shape the politics of mothers' employment.

The late nineteenth century was a critical period of political development. Mass political systems were taking shape, and the role of the state in
social life was steadily expanding. Religion was a significant source of political and social conflict in this period, particularly around the issue of who
should oversee the education of children and protect the well-being of families. These conflicts sparked a political mobilization in some countries over
the relative power of state, church, and competing religious groups. Patterns
of church-state relations and religious conflict had an enduring impact on
early family and educational policies, as well as the way religion would be incorporated into politics. In both France and Sweden, religious authorities
were subordinated to secular state ones, facilitating an active state role in
family policy and furthering the secularization of politics and social life. Secularization went furthest in Sweden, but religious forces would also play a
constrained role in French politics through much of the twentieth century.
In the Netherlands and the United States, by contrast, social conservatives
gained more influence over politics than in France and Sweden—although
by different means—and tried to shield the family from state influence while
also espousing traditional gender roles.

The resulting structure of political competition shaped how governments
responded to the rise of female workforce participation in the 1960s and
1970s. In France and Sweden, acceptance of an activist state in family affairs and the weak role of organized religion in politics created approval for
both wage-earning mothers and state policies to support them. Although
agreement on this was greater in Sweden and the policy shifts more radical,
pragmatic acceptance of this social change in France led to policies that
supported wage-earning mothers. In the Netherlands and the United States
there was stronger opposition to both government family policy and shifting

gender roles, reflecting in part the greater influence of organized religion on both politics and society. The result in the Netherlands was a continuation of the male-breadwinner model of public policy, while American policy makers encouraged private-sector solutions to work-family problems rather than try to reach agreement on whether or not public policy should encourage mothers' employment.

Since the 1970s, secularization and the growth of women's employment have further eroded the foundations of the traditional male-breadwinner model in all countries, creating pressure for policy reform. There has been both stability and change in this policy area, however. The stability reflects the constraining effects of economic slowdown in the post-Fordist era and the institutionalization of different approaches to the work-family issue. Particular policy configurations have shaped beliefs about mothers' employment that endure, creating a powerful force for the status quo—whether for universal supports to working mothers in Sweden, the more mixed model in France, or private solutions in the Netherlands or the United States. At the same time, however, continuing social changes have created new tensions and problems, opening up spaces for political competition around the needs of working mothers. As we shall see in the case of the Netherlands, the growth of women's employment and the crisis of Christian Democracy in the 1990s created an opening for new child care, parental leave, and work time policies designed to encourage women's employment. Even so, the continued emphasis in Dutch policy on facilitating maternal care and the reluctance to involve the state too much in the provision of child care show the enduring legacies of one hundred years of debates about gender roles and the boundaries between the state and the family.

The Social and Political Significance of Work-Family Policies

Child care, parental leave, and other work-family policies affect the lives of nearly everyone by shaping the experiences of childhood, parenthood, and employment. These policies influence how societies organize the care and education of young children, because they affect parental caring time and the availability of day care and early education programs. Access to child care also has consequences for women's employment. Some studies show that the availability and affordability of day care affects how likely mothers are to re-main in paid work, and the same is true for parental leaves that are neither too long nor too short and are reasonably well paid.[1] This is not to imply that work-family policies are or should be solely considered "women's issues," and there are efforts in a growing number of countries to increase the role of men in caring for children. Nonetheless, though men have increased their caring role in recent years, having children has virtually no impact on either men's participation in the labor force or their wages. If anything, the relationship is the inverse: having children correlates with higher wages for men.[2]

Many scholars argue that work-family policies have major ramifications for women's equality, autonomy, and social citizenship. The current gender-based division of labor in the home, in which women in two-income families are responsible for more than 70 percent of the "second shift" of child care and housework, affects women's political participation, activity in the labor force, and long-term earning potential.[3] Recent analysis has linked the wage gap in the United States almost entirely to whether female employees have children; controlling for age, education, and experience, childless women earn 90 percent of what their male equivalents do, whereas mothers earn 73 percent. This gap is smaller in France and Sweden owing both to wage compression policies and to more continuous patterns of women's employment.[4] Moreover, child care responsibilities reduce mothers' entitlement to such social benefits as pensions, health care, and unemployment insurance because these are often related to participation in the labor market. Mothers' dependence on husbands for these rights increases their vulnerability and susceptibility to poverty if they become widowed or divorced.[5] The feminization of poverty in some countries reflects the ineffectiveness of their welfare states—constructed around the assumption that most mothers would be full-time caregivers supported by working husbands—in socializing the costs of child rearing in an era of high divorce rates and growing numbers of single mothers.[6]

How states respond to the needs of families for child care may also affect the demographic future of these nations. According to some scholars, population stagnation in much of continental Europe reflects a failure to develop social services that would spread the burden of care across the larger society and support women in paid employment.[7] Ironically, in the more conservative states that have sought to reinforce traditional caring arrangements—Germany, Italy, Japan, Spain—women face a stark choice between paid work and family and therefore delay childbirth and/or have fewer children. Fertility rates are falling below replacement rates, and these countries now face a veritable demographic crisis. In France and the Nordic countries, which have done more to support mothers in the workforce, fertility rates are considerably higher, although high fertility rates in the United States complicate this story.[8]

Work-family policies now figure prominently on the political agenda of many Western countries. In Sweden, France, and the United States, political debates about these policies began in the late 1960s and early 1970s, and the issue has been on and off the political stage ever since. In recent years, Swedish efforts have focused on the responsibilities of fathers for the care of young children, while American policy targets the needs of poor single mothers. The Dutch discussion began later but intensified in the 1990s as governments began adopting measures to increase women's employment.

In addition to these domestic debates, there is growing pressure from international organizations to develop early education programs and policies to help women "reconcile" work and family. The European Union (EU) and the Organization for Economic Cooperation and Development (OECD) have been important agenda setters on these issues, calling upon their member states to increase the female labor supply in the name of both gender equality and economic efficiency.[9] The EU has set a voluntary benchmark for women's employment and provision of child care that the member states are supposed to meet by 2010. In addition, there is an increasing push at both the domestic and international level to promote early childhood education programs. As Jane Jenson and Denis Saint-Martin have shown, these initiatives have been promoted under the mantra of "social investment"—the need to enhance the productive capacities of the population.[10]

For comparative studies of the welfare state, employment policies toward mothers offer one way for scholars to evaluate the gendered impacts of welfare regimes. In recent years, much social policy research in history and the social sciences has sought to reinterpret the welfare state along gendered lines.[11] Many of these scholars have challenged existing gender-blind indicators of welfare regimes while developing new measures that capture the distinctive ways in which social programs affect women. Employment policies toward mothers are important because participation in the labor force is often crucial for social citizenship rights.[12] In even the most universalistic welfare states, entitlement to generous social programs requires time in paid work—and the more time, the better. As Ann Shola Orloff has aptly phrased it, before one can be decommodified so as to reduce dependence on markets, one must first be commodified so as to gain entitlement to social benefits.[13] Participation in the labor market can also be a means of reducing dependence on men. Thus, to the extent that welfare regimes take into consideration the distinctive needs of women workers for leave time and care services, they are more likely to receive the appellation "women friendly" from feminist scholars.[14]

At the same time, many feminists have argued that scholars and policy makers, in their drive to support women's employment, may simply be contributing to the devaluation of women's care work in the home.[15] From the beginning, feminist activism and theory sought to value women's activities by tearing down the boundary between the privileged public sphere and the neglected private sphere. However, motherhood and care work have generated thorny questions about women's interests. Do they lie in policies and social arrangements that glorify care work and support these activities, or in efforts to commodify or socialize caring responsibilities so that women can work for pay? In many countries, debates about mothers' employment have mobilized women on both sides of the divide, with some arguing for "wages for housework" that will value care and others lobbying for measures that promote women's employment.[16] This book does not take sides in this normative debate. Rather than adopt one definition of women's interests, this study looks empirically at how different actors and polities have defined these interests and how these visions have been enacted in the policies and programs of the welfare state.

The Diversity of Mothers' Employment Policies: Some Useful Definitions

A potentially wide range of policies affects mothers' employment patterns, ranging from anti-discrimination measures to state-provided child care to the incentives created by different tax and benefit systems. This study focuses mainly on child care, parental leave, and work time arrangements.[17] It also looks closely at some of the most significant programs that affect parents' decisions about child care and work. Comparing these policies is a complex enterprise, given differences in their actual meanings in different countries. Simply looking at the length of parental leave time or the percentage of children in public programs does not say enough about the real-world effects of these systems. For that reason, some definitions and interpretations are needed.

In the area of child care, it is important to distinguish between preschool and day care programs. Preschools are often part of the education system, and because their main objective is education, their schedules do not necessarily suit working parents. Many programs are part-time, but this varies cross-nationally. In France and Belgium, such programs are open for a full school day (often 8:30 A.M.–4:30 P.M. in France, 8:30 A.M.–3:30 P.M. in Belgium, with one day or afternoon free per week), and in some areas there are after-school programs that help round out a full working day. In Germany (particularly in the western *Länder*) and Austria, however, preschools usually close by lunchtime, and after-school care is minimal. As preschools usually follow the school schedule, there is also a lengthy break in the summer when there are no classes. Day care programs, on the other hand, exist almost entirely for the purpose of taking care of children while parents are working, so they usually fall within the jurisdiction of social services departments and are open for a full working day. The line between these day care services and preschool programs is often blurred and varies by country. The Nordic states lack this differentiation between care and education: programs for children from infancy to age six or seven (the mandatory school age) were originally developed under the auspices of social services agencies. Many of these programs had an important pedagogic component but also addressed the needs of working parents. The book will refer to all these services as day care, although in Sweden they are now called preschools (*förskola*) and the Swedish Ministry of Education now oversees all programs for children below the mandatory school age.

In all countries, the term day care generally includes both formal day care centers and family day care, where several children are cared for in a private home. The latter is usually a private arrangement between families and individual caregivers that is minimally subsidized (at most, through the tax

code) and often weakly regulated. However, a number of countries now reg-
ulate and fund family day care and conceptualize these services as part of
their day care system. In France, these *assistantes maternelles* are part of networks of family day care subsidized by public resources, and they are guaranteed paid vacations, sickness and maternity leave, and a certain wage level.
In Sweden, family day care is even more strongly subsidized and is overseen
by public authorities. France and Belgium, as well as Sweden and the other
Nordic states, include these programs in their statistical accounting of public child care availability, a convention this study maintains.[18]

Parental leave systems are also complex. Many countries have maternity
leave programs that are specifically for women, relatively short, and paid at a
high rate, such as 90 or 100 percent of a woman's previous salary. Parental
leave, if it exists, generally follows the period of maternity leave and is open to
both parents.[19] Usually these leaves are longer than maternity leave, but they
are not necessarily paid. In some European countries, parental leave is part of
the social insurance system and is treated as such. Work entitles parents to a
certain level of benefits, and this parental insurance is then paid out during the
time that one is at home caring for a child. Yet another form of leave, care
leave, can be distinguished from parental leave in that it usually is longer but
paid at a low rate, if at all.[20] Care leaves allow a parent to look after a child at
home for an extended period and are either unpaid or paid at a low flat rate for
two or three years. In both parental and care leave, it is important to distinguish the right to leave from work, on one hand, from the right to a benefit,
on the other, because these are often distinct entitlements.

Interpreting the impact of leave systems is still more complicated. From
the standpoint of maximizing parental caring time, longer and more generously paid leaves are preferable. From the perspective of promoting women's
employment, however, leave systems that are either "too short" or "too long"
may be detrimental.[21] Very short and poorly paid maternity leaves, for example, may encourage women to leave the labor market when they have a
child rather than put their infants in day care—something many parents do
not want to do. However, women who take very long leaves might find that
their jobs have vanished when they return, or that their employment status has
been downgraded. In all countries, women take the majority of parental and
care leave days. In France, 98 percent of people who take the extended three-
year care leave are women.

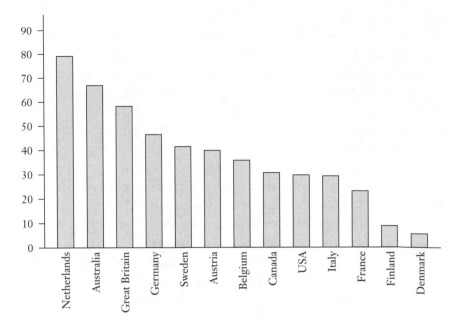

Figure 1.1   Percentage of employed mothers in part-time work (youngest child under age 6), 2002

SOURCE: OECD, *Society at a Glance: OECD Social Indicators* (Paris: 2005), 41.

These data are for women aged 15 to 64. Part-time work is defined as employment for fewer than 30 hours per week except in Australia, Sweden, and the United States, where it is defined as employment fewer than 35 hours per week.

A third set of policies that affect women's employment are measures that enable part-time work. Part-time work among women is widespread, particularly among mothers of young children, although it is more prevalent in some countries than in others (figure 1.1). In the United States, fewer than one-third of employed mothers with children under six work part-time, but more than 40 percent of Swedish mothers and 79 percent of Dutch ones do so. However, it is essential to clarify the meaning of part-time in different countries. In Sweden, parents of children under eight are entitled to work six hours a day, and many of them do, which results in their being classified as part-time workers. This is quite different from the situation in the Netherlands, where many women who work part-time are working fewer than twenty hours a week. Currently, 35 percent of employed Dutch

TABLE 1.1
Employment rates of women by age of youngest child, 2002

	Under 3	Aged 3–5
Austria	80.1	70.3
Australia	45.0	45.0
Belgium	70.4	67.4
Canada	58.7	68.1
Denmark	71.4	77.5
Finland	32.2	74.7
France	66.2	63.2
Germany	56.0	58.1
Great Britain	57.2	56.9
Italy	54.4	51.7
Netherlands	74.2	68.2
Sweden	72.9	82.5
USA	56.6	60.0

SOURCE: OECD, *Society at a Glance: OECD Social Indicators* (Paris, 2005).
These data are for women aged 15 to 64.

women work fewer than twenty hours a week, whereas only 6 percent of Swedish and 9 percent of French women are in equivalent forms of employment.[22] Another important difference is the degree to which part-time work includes the rights and benefits associated with full-time employment. Dutch law requires that employers treat part-time workers the same as full-time workers in terms of pay and benefits. In the United States, by contrast, part-time workers often lack entitlements to health insurance or a pension. One reason many employers hire workers for fewer than forty hours is that it enables them to classify workers as part-time and therefore to deny them access to company-provided benefits for full-time employees.

Cross-national comparisons of work-family policies are a delicate enterprise; seemingly comparable statistics often conceal considerable differences in what these policies actually look like in practice. The same is true of data on mothers' employment rates. The figures provided in table 1.1 on the employment of mothers with young children must be qualified. First, the table does not distinguish between part-time and full-time work. Although Dutch mothers at first glance appear to be in the labor force in higher proportions than French mothers, only 23 percent of French mothers with children under six work part-time, compared to 79 percent of Dutch mothers. In addition, the figures overstate the proportion of women who are actually *at work*.

In Sweden or Austria women on lengthy parental leave are counted as employed, whereas in France, Germany, and Finland women on care leaves are not, even though they hold on to their jobs while on leave. Although at first glance it appears that Austrian mothers work in very high numbers, more than half are on parental leave, and only a small proportion work full-time.[23]

Typologies of Welfare Regimes

One starting point for comparing how Western welfare regimes treat the issue of mothers' employment is Esping-Andersen's influential typology of welfare state regimes, which divides nations into three worlds of welfare capitalism.[24] *Liberal* regimes (Australia, Canada, United Kingdom, United States) privilege private social benefits and services while offering more residual public protections. Direct spending on social welfare is lower than elsewhere, but private provision of child care is often encouraged by such indirect means as tax breaks or regulatory measures.[25] The *Social Democratic* welfare states of the Nordic countries provide universal, equal benefits and services through direct public spending. Finally, the *conservative/corporatist* (or Christian Democratic) welfare states of continental Europe (Austria, Belgium, France, Germany, Italy, the Netherlands) are generous yet status-reproducing. Benefits often are linked to professional status, making labor market participation a particularly important source of entitlement. Following the principle of subsidiarity, in which social burdens are left to the lowest levels of society, these states also assume that lower levels of society—such as families or the voluntary sector—should provide for human welfare needs.[26] The Social Democratic regimes promote employment for all through active policy measures, and the liberal regimes do so through the stinginess of their social protections. The conservative welfare states have been passive, encouraging the dependence of unemployed men on social benefits and the dependence of women on men.

This typology is useful for identifying patterns in work-family policies but does not map fully onto cross-national differences in these policies. The Nordic regimes are often held up as models of gender egalitarian social policy, and they show clear similarities in their approach to mothers' employment. All have high rates of participation by women in the labor force (albeit often in part-time work), the result of explicit government policy to promote women's employment. In these work-oriented regimes, all adults are assumed to be working, and changes in tax and benefits systems since the 1970s have removed many of the disincentives to married women's employment.[27] Such measures have been matched by the development of public child care services and generous parental leaves tied to employment, both of which facilitate the balancing of work and family needs and obligations. Consistent with these welfare states' emphasis on public services, much child care is publicly run and provided by well-trained staff.[28]

These features make the Nordic countries a seemingly uniform cluster in their approach to work and family, but there are some significant differences between them.[29] As table 1.2 shows, the availability of public child care varies markedly: it is highest in Denmark and Sweden and substantially lower in Norway or Finland. The latter two countries also have developed extended care leaves of two or three years, creating incentives for parents—especially mothers—to leave paid work for a lengthy period while their children are young, whereas Sweden initially adopted and later repealed a similar measure.[30] In general, Sweden and Denmark have put the most emphasis on promoting mothers' employment, while Norway and Finland enable parents (mostly mothers) to take very long leaves from work.

The continental European countries are even more heterogeneous, and here Esping-Andersen's typology breaks down. Some countries fit the label of the conservative welfare state relatively well: Austria, (West) Germany, Italy, and, until recently, the Netherlands. Policy in these countries has strongly reflected the assumption that mothers are and should be at home caring for their children while they are young. Tax and benefits policies have long discouraged married women's employment, and the weak provision of social care services makes it difficult for mothers to work outside the home while their children are young. A religiously based notion of subsidiarity has justified minimal state provision for social care or early education while delegating these responsibilities to churches, other volunteer organizations, or local governments.[31] School schedules also are unhelpful for working parents, with the primary school day lasting only until 1:00 or 2:00 P.M. and few after-school programs available. In some of these countries, maternity leaves have been generous but short, while extended leave programs are very long and low paid. This nexus of policy measures encourages mothers to

TABLE I.2
Percentages of children in publicly funded services

Welfare state cluster	0 to 2-year-olds	3- to 5-year-olds (or until school age)
Social democratic		
Denmark	52	94
	▶ 9 (under 1)	
	▶ 78 (1–2)	
Finland	19.6	67
	▶ 1 (under 1)	
	▶ 36 (aged 1–2)	
Norway	28.7	82
	▶ 2 (under 1)	
	▶ 40 (aged 1–2)	
Sweden	43	91
	▶ 0 (under 1)	
	▶ 65 (aged 1–2)	
Conservative		
Austria	11	85.2*
Belgium	29.8	100 (hours of operation are 8:30–3:30; closed one afternoon per week)
France	≈ 38	100 (hours of operation are 8:30–4:30; often closed one day or afternoon per week)
	▶ 27% of children aged 4 months to 2-1/2 years are in child care	
	▶ 32% of 2-year-olds in preschool (2-1/2 and older)	
Germany	8.5	89.8 (2002)
	▶ 2.7 Western *Länder*	▶ 88.1* Western *Länder*
	▶ 37 Eastern *Länder*	▶ 105.1 Eastern *Länder*
Italy	7	98
Netherlands	29* (most attend 2 to 2-1/2 days per week)	89* (4- and 5-year-olds)
Liberal		
Australia	20 (receive child care benefit)	35 (in child care, receiving child care benefit)
Canada	5	53*
United Kingdom	10.8	29.4
United States	6	53*

* Indicates most children attend services for part of the day, or part of the week.

SOURCES: Australia: author estimates of the proportion of children receiving Child Care Benefit, from the Department of Family and Community Services, *2004 Census of Child Care Services* (Commonwealth of Australia, 2005); figures do not include preschool attendance; data for Austria, Belgium, Germany, Italy, Netherlands, and the UK are from European Commission, *Indicators for Monitoring the Employment Guidelines, 2004–2005*; France: Nathalie Blanpain, "Accueil des jeunes enfants et coûts des modes de garde en 2002," *Etudes et Résultats* 422 (August 2005), and *Repères et références statistiques sur les enseignements, la formation et la recherche* (Paris: Ministère de l'Education Nationale, 2003), 63; Nordic countries: NOSOSCO, *Social Protection in the Nordic Countries 2002: Scope, Expenditures, Financing* (Copenhagen, NOSOSCO 2004), 60–61; U.S. and Canada: Janet C. Gornick and Marcia K. Meyers, "Supporting a Dual-Earner/Dual-Carer Society," in Jody Heymann and Christopher Beem, *Unfinished Work: Building Equality and Democracy in an Era of Working Families* (New York: New Press, 2005), 398 (data from around 2000).

leave the labor market while their children are young and to reenter in part-time work.

France and Belgium represent a more mixed model of work and family policy, diverging from other continental European countries in a number of ways. One of the most striking differences is the significant role of the state in family and educational services. This contrasts with the notion of sub-sidiarity that is so important in Germany and the Netherlands. As table 1.2 shows, children aged three to six have universal access to state-funded (and often state-provided) preschool education, and a substantial proportion of two-year-olds are in the same programs. Moreover, France and Belgium of-ten have been more pragmatic on the question of working mothers, provid-ing assistance both to mothers in paid work and to those who stay at home.[32] There are extensive subsidies and services for day care and also subsidies for parents at home. Although it cannot be said the parents have a perfectly free choice in the matter, there is a range of options and possibilities.

The liberal English-speaking countries are a fairly coherent cluster in their approach to work and family, but there are some important differences between them. All offer minimal or no maternity or parental leave. The United States now entitles workers in firms with fifty or more employees to an unpaid leave of three months. In the United Kingdom, maternity leave was relatively short until 2002 when, prodded by EU requirements, the Labour government improved the right to both paid and unpaid maternity leaves. Public provision of day care is fairly minimal and consists of either subsidies for very-low-income parents or part-day programs for preschool children. The Blair government has made significant investments in early education programs in recent years, but the main focus has been on developing part-day services.[33] Australian subsidies for day care also have expanded considerably in recent years, but overall spending on child care is low compared to that in the Nordic countries, and much care is in part-time services.[34] In many of these countries, there is much sub-national variation, with some state or provincial governments offering a greater degree of public services.[35]

Despite the lack of public support, private market options sustain a rela-tively high level of women's employment in the liberal welfare states. In the United States, private firms were developing unpaid and, in some cases, paid leave arrangements for parents even before the 1993 Family and Medical Leave Act. Private child care is quite significant in many of these countries and has been expanding in recent years. The United States has a large market of for-profit day care services as well as an extensive sector of nonprofit programs.[36] Recent developments in Australia and the United Kingdom also point to an expanding private sector of services.[37] By contrast, most continental European and Nordic countries lack much of a private market for child care, owing to high minimum wages and rigorous regulation of private services. This makes unsubsidized services difficult to sustain, particularly in the case of for-profit programs that do not benefit from volunteer labor.[38]

Analyzing the Issue of Mothers' Employment Policy

One social science framework that seeks to interpret broad cross-national differences in welfare states is power resources theory. First elaborated in the late 1970s and early 1980s, this approach explains the creation, expansion, and nature of welfare states through the relative power of labor and capital.[39] Most scholars have operationalized labor power through the strength of Social Democratic parties, generating clear hypotheses about the role of political parties in shaping public policy. Strong Social Democratic parties and centralized unions have the political resources to enact their redistributive visions into public policy and thus create large and generous welfare states. Where leftist and labor power is weak and business power is great, welfare provision is stingier, less redistributive, and less likely to disturb the interests of capital. Greater nuance was introduced through the analysis of cross-class coalitions as well as other power-mobilizing groups. Esping-Andersen's typology has its foundations in power resources theory: each world of welfare capitalism reflects the power of liberal, labor, or conservative political forces.

A focus on leftist political power affords some leverage for explaining differences in work-family policies. Left parties have become champions of gender equality policies in many Western countries and generally favor public solutions to social needs. As advocates for the rights of workers, these parties have become defenders of the rights of female workers as well, favoring labor market regulations that enable parents to take parental leave. Many Social Democrats advocate universal, publicly provided services staffed by highly trained, and well-paid, public-sector workers. When these parties

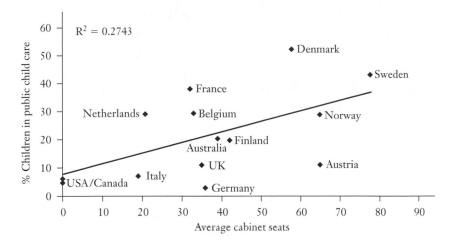

Figure 1.2   Social Democratic political power and public child care for children age 0–2

SOURCES: Figures on social democratic power are from Evelyne Huber, Charles Ragin, John D. Stephens, David Brady, and Jason Beckfield, Comparative Welfare States Data Set, Northwestern University, University of North Carolina, Duke University, and Indiana University, 2004. Child care data are from table 2.

Social Democratic power is a measure of the average percentage of cabinet seats held by Social Democrats, 1960–2000. The child care measure is the percentage of children under the age of 3 in publicly provided or funded programs as of around 2000–2001.

have pushed for public child care, their commitment to universalism and public-sector provision has shaped the form these services have taken. Strong unions also have kept wages and skill levels higher, impeding the development of a low-wage service sector that would enable a private market to develop.[40]

Beyond this, leftist political power cannot, by itself, explain patterns in mothers' employment policy. For example, as figure 1.2 illustrates, there is at best a weak correlation between the extent of Social Democratic political power and the availability of public child care. By 2000, public provision in Denmark was substantially higher than in both Sweden and Norway, even though Social Democratic parties have held cabinet seats less frequently in Denmark. Moreover, France has long superseded Norway and Finland in the development of public child care, despite the relative weakness of leftist political power. Finally, Social Democratic parties in Austria, (West) Germany, and the Netherlands hewed to the male-breadwinner model until at least the 1980s, and Austrian Social Democrats remain lackluster advocates of wage-earning mothers; the high level of Social Democratic power in Austria has not produced policies to encourage mothers' employment.

Left parties have not been inevitable champions of gender equality and mothers' participation in the workforce. Many such parties long espoused variants of "proletarian antifeminism" that viewed women's claims for gender equality as a diversion from the main source of oppression—class.[41] Moreover, throughout the 1950s and much of the 1960s, Left parties throughout the Western world embraced the traditional family model as a social norm and a goal of public policy. Such views resonated with many in their working-class base, for whom it was a sign of social and economic progress that women no longer had to toil in difficult jobs while raising young children. Although Left parties generally have moved toward supporting mothers' employment and gender equality policies, these shifts have occurred in different countries and at different times. We need to find a way to explain differences in the behavior of parties on the same end of the political spectrum across countries and across time.

The first step is to identify and explain the ideologies held by political parties with regard to gender relations and the family. By ideology, I mean a coherent set of beliefs, values, principles, or attitudes about social relations that is expressed in the political arena by parties or other dominant political groupings.[42] Ideology is distinct from culture, which is a more diffuse, general force not linked to specific groups or focused on particular political aims.[43] In addition, cultures usually contain a multitude of often contradictory strands and traditions, whereas ideologies possess a certain amount of internal consistency.[44] A focus on ideology is also distinct from purely ideational explanations, which often try to show the independent causal weight of ideas by distinguishing them from raw self-interest. The concept of ideology can encompass the complex intermingling of ideas and interests that often characterize political action. Not only do the dominant political groups in Western Europe—which are either class-based or religious parties— espouse a particular ideological vision that transcends the particular interests at stake in each debate, but the origins and enduring power behind these parties have been organized labor and organized religion. Ideas and interests go hand in hand when, for example, Social Democratic parties push a vision of class-based redistribution. In the United States, where the dominant divisions in politics have been those of class, religion, geographical region, and race/ethnicity, we can find a similar mix of self-interest and ideology at work.

Policies for working mothers lie at the intersection of distinct vectors of ideological thought. Programs that encourage mothers to work for pay are not straightforward gender-equality policies, which typically concern discrimination against women in the labor force or sexual violence, because these policies also are redistributive in nature, requiring governments to raise revenues and redistribute them from one category of people to another one. Child care and parental leave are not straightforward class-redistributive issues either because they also tap "values" questions about gender relations and the division of labor in the workplace and home. Thus, one can fully embrace the idea that the state should intervene in the economy but still believe that it should do so to enable men to support their families on one income. Another precondition for an active state policy in this domain is some acceptance of the state's role in shaping gender relations and family life. One may fully support changing gender roles but prefer that the state stay out of a person's private decisions in these matters. In short, to understand the ideological alignment of different political forces on employment policies for mothers, we need to understand their views on a wider set of questions: the relationship of states to the family, the relationship of states to markets, and the gendered division of labor. Beliefs on these underlying issues, as represented in ideologies, shape preferences in policies for working mothers. Although power resources theory can help explain the states-versus-markets dimension, we need other theories about the sources of ideologies concerning gender and the family.

One approach is to emphasize the power resources of women's movements. Gender egalitarian ideas have their origins in the second wave of the feminist movement that sprang up in Western countries in the late 1960s. As the case studies in this book show, feminist movements have had a clear agenda-setting effect, propelling child care, parental leave, part-time work, and other such policy ideas onto the political stage. Nevertheless, there is no clear link between feminist organizing, either inside or outside political parties, and the development of policies on mothers' employment.[45] Active feminist movements in Germany and the Netherlands failed to effect change in this area, but France has developed an array of supportive policy measures despite the fragmentation of its feminist movement. The United States has had one of the most significant feminist movements in the Western world, yet it has failed to produce a national child care policy or paid parental leave. As the case studies show, policies on mothers' employment often have the fingerprints of women all over them—particularly "femocrats" who work within the state to push feminist policy goals.[46] Yet, given the heavy redistributive requirements of these policies, mainstream political forces need to see an electoral payoff for acceding to feminist demands.

Another alternative is that social structural changes have generated pressures on welfare states that policy makers have sought to address. The growth of women's employment since the 1970s has injected new concerns and issues into politics in many countries. Although structural economic trends do not guarantee a political response, they can change the calculus of political actors. Employed women often show different political orientations from women outside paid employment, such as increased sympathies with feminism and, in some countries, a tendency to vote for Left political parties.[47] As we shall see in the case of Sweden, the rapid rise in women's participation in the workforce in the 1960s and 1970s created a new source of workers for unions to organize—and thus a new pool of possible voters for Social Democratic parties. Similarly, Left and Right parties in France competed over gender equality issues in the 1970s and sought to address the growing population of employed women. At best, however, changes in women's employment may put new issues on the agenda but do not guarantee a policy response. Starting from similar rates of women's employment, Sweden, France, and the United States all enacted very different policies in the 1970s. In short, leftist political power, women's employment ratios, and feminist organizing all fail—on their own—to explain patterns of work-family policies.

Organized religion is an important source of ideologies about gender roles and the family that has not been fully explored by welfare state scholars.[48] Many family sociologists have long noted the connection between religiosity and family morality and behaviors,[49] and studies of public opinion demonstrate the link between religiosity and conservative views on gender and family issues.[50] Historically, the two dominant forms of organized religion in Western societies—Catholicism and the various permutations of Protestantism—have espoused a patriarchal view of social relations, conveying in both doctrine and church organization that men are leaders and women are submissive followers. Moreover, the Roman Catholic view of marriage as a sacrament that exists solely for the purpose of procreation subordinates women within the family and to their reproductive role. Protestant views on these matters long upheld many of the same principles, although there are considerable differences between the various strains of Protestantism.[51] The dominant religions have adjusted to the widespread social changes that have produced individualized family relationships, lower fertility rates, and growing divorce rates, and some scholars link these very changes in church doctrines and/or practices to the secularization of Western societies.[52] Still, because many churches are the bearers of doctrines composed centuries and even millennia ago, they often perpetuate understandings of social relationships from the past and espouse traditional familial roles and behaviors.

Organized religions have sought to maintain their position as the dominant arbiters of community values and morality. The decline of religious power over the public sphere in the nineteenth century led to efforts by churches to preserve their role in the private one. This meant guarding the influence of religious organizations over child and family affairs. For example, given that churches and related sectarian organizations long had the predominant responsibility for children's education, the steady encroachment of the state into this realm turned schools into a source of political conflict. As I will show in chapter 2, the resulting conflicts shaped the development of educational systems and some of the early structures of the welfare state. Where religious forces maintained some degree of political power and could exercise their influence through the state, the conflicts were relatively minor or resolved to favor religious groups. Where these forces failed to gain such influence and were in an antagonistic relationship with public authorities, religious organizations sought to build their own centers of power and influence in society.

There also are contemporary examples of religious influence on public policy. In Western Europe, Christian Democratic parties have shaped conservative abortion and divorce laws, the nature of education systems, and spending on families.[53] At the macro-level, there is also a correlation between the strength of societal religiosity and the extent to which countries have developed public child care systems that serve to promote mothers' employment. Figure 1.3 shows the negative relationship between levels of

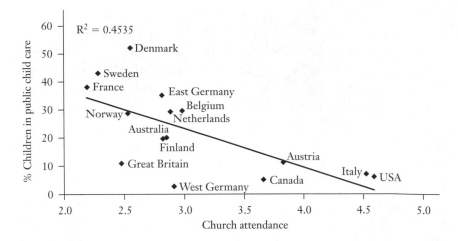

Figure 1.3 Church attendance and public child care for children age 0–2
SOURCES: World Values Survey. Child care data is from table 2.

Church attendance is the national mean of answers to the question "How often do you attend religious services these days?" "More than once a week" is 7; "never or practically never" is 1. Most church attendance data are from 2000, but for Australia, Norway, and West Germany they are from 1995–97, and for East Germany they are from the early 1990s.

church attendance and provision of public day care for several countries. Countries that have done the most to develop public child care services are the most secular, including many of the Nordic countries and France. As this graph suggests, secularization dampens an important source of conservatism with regard to women and the family.

Of course, this correlation says nothing about the particular mechanisms that link religiosity with public policy. It is puzzling to find such a relationship given the ongoing secularization of most Western societies.[54] Although rates of religious belief and practice first dropped to particularly low levels in the Nordic countries and France, there has been a similar trend in the Netherlands and the rest of continental Europe. The United States is one of the few countries to maintain high levels of religious practice and belief, albeit at lower levels than in the past. Clearly something more is needed to explain how religious institutions have influenced the development of policies on mothers' employment. This project does so by adopting a historical perspective on the development of public policy that enables us to see how past aspects of Western polities, societies, and their welfare regimes have a continuing influence on the contemporary politics of social provision.

The Temporal Dimension of the Welfare State

Viewing the welfare state as a historical construction enables us to trace how the political decision making and debates of one era influence the politics of social policy in later periods. In many countries, the welfare state has been a central feature of domestic politics for well over a hundred years and has affected politics in its own right. As students of path dependency have argued, social programs often shape the future politics of the welfare state by generating groups of beneficiaries that become strong supporters of the status quo.[55] More broadly, state programs can alter conceptions of the role of the state in social affairs. Once the state has expanded its authority into one realm, even those initially opposed to this expansion may come to believe that this area is properly the responsibility of the state—particularly given the growth of supportive social constituencies for this expanded state role. Finally, the policies and programs of the welfare state can affect patterns of social and political relations. Suzanne Mettler's study of the American welfare state shows how policies can be constitutive of notions about who should gain access to social citizenship rights.[56] We can posit a similar impact of social programs on gender relations, with some policies entrenching and reinforcing traditional gender roles and others helping to disrupt and restructure these most basic of societal relationships.

A temporal perspective on the welfare state also enables us to understand the political actors that affect social policy and how they have evolved over time. Many scholars now view the three decades following the Second World War as a key period in the development of the welfare state. However, the political forces shaping the welfare state during that time were hatched out of political cleavages of the late nineteenth and early twentieth centuries.[57] The politics of the welfare state after 1945 were influenced not only by the policy legacies of the previous era, but also by the political legacies of past conflicts and debates. The same is true in contemporary social politics: the dominant political groups have deep historical roots, yet have evolved in response to changes in their social constituencies. The policies and programs of the welfare state also have shaped these constituencies, reinforcing the ways in which past debates and decisions affect present-day politics.

Although attention to the path dependency of social programs is essential, it should not blind us to the possibilities for change. One significant criticism leveled at historical institutionalism is that it is unduly static, down-playing the potential for change. Kathleen Thelen suggests paying more attention to the complex realities of political phenomena, because political and social life is characterized by both stability and change—change that is at times, but not always, bounded by preexisting institutions.[58] A temporal perspective on the welfare state enables us to identify the mechanisms that produce stability in political or social arrangements and to observe whether change in those mechanisms gives rise to policy reform.

What is it that makes social policies stable and enduring? Social programs become embedded in the fabric of social relations, affecting citizens' behavior and expectations about their own lives and the state's responsibilities in ways that are slow to change.[59] For example, policies that support the male-breadwinner model influence the way people organize work and care, as well as their beliefs about what the state should and should not do in this area. Policies that fundamentally alter the gendered division of labor create new expectations about state responsibilities, generating pressure on politicians to fund programs such as child care or parental leave. The key lies in the constituencies for the political parties and the extent to which social policies reinforce or erode their sources of support.[60] Conservative parties generally are aided by programs that reproduce traditional gender roles and values, for these programs reinforce the constituency that is partial to their political vision.

At the same time, the social embeddedness of the welfare state is a source of dynamism and change. People inhabit a world that is bounded not only by the institutions of the welfare state, but by a larger set of economic, social, and cultural forces that can have a life of their own. Thus, despite male-breadwinner–supporting policies across the Western world, rapid economic growth in the 1960s and rising levels of women's education generated new social values and demands as women's participation in the labor market increased. The response to these demands was in no way guaranteed, but rising levels of women's employment put new issues on the agenda and spurred political competition over who could best meet the needs of this growing constituency. The irrepressible dynamism of complex societies often unsettles existing social and political arrangements, opening up space for new beliefs and demands.

How governments respond to these demands is likely to be shaped by both existing public policies and the structure of partisan competition. Faced with new problems, policy makers often reach for established repertoires of action, perhaps modernizing existing programs or services to fit new needs.[61] In addition, previous policies can affect current policy choices because they tend to generate both mass and bureaucratic constituencies with a stake in the status quo. In fact, sometimes the absence of past policies can create space for more innovation.[62] The structure of partisan competition also is an inherited feature of polities, reflecting the societal cleavages that give rise to the political parties, or factions within them, that dominate political life.[63] The nature of these political forces, their ideologies, and their strength in the political system affects how new social issues will be treated, namely through the way in which the parties compete around these issues. As the case studies will show, the rise in mothers' employment became a source of partisan competition in some countries but not others, reflecting the predominance of conservative ideologies about gender and the family in some places and their weakness in others.

The Politics of Mothers' Employment

This project focuses on three distinct time periods: the late nineteenth and early twentieth centuries; the era of welfare state expansion between about 1945 and 1975; and the period of welfare state "crisis" since the mid-1970s. Each era is marked by political and social phenomena that prompt policy change, but the periods are linked through the way in which debates and decisions in one time influenced those of the future. During the first period states were expanding their reach into social affairs, including the familial sphere. One of the most significant extensions of public authority was in education, although some states became engaged in other child- and family-related initiatives. The second period was one of high economic growth and expansion of the public sector. Although the male-breadwinner model initially informed public policy in all countries, by the late 1960s and early 1970s gender-equality issues had come onto the political agenda, and welfare states began to diverge sharply in the area of policies on mothers' employment. The third period is characterized by continuing changes in gender roles and the family as well as a dense thicket of policies and institutions affecting decisions about work and care.

In the late nineteenth and early twentieth centuries, women's subordinate role in society and the family was widely accepted, and the dominant debates of the day were not about how to support or encourage women's employment. Instead, one of the most significant questions in the domestic politics of all countries was the development of mass education systems. Because churches traditionally had responsibility for children's schooling, the spread of public education often generated conflicts between secularist and religious forces and/or between competing religious groups. Four patterns of church-state relations and religious divisions shaped these debates: (1) a clerical-anticlerical model in France, in which there were sharp clashes between Catholics and secularist Republicans; (2) church-state fusion and religious homogeneity in Sweden, which generated relatively minor religious conflicts; (3) biconfessional and clerical-anticlerical divisions in the Netherlands, with cleavages between Catholics and Protestants and between secularist and religious forces; and (4) religious pluralism in the United States, where the early separation of church and state and religious diversity produced a complex landscape of religious groups.

The nature and resolution of these conflicts had enduring consequences for both public policy and politics. In France and Sweden, we can see the beginnings of an activist state tradition in education and family policy. In France, the triumph of secular republicans over Catholics in the Third Republic produced an expansion of national state authority over schools and family affairs in an effort to bring children into the ambit of secular state influence. France developed pro-natalist family policies and a centralized education system that provided services for children as young as two or three years old. In Sweden, the fusion of church and state produced a similar (though relatively peaceful) transfer of authority over family affairs from religious to secular authorities. The central state assumed responsibility for matters of family morality and well-being, as evidenced by a centralized, state-run education system and policies early in the twentieth century that sought to expand women's legal and economic rights within marriage and to protect the rights of children. This encroachment on paternal power, made possible by the weakening hold of the established church on both politics and society, was indicative of the gender-egalitarian reforms to come later in the twentieth century.

In religiously diverse countries such as the Netherlands and the United States, opposition to allowing central state interference in the familial domain led to the emergence of a reticent state tradition in education and family policy. In the Netherlands, fierce conflicts among secularists, Protestants, and Catholics generated parties of religious defense that ultimately triumphed in the political sphere. These parties shaped education and early social services policy around the notion of subsidiarity so that religiously based voluntary associations would provide these services and thereby preserve their influence in child and family affairs. In the United States, the early separation of church and state and the country's extreme religious pluralism produced a desire to decentralize questions of morality and family life to the lowest levels of society. Because no one religion could claim a position as the national or even state-level arbiter of community morals, family-related issues came to be determined at the local level. Thus, education remained the responsibility of local communities and slowly came under the reach of state governments, although substantial local control was preserved.

The larger political consequence of these historical conflicts was to influence how religion was incorporated into modern polities and thus the role it would play in shaping ideologies about gender and the family. In France and Sweden, the subordination of religious forces to secular ones weakened a source of conservative gender ideologies and an opponent of state family policies. The change was more complete in Sweden than in France, but secularization advanced more quickly in both these countries than in the rest of continental Europe, and religiously based parties came to play a fairly weak role in politics. Both also maintained an activist state role in family affairs, as evidenced by centralized education systems and active family policies. Rejecting the subsidiarity model found in most continental European countries, the central state in both Sweden and France assumed direct responsibility for child and family well-being.

In the Netherlands and the United States, religious pluralism was a source of continuing religious vitality, although its impact on politics in the two countries differed. Christian Democratic parties became the dominant force in Dutch politics through most of the twentieth century. Religion had a more diffuse role in the United States, becoming a touchstone of political life without generating any religiously based parties. In both countries, there was an enduring belief in leaving family-related affairs to lower levels of society and entrusting local governments or volunteer organizations (and, later, for-profit organizations) with the responsibility for many child- and family-related services. Conservative gender ideologies also maintained a significant foothold in politics, although these values were more hegemonic in the Netherlands. In the United States, a strong liberal tradition and commitment to individual self-determination created more room for changing gender roles. Still, throughout the twentieth century, the periodic mobilization of conservative religious movements in the United States usually has come in reaction to government policies affecting children, families, and gender relations.

Ideologies about gender roles and the acceptability of national family policies played a crucial role in shaping how governments responded to a new social pressure in the 1960s and 1970s—the rise in the number of working mothers. In Sweden, secularization and the lack of religiously based parties created a favorable environment for policies that undermined traditional gender arrangements. The politically powerful Social Democratic Party was essential for this transition in the welfare state, yet the party's own shift on this issue was facilitated by the absence of a religious cleavage that could fragment the working class and politicize gender and family questions. Swedish policy sought to eliminate the male-breadwinner model, transforming Swedish society into one of universal breadwinners in which all parents were also in paid work. In the Netherlands, the hegemony of religious parties and strength of religion in society impeded such a shift: Christian Democratic notions of subsidiarity and traditional family arrangements continued to guide public policy. Male-breadwinner and female-caregiver ideals were so hegemonic in society and politics that even Dutch Social Democrats hardly challenged them.

Secular center-right parties dominated politics in France during the 1960s and 1970s, and they responded with pragmatism to shifting gender roles and labor market needs. Although they did not adopt transformative public policies, as the Swedish Social Democrats had done, they did support policies to help wage-earning mothers. These measures, combined with the nearly universal preschool system, created a supportive environment for working mothers. In the United States, centrist Republicans initially behaved in a similar fashion when they joined Democrats in advocating a greater federal role in supporting working mothers and assuring early-education programs for young children. Their efforts ultimately failed in the face of a conservative attack on federal family policy. Throughout the 1970s, continuing efforts to expand the federal role in this area faced a growing mobilization of social conservatives against changing gender roles and federal involvement in family affairs. Instead, policy measures sought to encourage private markets to solve the needs of working parents, thereby decentralizing responsibility and delegating debates over this question to local communities and families themselves.

Since 1975, the policy choices made in these earlier periods have influenced the way states cope with both economic crisis and political change. Economic stagnation and high unemployment in many countries have created an unfavorable environment for policies that encourage mothers' employment. At the same time, Western countries have experienced significant political changes with the erosion of the social cleavages and political alignments that had defined party systems for decades. In many countries, this has led parties to reach out to new constituencies, such as women, for whom changes in gender roles and family life created new identities and needs. Their expectations and preferences have been shaped in part by the existing policy context.

The transformation of Swedish society into one in which all parents were working created political pressures for expanded access to public child care. Because of the difficulty of meeting these demands in the immediate term, however, government policy also repeatedly increased the length of parental leave as a way to divert pressure from the child care system and to respond to demands of conservatives for more parental caring time at home. The end result is a system in which all parents have the supports and services they need to remain in paid work, although they may spend a substantial amount of time at home during the first year and a half of a child's life. In France, government policy since the 1970s neither sought to nor succeeded in transforming French society into one of universal breadwinners. With economic pressures on the welfare state and continuing divisions between mothers at home and mothers at work, governments of both the Left and the Right moved toward developing lengthy care leaves rather than promoting a universal child care system for children under three.

The American trajectory was distinct because of the development of private markets. Tax subsidies and regulatory policies have encouraged private child care and parental leave alternatives, which began developing in the 1970s. Although access to private services and benefits has been unevenly distributed throughout the population, these alternatives have addressed the needs and demands of many middle-class parents. This, in turn, has undermined the push for expanded federal policies in this area. There have been expansions in child care services for low-income families, but these have been scrupulously means-tested and kept out of the reach of families above the poverty level. As child care policy has become increasingly dominated by the goals of welfare reform, most parents ineligible for assistance have sought solutions in the private sector.

The lack of affordable private services in the Netherlands and the absence of paid parental leave created difficulties for the small but growing number of working mothers. As in all Western countries, women's participation in the workforce continually expanded during the 1970s and 1980s, creating new openings for political parties that could successfully address their concerns. Labor unions and the Social Democratic Party slowly moved toward supporting the demands of working women, and by the 1990s there were new debates about the demographic unsustainability of the welfare state and the importance of "activating" women's labor. Combined with the decline of the Christian Democratic Party in the 1990s and the very rapid secularization of Dutch society, the moment was ripe for policy change in the 1990s. A series of measures sought to make child care, parental leave, and part-time work available to parents so as to encourage more mothers to maintain their attachment to paid work.

This represents an important instance of policy change, but there is also a good deal of continuity in Dutch work-family policies. Reluctant to involve the central state in providing child care, governments of different ideological stripes have instead sought to subsidize private alternatives. In addition, the main thrust of Dutch policy encourages extensive part-time work for women in order to preserve extensive maternal caring time. In this way, policy makers have trod cautiously around deep-seated values about the importance of maternal care for young children. Clearly, Dutch policy has changed, but we can still see the weight of the past in contemporary work-family policies. In this, Dutch policy today represents an example of change that is bounded by the institutional and political legacies of the past.

The Organization of This Book

The next two chapters examine the foundations of contemporary politics around work and family issues. Chapter 2 analyzes politics and policy in the nineteenth and early twentieth centuries, tracing the origins of policies regarding mothers' employment to the way religion shaped political development in four countries. Chapter 3 covers the first three decades after the Second World War, a period of rapid welfare state expansion. The chapter focuses in particular on the 1960s and early 1970s, when states began to diverge in their policies and programs for working mothers.

Chapters 4 and 5 look at the evolution of work-family policies since the 1970s, showing how economic slowdown, political change, and past policy decisions intersect to shape the contemporary politics of work and family. Chapter 4 traces the diverging paths of French and Swedish policy, while chapter 5 shows how the private model in the United States has undermined efforts to expand the state role in family policy. Chapter 6 then considers whether there have been openings for policy change in the 1990s, given improved economic growth in many countries and the continued rise in women's employment. Taking the example of the Netherlands, the chapter assesses the impetus for policy reforms in the 1990s and the extent to which these reforms represent a departure from past policy.

The final chapter briefly summarizes the arguments developed in the preceding chapters and their implications for the study of the welfare state. It also draws some lessons for American debates about work and family.

CHAPTER TWO

The Religious Origins of the Gendered Welfare State

Historical studies of the welfare state often focus on the role of class politics in shaping the origins of social policy. Certainly, the Industrial Revolution influenced the foundations of the welfare state in the late nineteenth and early twentieth centuries, as it spurred the development of class consciousness and resulting growth of labor unions and Left political parties that would champion redistributive programs. Less attention has been paid to the mobilization of religious identities during this period, which in some countries was a major source of political conflict. In much of Western Europe, there were heated disputes between secularist and religious forces, or between different religious groups. Ethnoreligious conflict also was a mainstay of American politics during the latter half of the nineteenth century. Coming during the construction and expansion of the nation-state and the development of early democratic politics, these divisions exerted a lasting influence on the structure of state institutions and the cleavages underpinning politics in most countries.

This chapter explores how religious divisions affected political development in the late nineteenth and early twentieth centuries and the consequences for gendered dimensions of the welfare state. Religious conflict played out over numerous issues. A central area of dispute concerned the expanding role of the state in public education—a hitherto privileged realm of churches. The push for secular, state control over this area fueled conflicts between religious and secular forces and between competing religious groups. The intensity of these conflicts reflected the larger issue at stake: what would be the relative power of religious and secular authority in shaping children's socialization, and with it the social mores and values of a nation? Although education was often the spark that ignited these conflicts, political actors were grappling with more fundamental questions of what role religion should play in politics and where to draw the boundaries between the state, religious civil society, and the family. The nature and outcome of these conflicts had enduring significance for the politics of mothers' employment, shaping both the way religion was incorporated into modern political systems and key features of early welfare states.

There were four distinct patterns of religious practice, religious divisions, and related political conflict. In France, fierce clerical-anticlerical conflict crystallized around the question of education and reverberated across French politics and society. Anticlericalists ultimately gained the upper hand in these struggles, but Catholicism continued to be an important social force and basis of political contestation. Sweden was characterized by weak religiously based conflict owing to its religious homogeneity and the early fusion of church and state. Religion did not become the source of a significant cleavage in politics, and Swedish society secularized at a rapid pace. The opposite was true in the Netherlands, where there was a strong political mobilization around religion because of conflicts between secular and religious forces and between Catholics and Protestants. By the start of the twentieth century, religious groups had allied against secular liberals, ensuring their preeminence in Dutch politics and society for decades to come. Finally, the United States is characterized by tremendous religious diversity, the early separation of church and state, and strong, societal religiosity. Religion exerted a diffuse effect on politics, and powerful impact on society, without becoming an explicit line of division in the political system.

These patterns of political contestation over religion influenced early public policies for women, children, and families in a way that was indicative of emerging ideologies about the relationship between the state and the family. In France, clerical-anticlerical competition over children and families led to an extension of secular state responsibility—particularly in the area of education, but also in other forms of family policy. One immediate consequence was the inclusion of early education programs for children in the national education system, which institutionalized preschools as a responsibility of the central state. In Sweden, a similar extension of state authority over the family was effected through entirely different means. The fusion of church and state essentially transferred responsibility for family affairs from the church to the state, while the early secularization of Swedish society reduced the influence of conservative social values over both society and politics. Lacking competition between the state and religious civil society over education or welfare, Sweden did not see the same expansion of services for children as did France. Instead, the state adopted a series of measures to undermine the patriarchal family and promote the rights of women and children as individuals.

In the Netherlands and United States, the state was more reluctant to intervene in the sensitive area of the family, although this reticence took different forms. In the Netherlands, conflicts between religious and secular forces and among denominations themselves produced a flourishing civil society and political mobilization around religion. The success of religious groups in these conflicts and their ascent into political office ensured that public policy would not disturb the patriarchal organization of the family. It also meant that religious organizations would maintain their influence over educational and welfare programs by receiving public funds to provide these services. In the United States, the early separation of church and state and extreme religious pluralism produced a will to devolve responsibility for education and family matters to local communities. No one denomination had the strength or numbers to serve as the national guardian of social values. Instead, potentially polarizing conflicts over education and the family were decentralized to lower levels of society, creating a lasting aversion to federal family policy for any but the poor.

In the long term, these patterns of conflict affected how religion was incorporated into political systems and shaped the parties, factions, and lines of political contestation that developed in each country. Religious cleavages were largely absent from the Swedish party system, and politics became highly secular. The opposite was true in the Netherlands, where religious parties dominated Dutch politics through most of the twentieth century. In France, religious groups struggled to gain a foothold in politics, yet Catholicism remained an important social force that championed a conservative vision of the family. Finally, in the United States, religion's influence over politics and society was diffuse yet powerful.

Religion and Political Development

Why must we go back to the late nineteenth and early twentieth centuries to make sense of the contemporary politics of child care and policies on mothers' employment? For one thing, the roots of modern political parties and ideologies lie in this period. As Seymour Martin Lipset and Stein Rokkan show in their seminal work on political development, nineteenth-century cleavages and conflicts in Western Europe formed the basis of political parties and systems that were in place by 1920.[1] The U.S. trajectory was somewhat different and normally is analyzed in terms of the fourth party system of 1896 and the fifth party system that arose during the New Deal.[2] In both Western Europe and the United States, party systems were "frozen" in place beginning in the 1920s or 1930s, with predictable parties, ideologies, and voter orientations rooted in the traditional cleavages of class and religion. These political forces oversaw the expansion of the public social provision between 1945 and 1975, when the heyday of the traditional party system corresponded with the "golden age" of welfare state expansion.[3]

These political groupings also embodied certain ideals and values about gender relations and the family that affected their response to the question of mothers' employment. To understand the ideologies driving public policy in this area, we need to explore the impact of religion on political development. Religion has played a fundamental role in shaping social values about gender and the family. For centuries, Christian churches in Western societies defined the structure, meaning, and morality of family life for the great majority of people. This had particular implications for the status of women and children. The patriarchal family has its roots in Roman law, but the moral prescriptions of Catholic and, later, Protestant churches upheld the subordination of women and children to the male head of household. The Catholic church emphasized the family as an organic, indissoluble unit, whereas the Reformation brought a more individualistic perspective on marriage as the union of two persons who are individually accountable to God. The Reformation did not bring immediate changes in the status of women, however, who were subject to strict codes of behavior. More generally, churches viewed themselves as the arbiters of community morality. This was one reason they took an important role in the education of children—to assure that children would be brought up according to religious precepts and thereby become both good members of the community and faithful adherents to the church.

Although many countries experienced a gradual secularization of political authority beginning in the Renaissance, the century following the French Revolution brought direct, sharp challenges to the power and influence of organized religion in many countries. The revolution was a direct assault on both the monarchy and the Catholic church and it reverberated beyond French borders. The anticlerical mobilization was matched by a counter-mobilization of religious forces, shaping the dominant political organizations of the day and fueling debates about church-state relations. Not all countries experienced this level of acrimony around religious issues. In Sweden, religious homogeneity diminished the intensity of these conflicts. In the United States, church and state were separated with the founding of the country, which weakened anticlericalism and decentralized religious conflicts to states and local communities. In all Western countries, the spread of secular values and the extension of state power in the nineteenth century raised questions about the role of religion in both society and the public sphere.

In most countries, such debates did not have immediate ramifications for the situation of women or the issue of mothers' employment. Some improvements in women's legal status grew out of secularist challenges to traditional views of the family, as when the French revolutionaries overturned the ban on divorce. Marriage became an increasingly secular institution, and women slowly gained increased legal rights of personhood—particularly, as we shall see, in Sweden and other Nordic countries. However, the belief that women's primary sphere was the home was scarcely contested; many men and women shared the view that women were defined by their biological capacity for motherhood.[4] Rather than challenging the traditional norms of motherhood and domesticity that defined women's roles, these values intensified in the nineteenth and early twentieth centuries. Moreover, in most countries, public provision of social welfare in the nineteenth century was minimal, with limited interventions on behalf of certain categories of people. Although some favored the expansion of public child care to help poor mothers at work, the idea of a widely available child care system was unthinkable. Women in trade unions and Left parties sometimes espoused more radical visions about the need for women's economic independence, but maternalist reformers, rather than promoting the idea of mothers' employment, often pushed for subsidies to enable mothers to be at home.[5]

Debates about the relationship between religion and politics and between state and family crystallized around education. One of the greatest expansions of governmental authority in this period was in mass education, a move that reflected the imperatives of the creation and consolidation of the nation-state. Because education was an age-old prerogative of churches, this raised questions about whether religious forces would maintain influence in this sphere or lose it to secular authorities. More fundamentally, a state-run mass education system threatened to involve secular state authorities in the intimate lives of families by influencing the socialization of their children. The education issue came to dominate domestic political life in many Western countries, producing fierce conflicts and the political mobilization of religious and secularist forces. As Lipset and Rokkan described in their classic work on political cleavages,

> The development of compulsory education under centralized secular control for all children of the nation came into direct conflict with the established rights of the religious *pouvoirs intermédiaires* and triggered waves of mass mobilization into nationwide parties of protest. To the radicals and liberals inspired by the French Revolution, the introduction of compulsory education was only one among several measures in a systematic effort to create direct links of influence and control between the nation-state and the individual citizen, but their attempt to penetrate directly to the children without consulting the parents and their spiritual authorities aroused widespread opposition and bitter fights.[6]

Not all countries experienced such acrimony over the education question. Differences in the degree of conflict between religious and secular groups and in the way these conflicts were resolved influenced early structures of the welfare state, ideologies about the relationship between the state and the family, and the ways in which religion was incorporated into political life.[7]

France: Clerical-Anticlerical Conflict and the Origins of an Activist State

Nineteenth-century France was divided into two worlds: one resolutely monarchist, proclerical, and reactionary, and the other just as determinedly anticlerical and republican. Since the French Revolution, the Catholic church's defense of the monarchy and hereditary privilege earned it the lasting enmity of the revolutionaries and their political descendants. Throughout the nineteenth century, the church was associated with political movements to restore the monarchy and with the reactionary regimes of the Restoration (1815–1830) and the Second Empire (1851–1870). Clericalism and anticlericalism became the source of deep and enduring cleavages in political and social life.[8]

These conflicts reached their apogee in the late nineteenth and early twentieth centuries, with education serving as the privileged terrain of dispute.[9] Schools had long been the prerogative of churches in France, and religious congregations expanded through much of the nineteenth century to provide educational services, often funded by local governments. Faced with a loss of power in the political sphere, religious groups saw these services as a means for maintaining their influence over future generations of French citizens. This view brought them into conflict with anticlericalists, who wanted schools that espoused their own republican values.[10] Republicans also believed education was central to the socialization of the citizenry into a common identity and set of moral values. Conflicts with the clergy over education intensified in the latter part of the nineteenth century and came to dominate domestic political debates.

With the founding of the Third Republic in 1879, secular republicans gained the upper hand over Catholics in these disputes and immediately began constructing a centralized public education system. Schools were made legally obligatory for children between the ages of seven and thirteen, and tuition was eliminated. Other legislation sought to break the traditional reliance of school systems on congregations by requiring all departments to have secular teacher training schools, making all school buildings secular, and requiring public school personnel to be laypersons.[11] By the early twentieth century, more radical republicans had gained power, and they intensified efforts to uproot the clergy from the education system.[12] A 1901 law on associations required all congregations to seek formal approval from the state or risk dissolution and exile of its members. By 1903, more than 10,000 congregation schools run by unauthorized religious houses were closed. In 1904, another law forbade members of any congregation, authorized or not, from teaching.[13] In 1905, the government enacted the formal separation of church and state, ending the 100-year-old concordat between Napoleon and the Holy See. Henceforth, religion would be purely a private affair, receiving no subsidy or other support from the state. Private, Catholic schools could continue to exist, but without public subsidy.[14]

The larger significance of these struggles over education lay in the ascent to power of anticlerical republicans, which was the preeminent political force throughout the Third Republic (1879–1940). Although republicans were divided between conservative, centrist, and more radical factions, they shared a commitment to a national, secular education system.[15] Secularism became a founding principle of the French Republic; the notion that religion has no place in the public sphere has lived on to the present day, interrupted only by the authoritarian clericalism of the Vichy regime. This is not to say that Catholics entirely lost influence over French society and politics. Catholicism continued to be a vital social force in some areas of France and a source of political mobilization against the policies and practices of republican governments. The clerical-anticlerical cleavage continued on in French politics even as religious forces struggled to create a viable political actor that would return them to political power.

Religiously based political competition and republican political hegemony had a number of implications for the development of child and family policies. First, the suppression of religious congregations in education was part of a larger process by which the central state would displace religious organizations as the provider of many social and educational services. As the discussion of the Netherlands will show, where religious forces maintained political influence, they worked to protect the role of a religiously based voluntary sector as an intermediary layer between the state and the family. The weakness of these forces in France produced the opposite effect, as republicans sought to forge a direct relationship between the state and the individual. State suppression of voluntary associations dates back to the Revolution, and France was one of the last European countries to grant the right to freedom of association. Even this more liberal 1901 law restricted the activities of religious congregations.[16] As a result, France did not develop the strong, Catholic civil society found in much of continental Europe. Certain parts of France (such as Normandy and Brittany) had a religious subculture that included Catholic voluntary organizations, media, sports clubs, and so on.[17] In the rest of France, however, such organizations were few, reflecting the weak reach of Catholicism into many parts of the country.

Second, by weakening these intermediaries between the state and the nation's children, the republican education laws signified a new degree of direct state involvement in the lives of children and families. Requiring all children to attend school and learn a curriculum defined by state bureaucrats was already an impingement on paternal authority. What was of particular importance was the fact that programs for young children—the preschools for children between the ages of three and six—also were included in the new education system. These programs had been provided by charities and some local governments through much of the nineteenth century, the two often working in collaboration.[18] Because the programs had an educational mission, they became caught up in the fight between secularists and clericalists in the latter half of the nineteenth century. This competitive struggle produced a rapid increase in the number of preschools as both sides sought to draw children into their own services.[19] Hastily increasing their provision of these programs, Catholic congregations gained a hegemonic position in the care and socialization of pre-primary-aged children by the mid-to-late nineteenth century.[20]

Because republicans were determined to leave no element of mass education in the hands of Catholics, these programs for young children also were incorporated into the secular national education system in the 1880s and named *écoles maternelles*. Newly appointed state inspectors overhauled the schools' pedagogy to bring them in line with republican principles. Parents were not required to send their children to the *école maternelle*, but they were free, secular, and supposed to be available to families who sought them.[21] As with the primary education system, preschools served a working-class population and provided needed care for children during the day. They therefore embodied both educational and care-giving aspirations, even though government officials highlighted their educational mission.

Clerical-anticlerical conflict had less immediate effects on the other main form of child care in this period—the *crèches* (day nurseries) for children under the age of three—owing to divisions among republicans about the role of the state in social welfare. Although most republicans agreed on the importance of publicly run secular education, many were economic liberals leery of excessive state intervention in the economy.[22] The lack of agreement on these matters meant that public welfare remained the responsibility of local governments, and so the balance of religious charities and secular public authorities in the provision of these services varied by region. In some localities, public authorities shut down religiously run programs and attempted to create secular equivalents, while in others the state and religious charities had a more collaborative relationship.[23]

The development of the *crèches* depended largely on these localized arrangements and failed to become part of the national dispute over the influence of church and state in the lives of children. In contrast to the preschools, the *crèches* were seen as welfare programs devoid of educational content. Through much of the nineteenth century they had been run by religious charities, often with the aim of supervising the behavior of the poor mothers who used these services while working.[24] By the 1880s, the hostility of republicans toward charitable organizations led to the closing down of religiously run *crèches* in some regions of France, whereas municipal governments in other areas developed secular services alongside the religious ones, using public funds to support the latter.[25] More generally, the lack of agreement on whether these services were actually good for children and whether the state should be engaged in this kind of activity precluded the kind of national public involvement that was devoted to education. Throughout the Third Republic, it would be largely left to employers, municipal governments, and charities to decide whether they wished to create these programs.[26]

Although the *crèches* did not become a priority of national elites, the climate of clerical-anticlerical divisions and competition shaped the expansion of state authority over the family in other ways. The family had long been a central concern in Catholic social thought, and by the early twentieth century, a Catholic family movement began to take shape around the defense of the family against secular schools and moral decline.[27] Some Catholics argued that the French revolutionaries had sacrificed the family on the altar of individualism, with their secularization of marriage, liberalization of divorce laws, and weakening of paternal authority. As evidence of the crisis in French families, they pointed to declining birth rates that threatened the national security and economic vitality of the nation. By heaping scorn on large families and promoting a secular state, they argued that republicans had produced a crisis in both the family and fertility rates that could be redressed only through re-Christianization.[28]

Such claims touched a raw nerve. Alarm had been growing about the expansion of the German population and relative stagnation of the French one since the Franco-Prussian war of 1870–71.[29] Fears of depopulation endured and intensified during the first three decades of the twentieth century, putting republicans on the defensive. The republican response was pro-natalism—a patriotic, secular doctrine that aimed to promote the growth of the French population. In an attempt to stave off Catholic criticism, republicans developed a secular, rationalist view of the family.[30] Thus, though the Catholic family movement put moral decline at the heart of their analysis, the lawyers, physicians, demographers, and other scientists on the republican side focused their attention on the causes of infant mortality.[31] For them, the answer to the population crisis was not in greater levels of religious faith and practice, but in improved resources and services for families.

Pro-natalist fears and this republican vision of the family ultimately helped produce an expanded role for the state in the lives of French families.[32] In the first decades of the twentieth century, governments adopted a host of measures to encourage reproduction, protect infant health, and redistribute income to large families. Of particular significance for women's employment was the creation in 1913 of a mandatory, paid maternity leave for mothers working in the industrial and commercial sectors.[33] The Catholic family movement often criticized government policy, but republicans and Catholics were able to agree that the family should be a central priority. One especially important development was the extension of family allowances to most workers—a process that built on an existing set of employer-provided benefits to families but sought to expand them to more families.[34] These policies, which became one foundation of the French welfare state after 1945, revealed how the family remained a central category of social and policy analysis, albeit in a laicized form.[35]

In sum, we can trace the roots of the activist French state in matters of children's education and the family to clerical-anticlerical conflicts and political competition over a century ago. What were the implications of this situation for women? On the one hand, women undoubtedly gained from the various benefits and services put in place for children. Both preschool and primary education served mostly working-class children during this period, and the availability of these free services helped mothers during the day. Moreover, women also profited from maternity leave benefits, family allowances, and health services for mothers and children, all of which were made possible by heightened concern over depopulation.

It is difficult to determine what effects these disparate programs and services had on women's employment. Many have noted the high rates of women's workforce participation in France relative to that of women in other countries, a phenomenon that has deeper economic causes but that may have been reinforced by access to free preschools and maternity leaves.[36] It also is notable that, despite calls by Catholics for mothers to devote themselves exclusively to raising children, policy makers never adopted laws barring married women from employment during the Third Republic. They sought instead to encourage forms of work for women that fit better with their maternal duties.[37] Although family allowances could enable families to live on one income, they were not accompanied by measures to compel mothers to quit the labor market, an omission that revealed a pragmatic recognition of how many families relied on women's paid labor to survive.

With the family as the dominant category of analysis, however, there was little concern with the individual rights and concerns of women per se. Family policy was oriented most strongly around the needs of the child; limited attention was paid to women's rights.[38] Repressive legislation against abortion and contraception made clear that policy makers tended to view French women as mere vessels to bear babies for the state.[39] There also was only minimal state intervention on behalf of women as individuals in this period. Secular republicans did make some attempts to fight Catholics on the subordination of women to the family. Reforms in the first decades of the Third Republic brought a number of significant changes in family law, such as the reestablishment of divorce (albeit under limited circumstances), allowing women to deposit money in savings accounts without male authorization, and the principle of married women's right to earn a salary. However, many patriarchal elements of the Napoleonic code remained on the books for decades.[40] Republican secularism created a willingness to challenge the authority of the Church on the socialization of children and family morality, but this did not make republicans into champions of feminist causes, such as suffrage.

The republican men who dominated politics during the Third Republic viewed women as hopelessly under the sway of the Catholic church. The widely held view was that women were more religious than men, and there is some evidence to support this.[41] For anticlerical republicans, this was all the more reason to make sure that children received a secular education as early as possible, but it did not produce much interest in extending women's political rights. If women were granted suffrage, it was assumed they would vote for Catholics, endangering not only the republic but the political careers of many anticlerical politicians.[42] Women were not taken seriously as a constituency, and arguments to improve the status of women in society often fell upon deaf ears.

Secular republicans won their battles with religious forces in France. Both pre-primary and primary education became a public service, and the congregations that had traditionally run these programs were barred from any role in the education system. Removing congregations from their historical role was symptomatic of the efforts of the French state to usurp church responsibilities in the area of children and families. Widespread acceptance of the state's role in the lives of children and families was to be a crucial precondition for policies to support women's employment.

Sweden: Church-State Fusion and Early Secularization

Although the Swedish state also came to assume a preeminent role in child and family policy, the dynamics differed markedly from the French case and produced different forms of intervention. A more peaceful process of secularization impeded the mobilization of religious identities and polarizing conflicts that occurred in France, which in turn reduced competition over education and the family, enabling the state to more easily assume responsibility for these areas while limiting the growth of a religiously based civil society. In addition, although the Swedish National Church espoused conservative gender ideologies, the growing individualism brought by secularization impeded the kind of familialist policy orientation that marked French public policy. The family became a major concern of Swedish policy, but this did not come about at the expense of the individuals within it. While French family policy focused its energies on the health and education of children, Sweden became a pioneer in efforts to improve the legal and political status of women.

When the Reformation came to Sweden in the sixteenth century, Lutheranism became the official religion, but in this case the state gained the upper hand. Unlike the Catholic or Calvinist churches of continental Europe, which retained a greater degree of independence even as they were intertwined with the reigning political powers, the established Lutheran churches of Scandinavia were more thoroughly subordinated to monarchical authority.[43] The Lutheran church became an extension of the state apparatus, while the clergy became civil servants with both religious and non-ecclesiastical duties. In addition, with their monopoly over religion backed by monarchical power, the national churches did not depend on a societal mobilization of religious identities for their survival. One consequence was a relatively open religious culture that contrasted with the insular orientation of the more autonomous churches in continental Europe.[44]

In Sweden, these aspects of church-state relations contributed to the weakening hold of churches over both society and politics. Students of secularization often argue that established churches have difficulty staving off institutional decline, in part because they depend heavily on the whims of political authority. In Sweden, the state paid for the construction of churches and salaries for clergy. When this assistance was lacking, as it often was, the infrastructure of religious institutions declined, and the church lost influence over the public.[45] In addition, the Lutheran church's monopoly over religion and the weakness of religious divisions led to complacency and a lack of spiritual intensity. The established church became a mere bureaucracy.[46] Most people remained members of the established church, but actual church attendance plunged.[47]

Religious homogeneity and the clear subordination of religious to civil authority also minimized the development of religious cleavages in Sweden.[48]

Over the course of the eighteenth and nineteenth centuries, political authority was gradually secularized. Although at times the national church fought these developments, Sweden was generally spared the strife caused by the religious question in the rest of Europe.[49] The most significant religious disputes came out of revivalist movements that criticized the lack of emotion and vigor in the established church.[50] However, divisions among these critics, and the fact that many were arguing from their position within the Lutheran church, prevented them from becoming a unified political force that could fuel the kinds of passions unleashed by religious conflict in France or the Netherlands.[51] In addition, revivalist movements shaped political liberalism in Sweden, thereby mitigating the tendency toward an anticlerical or antireligious stance in politics. Swedish liberals often were critical of the form religion took rather than adopting the anticlericalism of the French republicans. Instead of the negative spiral of attack and counter-attack that France experienced, Sweden underwent a relatively peaceful process of secularization as religion came to play an increasingly marginal role in both society and politics.[52]

This pattern of church-state fusion, weak religious cleavages, and advanced secularization facilitated the expansion of state responsibility for children and families. With the fusion of church and state, the traditional responsibility of churches for family well-being was essentially transferred to the state. Religious actors initially maintained their involvement in family matters as state officials but gradually lost this influence with the secularization of the public sphere. This loss of influence is evident in the development of mass education. School administration thoroughly fused secular and religious authorities, because diocesan boards were above the school boards and oversaw the development of the education system through the nineteenth century.[53] However, as education was progressively secularized during the twentieth century, the Swedish National Church was edged out of its traditional role.[54] Although conflicts sometimes flared up between Lutherans and secularists, these disagreements in no way replicated the heated, polarizing disputes that occurred elsewhere in Europe.

Education policy was symptomatic of the relations between the state and social forces that would later be established in other areas of the welfare state. Increasingly in the twentieth century, policy makers would opt for state-led solutions to social issues, rather than leaving responsibility to charitable associations and actors. Although Sweden developed a rich network of voluntary associations in the area of culture or recreation, these organizations would play only a limited role in providing social welfare services.[55] The lesser degree of voluntary-sector activity also reflected the lack of religious cleavages and the fusion of church and state. As Estelle James has commented, "The Church of Sweden is, in effect, part of the Swedish government and as such could hardly become the source of entrepreneurship for a competing non-governmental sector."[56] As in France, the state developed an active role in child and family policy (although the French state often was more antagonistic toward civil society). In Sweden, there was mutual acceptance of the division of labor between state and civil society—with the former taking responsibility for education and social welfare.[57]

Although Sweden came to resemble France in its activist approach to children and families, Swedish policies took a different form. One difference lay in the absence of publicly run, widely available preschool programs, like the French *écoles maternelles*. In the nineteenth and early twentieth centuries, bourgeois reformers established some infant schools and day nurseries for the children of poor families, and some middle-class children attended part-day kindergartens.[58] These services remained extremely limited, however, developing neither in the voluntary sphere nor through state initiatives.[59] The lack of interest in early education could, to some degree, reflect the rural nature of the country and the long distances that children would have to travel. Even after industrialization and urbanization, though, there was little change in the availability of these programs. Until the early 1970s, Sweden had the lowest percentage of children in preschool education of almost any Western country.[60]

The weak development of early education programs reflects the lack of competition between religious and secular forces around the education of young children. Without serious contestation over state responsibility for these schools, there was no imperative to extend the education system beyond six- or seven-year-old children—the age at which primary school began.[61] French children could attend publicly funded schools by the age of two-and-a-half; the age of entry in Sweden was seven. Voluntary associations made some effort to provide kindergartens, but these were limited initiatives intended to provide middle- and upper-class parents with stimulating educational programs for their children. Charging fees and open for only a few hours a day, these programs were far from the free, publicly run programs available in France.[62]

State activism was shaping gender and familial relations in legal and other policy changes at the start of the twentieth century. Sweden was a pioneer in the development of family laws that assigned equal status to men and women.[63] Already by the end of the nineteenth century, Sweden had established the rights of married women to dispose of their property. Marriage reform laws in the first three decades of the twentieth century made spouses fully equal in marriage, raised the marital age (so that women would be fully independent before entering into marriage), allowed divorce by mutual consent, and made husband and wife equal property owners.[64] These changes were spurred by elite concerns about declining fertility. It was hoped that improving marriage in the eyes of women would lead to increased rates of marriage and child-bearing.[65] Another sign of the interventionist state came with a 1917 law that required men to recognize children born out of wedlock. Few other European countries at the time forced men to take responsibility for the fruits of their sexual activities.[66] By the 1940s, Sweden also had decriminalized homosexuality and liberalized abortion law; it was to be decades before other Western countries adopted similar reforms.[67]

The Swedish reforms were notable for a number of reasons. First, the reforms signified the penetration of the state into the private realm of family life. The general acceptance of these reforms signified a high degree of agreement that the state could engage in a restructuring of familial and gender relations in the name of larger social objectives. In addition, the individualization of women and acceptance of their having equal rights revealed the declining strength of religion. The Swedish Lutheran Church opposed the marriage reforms but had little influence by this period. The church apparently had few allies in politics either, as the reforms were not terribly controversial and passed without strong opposition.[68] By the early twentieth century, "rationality and science gradually came to replace religion as a base for legislation and moral legitimacy connected to marriage and sexuality."[69]

This growing recognition of women as individuals, and not as subordinates to husbands and families, was reflected in the development of early welfare state provisions, such as the old-age and disability insurance programs created in 1913. In most countries, women were either not entitled to these programs at all or got some entitlement through their husbands. In Sweden, women were individually entitled to these programs through their citizenship and not by their status as wives.[70] Although other elements of the early Swedish welfare state presumed and reinforced women's dependence on men, these early citizenship-based entitlements mitigated this dependency and, at least theoretically, held up women as individuals, independent of their familial relations.

Although the potential for an active state role in family policy was evident earlier in the century, population anxieties in the 1930s and 1940s reinforced state activism in family affairs. Sweden's birth rate had been declining for some decades, and by the early 1930s was the lowest in Western Europe.[71] Public authorities' response was not to plead for moral regeneration and a return to traditional values, but to convene a royal population commission that would scientifically evaluate the causes of and remedies for population decline. Following the policy recommendations of this and a future commission, Sweden created marriage loans to newlywed couples, built housing for large families with low incomes, gave free obstetric services to mothers, built child health centers, and, in 1948, created a national system of family allowances. Abortion was liberalized and contraception made more accessible on the grounds that giving people control over their fertility would encourage them to reproduce, and an income maintenance program was created for solo mothers.[72] Although the focus of family policy was on children's well-being, other measures improved the individual rights of women.

Early policy and legal changes indicate how an increasingly secular state was disrupting traditional, familial relations to promote the improved status of women. We can see the potential for state intervention in reshaping gender relations and affecting family life, although this had not yet taken place through the development of public child care or preschools. Although these services remained underdeveloped, legal reform and social entitlements affected the balance of gender relations and contributed to the individualization of women. Sweden's secular politics and society, combined with a tradition of statism in family policy, brought even greater changes to gender relations and family life in the 1960s and 1970s.

The Netherlands: Biconfessional Divisions and the Triumph of Religious Forces

Nineteenth-century Dutch society was split not only between religious and secularist forces, but also between competing religious denominations. Since the founding of the Kingdom of the Netherlands in 1814, the country has been divided between Protestants and Catholics, with Catholics constituting a large minority of between 35 and 40 percent of the population.[73] Most Protestants belonged to the Dutch Reformed Church, a Calvinist church that, by the nineteenth century, was fairly moderate in its theological doctrine. However, schisms within Dutch Protestantism gave rise to a vigorous orthodox movement that became an important actor in Dutch politics. Finally, as in the rest of Europe, the Enlightenment and the French Revolution generated a secular, rationalist challenge to organized religion. Liberals were the champions of this worldview and had grown into a powerful political force by mid-century.[74]

As in France, conflicts between these forces crystallized around education. Since the occupation of the country by Napoleon, the Netherlands had developed a centralized, state-run education system that transmitted the tempered form of Protestantism practiced by the ruling elites. The establishment of private schools required state permission, which especially constrained the growth of Catholic schools. When the 1848 constitution removed that requirement, the numbers of private schools increased, even without public funding.[75] However, the real challenge to the state-run system came from Orthodox Protestants, who objected to the vague Protestant curriculum of the state schools, and from liberals, who wanted a fully secular system. A liberal education law in 1857 made all state-run primary schools religiously neutral. This spurred an increase in the number of private schools founded by religious groups that, while receiving no public funds, were still subject to state regulations. A liberal education bill in the 1870s increased teachers' standards and salaries in an attempt to raise the cost of primary education for the non-state sector.[76]

By this time, there was a growing social and political mobilization around the "schools struggle," led by Orthodox Protestants. These were Protestants who had split from the Dutch Reformed Church and wanted the freedom and funds to set up their own schools. The leading figure of the day was

Abraham Kuyper, an Orthodox Calvinist who successfully mobilized political elites, clergy, and ordinary people to the cause. Catholics also opposed the move toward secular schools, but they lacked the political power of the Orthodox Protestants. They gained influence when they set aside historic grievances with Protestants and joined the push for publicly funded, privately provided schools.[77]

This alliance between Catholics and Orthodox Protestants enabled religious forces to triumph in the conflicts over education and gain a lasting hold over Dutch politics.[78] In 1887, Catholics and Orthodox Protestants won political power and enacted their own education bills. An 1889 law allowed non-state schools to have one-third of their costs covered by the state.[79] Over the next few decades, liberal and religious parties traded power, and subsidies for non-state schools expanded but remained incomplete. Finally, agreement was reached on the principle that all schools, public and private, should receive equal public funds. This agreement was enshrined in the constitution of 1917 and not only became the foundation of the Dutch education system, but also was part of the consociational settlement that has governed Dutch politics ever since.[80] Religious and other groups would be free to develop their own schools and welfare services and would receive public funds to do so:[81] schools would be publicly financed but largely privately run, often by religious organizations. Since the 1930s, roughly 30 percent of children have been in publicly run schools, compared to around 70 percent in the private system.[82]

The nature and resolution of these conflicts had numerous implications for Dutch educational and family policies. First, as in France, competition between religious and secular forces produced an expansion in the services available for children, including services for young children. Beginning in the mid-nineteenth century, religious organizations were founded to provide welfare and education services, including infant schools (*bewaarscholen*) for children aged two and above.[83] The result was an overall expansion of the programs available. The percentage of children in preschool programs was close to that of France; by the turn of the century, one-third of children between the ages of three and six were in either secular or religious programs, compared to 37 percent of similarly aged French children.[84] Access to preschool programs continued to grow in the twentieth century, particularly because there was great pressure on educational authorities to respond to any parental demands—otherwise, children might be forced to attend a school not of their parents' choice, which could reignite conflicts.[85]

The political strength of religious groups also shaped the way in which educational and social services were provided. Since the consociational settlement of the early twentieth century, voluntary organizations have played an intermediary role between the state and the family in the delivery of publicly funded services.[86] This system has its origins in religious thought and can be contrasted with the centralization championed by Left parties and, at certain points in history, by European liberals. For Catholics, voluntary-sector provision of education and social services is one dimension of the principle of subsidiarity, which does not foreclose state action but favors delegating educational and welfare services to lower levels of society. The Orthodox Protestant notion of "sovereignty in one's circle" is considerably more antistatist in that it holds God up as the highest authority, denying that authority or power to the state.[87] Yet, although the Orthodox Protestants often opposed social legislation, they still accepted public funds for the private provision of welfare and educational services. Between the 1880s and the Second World War, the number of voluntary organizations providing these services expanded rapidly. In the mid-1880s, there were around 200 voluntary associations created per year; by 1915, this number had jumped to 1,600 per year.[88]

With the rapid growth of the voluntary sector, Dutch society became "pillarized" into roughly four subcultural worlds: Catholic, Protestant, socialist, and liberal.[89] Each pillar consisted of, among other things, schools, sports and leisure associations, trade unions, and newspapers. The provision of social services also came to reflect this pillarization, with state funds flowing to associations from the different pillars that would actually provide the services. Voluntary organizations came to play a vital role in the organization of the Dutch welfare state, unlike the French or Swedish.[90] The creation of these self-enclosed worlds also promoted the transmission of the ideas of each group to current and future generations of their community. One consequence was a continuing high level of religiosity as people within the religious pillars absorbed the ideas and values of the surrounding community.

The strength of societal religiosity and the hegemony of religious forces in Dutch society helped preserve women's traditional roles. The place of women in the labor market was extremely limited compared to other

European countries at the time; in the early twentieth century, only 8 percent of married women were in paid employment, compared to 20 percent in France.[91] Although low rates of female workforce participation also reflected the slow pace of industrialization, conservative religious doctrine contributed to the strength of conservative gender ideologies in Dutch society. Catholics and Orthodox Protestants shared a rejection of liberal individualism and saw the family as the core unit of society. They therefore opposed policies or legal changes that would empower women as individuals, and women were denied legal personhood until decades after the Second World War.[92] For religious conservatives such as Kuyper, this was justified by women's natural vocation as mothers. As he wrote in 1914, "I base my premise on this state of affairs, which we did not create, but which was imposed upon us by God, that the Woman is not equal to the Man in public life."[93]

In the Netherlands, religiously based conflicts over education and the way in which they were resolved had a lasting effect on beliefs about the relationship between the state and the family. Because no one group could prevail and impose their vision of community and familial morality, the compromise was to support all groups that provide services within their own community. Publicly financed, privately provided programs became the norm in the Dutch welfare state. At the same, however, the hegemony of religious forces in Dutch society and politics was such that they sustained a patriarchal vision of gender roles and family life. Because of the power of religion in Dutch politics, this model was slow to change through much of the twentieth century.

The United States: Religious Pluralism and the Separation of Church and State

The roots of America's limited family policies lie in the tremendous religious diversity of the country and the early separation of church and state. This religious landscape contributed to the decentralization of matters of family morality and children's education to states, local communities, and the voluntary sector. Church and state were separated at the national level with the founding of the country in the late eighteenth century, making the United

States the first Western nation without an established church. The reason for the separation was neither anticlericalism nor a determination to eliminate the influence of religion in society, although the ideals of the French Revolution influenced Deists such as Thomas Jefferson. Rather, many realized that, given the colonies' religious diversity, no one denomination could impose itself as the sole religious authority, and that any effort to do so would create a repressive government.[94] In addition, nonconformist Protestant sects from England and other parts of Europe comprised many of the early settlers. Not only had they suffered as religious minorities living under an established church, but they also viewed faith as an intensely private experience. Their "radical individualism" also informed the drive for disestablishment and assured that the separation of church and state would extend beyond the federal government.[95] Although a number of states initially maintained links to one denomination, by the 1820s these ties were severed, and most churches held a purely private status.

The separation of church and state benefited organized religion, which thrived throughout the nineteenth century.[96] Protestant sects multiplied and grew in strength, while immigration from Germany, Italy, and Ireland swelled the numbers of Catholics in some parts of the country. Religion continued to be a vital element of American life as the Puritan spirit "roamed free" in society and a general Protestant outlook infused American politics.[97] Religious diversity contributed to the growth of civil society, the dynamism of which was a notable feature of the nineteenth century.[98] However, given the large number of denominations, voluntary organizations could not aggregate into peak organizations and pillars as in the Netherlands. Instead, the United States developed a decentralized and diverse community of charities, clubs, and associations that was largely independent of public funds.[99]

This complex and diverse religious landscape shaped family- and child-related policies in two conflicting ways. First, the separation of church and state contributed to a powerful strand of American political thought that favored localized power and control. The federal government generally avoided involvement in either the practice of religion or in what was intertwined with religious morality—the family. Family law remained a state government prerogative and took on substantial variations owing in part to the religious climate in which the law developed. The extreme decentralization of the American education system also is indicative of the belief that decisions about what values to inculcate in children should be determined at the local level. Most schools began as church-run or religiously based programs with extensive parental involvement. The role of national authorities in the development of the education system went no further than the provision of land grants to states, which they sold to pay for the development of schools.[100] State governments often assumed responsibility for school systems that had already developed locally.[101]

At the same time, however, the vitality of the Protestant sects and the tendency toward periodic religious revivals drove social and political movements rooted in religious identities. "Piestist" Protestant sects such as Baptists, Methodists, Congregationalists, and Presbyterians often displayed little compunction about intervening in the moral affairs of others.[102] From the abolitionists to the common school movement to the Prohibitionists and Progressives, these movements embodied a crusading spirit that could justify an expansion of public authority. Thus, the essential contradiction about the early separation of church and state in America is the fact that a moralizing, religious fervor frequently plays a significant role in American politics.[103] Since the nineteenth century, there has been an ongoing tension between these impulses—pluralism and decentralization of faith and related matters to the local or individual level, versus the drive to define and impose one moral standard for all.

These competing visions clashed in the nineteenth and early twentieth centuries over the expansion of the public education system. Anglo-Saxon evangelical Protestants were at the forefront of the movement to create a "common school" that would be public and available to all children within a certain age range.[104] This would mean greater state responsibility for school systems; it also implied some societal consensus about the values taught in these schools. One motivation of the common school movement was to counter the effects of immigration—particularly that of Irish, German, and Italian Catholics—on American identity.[105] Schools were not only to provide basic learning to children, but also to impart a set of common, American values. For many, there could be no other source for these values than the Protestant religion that they believed formed the bedrock of American society.[106] Rather than strip the public schools of religion, many common school advocates preferred that a nondenominational Christianity be taught. Horace Mann, the leader of the common school movement, advocated that children read the Bible without comment from their teachers—any biblical teaching would be at Sunday schools chosen by parents.[107]

Reading the King James Bible without comment might provide a common denominator among the diverse Protestant sects, but it was anathema to many Catholics. Not only did they object to the Protestant dimensions of the "nondenominational" public schools, but they also wanted curricula that explicitly reflected their own faith and values. Moreover, Catholics had benefited from the highly localized nature of the American education system because they often worked out agreements with local governments to provide funds for Catholic schools. The common school movement threatened to cut off public support for these programs and either force children into the public schools or collect taxes from parents who were paying for private education.[108]

The resulting battles between Catholics and Protestants shaped the evolution of the American education system and reinforced antistatist ideologies about child- and family-related policies. During the second half of the nineteenth century, ethnoreligious conflicts around education dominated local politics in some parts of the country.[109] The outcome of these disputes was neither the publicly funded, privately run schools found in the Netherlands, nor an extension of centralized control as occurred in France. Although public education expanded and was made more uniform in this period, strong resistance to centralized authority over education meant that local communities maintained financing and involvement through school boards.[110] One consequence of local control was that many public schools continued to use the Bible, have prayer in schools, and conduct other religiously based instruction per local preferences. A Supreme Court ruling banned such practices only in 1947.[111]

The American education system did not follow the French example of including younger children in the public schools. In some parts of the country, conflicts between religious groups spurred competition over certain kinds of child-related services and thus facilitated their expansion. In New York City, Catholic and Protestant child welfare organizations proliferated to assure the placement of orphaned children with families of the same faith.[112] By the mid-nineteenth century, Catholic churches across the country were determinedly constructing a parochial education system that would provide the needed services for their own children.[113] However, Protestants were content with the education system that they had and generally did not have to fear that their own children would be forced to attend a Catholic school. There was therefore little imperative to expand the public system to encompass younger children.

Throughout the nineteenth century, in fact, children below the age of five or six were progressively excluded from public education. Previously, three- or four-year-old children could be found in local primary schools, and special infant schools had been created in some cities.[114] By the nineteenth century, however, there was a growing backlash against the infant schools. With the spread of the bourgeois Victorian ideal of family life, many school advocates argued that young children belonged at home with their mothers. Not only were infant schools shut down, but young children were excluded from primary school systems.[115] The one relatively successful effort to extend the education system down to younger children came through the kindergarten movement.[116] These programs spread through the efforts of maternalist reformers in the latter quarter of the nineteenth century, slowly becoming incorporated in public education systems. By the turn of the century, kindergartens had gained wider support as a means of Americanizing new immigrants.[117] The expansion of these programs occurred in a decentralized fashion, however, and these schools had to compete with the regular primary school for funds. By 1912, only around 9 percent of kindergarten-aged children were in public kindergartens.[118]

The larger consequence of ethnoreligious conflicts in this period was that they produced a renewed determination to maintain local control over education and other family-related policies. The late nineteenth century and first decades of the twentieth was a period of ongoing conflict over the reach of state and federal power. Progressive reformers were often on the side of more interventionist public policy to redress social problems, although there also were strands of antistatism within the reformist camp. Nativist sentiment reinforced the call for greater government involvement in social issues because education and a range of social welfare programs were to ensure the Americanization of immigrants. However, the Progressives' drive to expand state authority over education, maternal and child health, and other family-related policies ran up against powerful opposition rooted in the ethnoreligious pluralism of American society.[119] Of course, opposition to expanded federal power encompassed a wide range of groups, ranging from corporations and other free market advocates to states' rights defenders in the South. To this coalition religious forces added intensity and vehemence on federal family policies and helped block government expansion in this area. Federal authority would ultimately increase in the decades following the New Deal, but family-related policies were still extremely circumscribed.

One example of the limits on family policies was the fate of initiatives during the 1920s to create a federal bureau of education, develop federally funded child and maternal health services, and impose restrictions on child labor. Catholics were particularly strong opponents of these initiatives, which they associated with the interventionist designs of the Progressive movement.[120] Catholic resistance to federal involvement in local affairs crystallized in the 1920s around the proposed federal education department. Many Catholics also opposed an amendment barring child labor and the Sheppard-Towner act, a measure that offered federal matching funds to states so that they could provide information on nutrition and hygiene to pregnant women and new mothers. The latter represented the threat of a federal movement to promote birth control, a prominent theme of some Progressive reformers.[121]

There were other powerful conservative currents taking shape at the grass roots—antisuffrage, anticommunist conservative groupings that were involved in the Red Scare of 1919–20 and red-baiting through the 1920s.[122] One strand of the "100 percent American" movement was a growing number of fundamentalist Protestants who had split off from the mainstream denominations. Although it originated in doctrinal disputes, the rift was deepened by the Scopes trial in 1925, over the teaching of evolution in public schools. The issue spurred the growth of a number of fundamentalist organizations, making the 1920s one of those periods in American history marked by a strong religious mobilization.[123] In the 1920s, these various currents of anti-statism came together to successfully lobby against the Sheppard-Towner act, child labor amendment, and federal education department.

Antipathy to federal family policies was so deeply rooted that there was little consideration of family benefits or other broad-based family policy measures among the New Deal Reformers. A few scattered voices argued for a system of generalized income support that took into account family size and thus family need.[124] Such systems were being instituted in Western

Europe at this time or would be part of the expansion of the welfare state after the Second World War. In the United States, the strongly held view both before and after the war was that such policies interfered in the private sphere of the family. Efforts in the 1950s to develop a national system of family allowances repeatedly failed.[125] A common argument against these measures was that they sought to promote increases in the birth rate, which represented a degree of social engineering that was unacceptable to many.[126]

At the same time, however, government involvement in the lives of a particular set of families—those living well below the poverty line—was well established by the 1930s. Progressive activists often had made it their business to moralize their charitable charges. One of the major accomplishments of maternalist reformers were mothers' pension programs, which employed "suitable home" tests and other ways to scrutinize the moral fitness of recipients.[127] The Aid to Dependent Children program established in the 1930s maintained these stigmatizing elements in the hope of discouraging single motherhood. State-run child welfare systems also intervened in family life in the name of protecting child well-being. Once families were labeled dysfunctional, the arm of the state could reach into this most personal sphere. The most extreme form of intervention in people's private lives was the forced sterilization, in some states, of the poor, incarcerated, mentally ill, or those otherwise deemed genetically "unfit."[128]

On the whole, however, the majority of families were left to do as they wanted with the financial means they had; unless families reached a particular level of desperation, there would be no state assistance but also little state meddling with their affairs. This also meant that fixed gender roles were not inscribed as explicitly in the programs of the welfare state as they were in the Netherlands, Sweden, or France at that time. Certainly, the social security system was structured along male-breadwinner assumptions. The closing of wartime day care centers after the Second World War and the establishment of mandatory joint taxation of income also created financial obstacles to married women's employment.[129] A host of local practices, such as the firing of women after marriage or pregnancy, often went unchallenged. However, there were fewer direct subsidies of the male-breadwinner family than in the European welfare states of the time. Traditional family roles were widely assumed, but they were not codified in the programs and policies of the welfare state to the same degree.

Religious Divisions and the Politics of Mothers' Employment

Historic patterns of religious cleavages and church-state relations had last-ing consequences for the politics of mothers' employment. One effect was institutional: this period saw the development of early family and educa-tional programs that embodied beliefs about the relationship between the state and the family. Embedded in policy-making machinery and in institu-tionalized relationships between the state and religious civil society, these beliefs influenced responses to new policy issues later in the twentieth cen-tury. These early debates also shaped ideologies about gender roles and the family by influencing the way in which religion was incorporated into polit-ical life, strengthening conservative ideologies for decades to come.

THE LEGACIES OF EARLY PUBLIC POLICIES FOR CHILDREN AND FAMILIES

By the 1930s, Sweden, France, the Netherlands, and the United States were developing distinct approaches to child and family policy that reflected ei-ther an activist or a reticent state role in family life. These approaches to the family live on through the institutional apparatuses being established in this period and in the wide consensus forming among the political class about the responsibility of the central state for the family. A more direct policy legacy comes from the nature of early childhood education systems, the roots of which lie in this period. These systems generated constituencies of parents and providers that would support the expansion of these programs, although the ability of preschools to help working mothers has been complicated by their conceptualization as educational services.

In France and Sweden, the central state had assumed a direct role in child and family policy by the start of the twentieth century that became institu-tionalized in state policy and accepted across the political spectrum. In France, this commitment was evidenced by the centralized public education system, which offered services to children from the age of three.[130] The state also was assuming greater responsibility for the well-being of younger chil-dren, although this was less embedded in the structures of the French state. It was only after 1945 that a universal system of maternal and child health was established and the national government assumed oversight for the fam-ily benefits system. However, by the interwar years there already was wide agreement among the political elite that the state should reduce the financial burdens on families and promote children's health and welfare.[131] Similarly, in Sweden there was widespread acceptance among political elites that the state bore responsibility for the well-being of the nation's families.[132] As in France, Sweden had created a centralized education system run by a national education ministry, although public schools were open only to children aged seven or older. During the 1930s and 1940s, the state's responsibility was extended to maternal and child health, income supports to families, housing, and other forms of assistance, including some measures to help single mothers.[133]

In the Netherlands, there was considerably greater aversion to the notion of a national family policy; responsibility for family affairs was left instead to voluntary associations in each subcommunity in Dutch society.[134] Although education was nationally funded and the central education ministry made sure that all schools met certain standards, the majority of schools were run by private, nonprofit entities.[135] The voluntary sector also had a guaranteed role as provider of publicly funded welfare programs, leaving an intermediary layer between the state and the family. The idea that child and family policies should largely be the responsibility of the subcommunities, and not the national government, was not simply a widely shared belief among political elites: it was central to the constitutional settlement of 1917, which put an end to decades of religious strife. This approach to family policy was thus entrenched in Dutch politics and shaped responses to a range of family-related issues throughout the twentieth century.

The United States had engaged in a significant expansion of federal bureaucratic capacity by the Second World War, but this did not include widely available benefits or services for families. The New Deal focused on the issues of old age and male unemployment, and there was no support for, or even any consideration of, European-style family allowances or other universalist measures for families.[136] As a result, the United States did not develop the institutions or agencies that could be a force for expansive family policies later on. The one agency responsible for children's policy—the Children's Bureau—had lost power since the repeal of the Sheppard-Towner act and was even excluded from administering the New Deal's means-tested program for families, Aid to Dependent Children.[137] In the decades following the Second World War, the bureau's influence continued to decline.[138]

In addition, the public education system remained highly decentralized, with limited involvement of federal authorities.

The one exception was the temporary expansion of federal involvement in preschool programs during the 1930s and 1940s. The Emergency Nursery School program of the 1930s offered federal funds for preschool education as a way to put unemployed teachers, janitors, and other school officials back to work. The funds continued to flow in the 1940s to provide services for women working in wartime factories. However, as Sonya Michel's analysis shows, these programs were not integrated into state education bureaucracies, but were controlled by temporary agencies—first the Works Progress Administration during the New Deal, and then the War Public Services Bureau after 1943.[139] Lacking a strong institutional base, these preschools were closed after their short-term purpose was achieved, despite the protests of women in some cities to keep them open.[140] The expansion of publicly funded preschools and kindergartens in the postwar era was slow because most programs were run by private nonprofit or for-profit organizations, usually without much public funding.[141]

The fragmented early education system in the United States contrasts markedly with the integration of preschool education into the national education ministry in France. Although these programs were not obligatory, French officials came to view the preschool as an essential aspect of the education system and to believe that parents had a right to these programs as much as to the primary schools. In addition, the inclusion of these programs in the education system meant that the teachers staffing these programs would be civil servants, trained and paid much like their counterparts in the primary schools. They would therefore share the strong professional identity held by French primary and secondary school teachers.[142] This highly unionized and politically active group continually pushed for the expansion of the preschool system.

The impact of preschool systems on later policies for mothers' employment was complicated by the largely educational orientation of these programs. Preschool teachers and advocates often sought to distance themselves and their services from custodial day care. Education was seen as a valued service for children of all socioeconomic strata, but day care was stigmatized by its association with charity and poverty.[143] Because many in the preschool community opposed mothers' employment as harmful to children's well-being, they kept the opening hours limited so that early education programs would not induce mothers to work outside the home.[144] In France, this had less impact owing to the long school day (often 8:30–4:30, closed one day or afternoon per week). Still, preschool teachers opposed changing the school hours or their own jobs to try and keep their profession from degenerating into mere "care giving" rather than education.[145]

The conservatism of many in the preschool profession meant that entrenching early education as the dominant form of services for children aged three to six would not always help working parents. Dutch preschools expanded rapidly after the Second World War as part of the educational system, which was necessitated by the way the schools conflict was settled earlier in the century. Because children had the right to attend a school of any denomination, once a given number of parents requested the creation of a school, the state had to build one or else risk reigniting conflicts over education.[146] Thus, by the 1960s, the Netherlands was one of the few countries in Western Europe that did not suffer shortages in the preschool sector. As chapter 3 will describe, however, reforms in the 1950s rendered these services considerably less helpful for working parents by raising the entrance age from three to four, forbidding children to stay during lunch, and shortening school hours.[147] By matching the structures of the primary education system, preschool education became less amenable to the needs of working parents.

In Sweden, the *absence* of a significant preschool sector shaped the course of child care policy in the 1960s and 1970s by weakening the constituency of conservative voluntary organizations and preschool educators that opposed full-time preschools. This small sector of Swedish preschool educators fought in vain against government moves to promote full-day child care over the part-time preschool in the mid-1960s.[148] Pushing the teachers' concerns aside, Swedish policy makers abolished state support of part-time nursery schools and put new requirements in place that child care centers had to be open for at least five hours a day and provide cooked food and nap facilities in order to receive state reimbursement.[149] Rather than perpetuate the division between day care and early education programs found in most countries—with their different schedules, staffing, and curriculum—the Swedish state began developing a unified set of services for all children below the mandatory school age that combined educational and care-taking functions. Chapter 3 will discuss the forces driving this new policy, but the lack of an entrenched sector of early education programs helped make this unified approach possible.

Religious cleavages shaped the ideological structure of party systems in Western Europe by influencing the constituencies, ideological orientations, and competitors of political parties. In the United States, these effects are similar but are complicated by the coalitional nature of American parties; factions within the parties came to espouse particular views on social and moral questions and to vie for influence over these issues. In both the United States and Western Europe, these political parties and factions held distinct values regarding gender roles and the appropriate relationship between the state and the family. As chapter 3 will show, these ideological orientations came to play a major role in shaping child care and other work-family policies during the welfare state's golden age of expansion.

One of the most important consequences of religious mobilization during the nineteenth and early twentieth centuries was the creation of parties of religious defense. In the Netherlands, the schools' struggle produced a widespread mobilization of Protestant and Catholic forces, and the formation of religiously based political parties that dominated Dutch politics through most of the twentieth century.[150] The ideological orientation of these parties reflected their constituency of religious voters, a constituency that often crossed class lines. Christian parties often supported redistributive policy—which appealed to their working-class voters—while also seeking to preserve traditional familial and gender relations. In the decades following the Second World War, the Catholic party played a significant role in developing a model of social provision that reinforced the male-breadwinner family.[151]

In Sweden, the relative lack of religious conflict meant that there was little political mobilization of religious groups. Not only did religion fail to become a major cleavage in Swedish politics, but the early and continued secularization of Swedish society attenuated the strength of religion in Swedish politics as a whole.[152] Although conservative parties continued to get a high percentage of the religious vote, the overall pool of religious voters shrank dramatically in the first half of the twentieth century. By the

1970s, Sweden was one of the most secular countries in the world, and religious parties played nearly no role in politics.

Christian Democratic parties also failed to develop very successfully in France, although for different reasons. Catholics had lost many of France's major political clashes around religion, and for many years they experienced the repression of their schools and voluntary associations. The resulting hostility of many Catholics to the secular republic made them slow to accept representative government. The marriage of Christianity and democracy so essential to the formation of Christian Democratic parties was slow and problematic.[153] Catholic influence over politics was not entirely eliminated, however; a Catholic subculture persisted in some regions and gave rise to conservative family associations. These associations gained some influence after 1945, yet were unable to monopolize political debates about family policy or mothers' employment. The religious cleavage, though not eliminated, was submerged and lacked clear representation in French politics.

The fact that religion did not become the basis for any one political party in the United States did not remove religion from politics. Since the nineteenth century, the role of religion in public life has shifted between two poles. On the one hand, the separation of church and state formally removed religion from the public sphere and decentralized questions of family morality to the local, or even individual, level, affording individuals a good deal of freedom to determine their own faith, moral code, and way of life. One implication for gender relations was that there was room for women to develop their independent identities and lives. Certainly, traditional notions of women's roles were prevalent through much of the twentieth century. Yet, relative to Western European countries, the ideology of the dominant political parties was not dedicated to reinforcing these roles.

On the other hand, the vitality of American religion is such that it repeatedly spills over into the public sphere. From the abolitionist and temperance movements of the nineteenth century to the civil rights and school prayer movements in the twentieth, religiously based movements have played a periodic yet significant role in American politics. Of particular relevance for gender and family issues has been the political mobilization of evangelical or fundamentalist political groups that espouse conservative social values. These groups have never been able to dominate American politics, but they have often served as an important coalition partner in particular policy campaigns.

Since the 1970s, conservative religious groups have come to play an increasingly important role within the Republican Party in defining stances on gender- and family-related issues.

The different ways in which religion was incorporated into political systems had larger consequences for the nature of party competition. In Sweden, the absence of a cross-cutting "values" cleavage based on religion meant that the working class was more unified than in continental Europe. The lack of a values cleavage enabled the Scandinavian Social Democrats to construct a more unified political base. We also can view the lack of religiously based mobilization as enabling the greater centralization of the Scandinavian states, something that would be advantageous for Social Democrats. Across Europe, Left parties often favored state intervention over subsidiarity or deference to civil society, and the Scandinavian Social Democrats were better able to realize this vision.

In the Netherlands, a cross-cutting religious cleavage fragmented the working class, which meant that Social Democrats faced constant competition with religious parties for the working class vote. One result was that the Left adopted an accommodationist stance toward the churches, seeking to woo religious workers by toning down their traditional anticlericalism. Moreover, given the strength of moral conservatism in Dutch society, the Left party could hardly serve as a font of radical ideas on gender and the family. By contrast, the French Left maintained its traditional anticlericalism throughout the twentieth century. Since the Dreyfus affair, the French Socialist Party resolutely embraced a pro-republican, anticlerical stance, an attitude that made the Left more suspicious of the familialist public policies championed by Catholics. Ultimately, French Left parties, in a departure from the conservatism of Left parties in countries such as Germany and the Netherlands, became champions of women workers.

In the United States, the impact of religious conservatives reverberated beyond the constituency of sympathetic voters. These groups played a central role in the realignment of political forces in the 1970s, when the Democratic Party became the party of feminism and civil rights and the Republican Party abandoned its previous support for both. In the process, social conservatives successfully politicized a host of gender- and family-related issues. As a result, efforts to expand the welfare state on behalf of working mothers faced fierce controversy over gender roles and whether the national government should be involved in family affairs. In response, policy makers fell back on a well-worn approach to contentious family issues—decentralizing them to lower levels of society such that families would make their own determinations about work and family with little direct assistance from public authorities.

Conclusion

Through much of the nineteenth century, one of the major issues in Western countries was the role of organized religion in society and politics. In many countries, the expansion of state authority and development of democratic political systems spurred religious groups to mobilize in an attempt to protect their interests in the political sphere. As this chapter shows, different patterns of church-state relations and religious cleavages influenced the shape of these forces and their lasting influence. The resolutions of these disputes also shaped conceptions of state responsibility for the family. Although secular-religious conflicts differed in both Sweden and France, both arrived at a similar end point—the expansion of central state responsibility for children's education and family well-being. In the United States and the Netherlands, different patterns of religious pluralism led to the decentralization of authority over child welfare and family morality to lower levels of society. This decentralization went much further in the United States than in the Netherlands owing to the direct influence of religiously based political forces over politics in the Netherlands. In both countries, however, a rich sector of voluntary organizations formed an intermediary layer between the state and society, providing many child- and family-related services.

As the succeeding chapters show, these cleavages over religion had an enduring influence on the politics of social provision. Both the early policy structures put in place and the nature and power of organized political forces affected the development of the welfare state in the post-1945 period, shaping the gendered contours of the welfare state in ways that either reinforced or undermined the male-breadwinner model of social relations.

Employment Policies for Mothers During the "Golden Age" of the Welfare State, 1945–1975

Scholars often describe the three decades following the close of the Second World War as the "golden age" of the welfare state. As rapid economic growth and high employment rates filled state coffers with tax revenues, governments built large and generous welfare states that aimed to meet a range of human needs. There was tremendous optimism about the ability of state policy to smooth out business cycles and cushion the population from the various risks to health, income, and well-being. Particular assumptions about gender relations also permeated the politics and societies of this golden age. Political parties from across the ideological spectrum endorsed the notion of men as breadwinners and women as full-time caregivers, a model of family life that the welfare state sustained and reinforced. Nearly all parties presumed that full-time maternal care was best for children and that social policy should help men support their families on one income.

By the late 1960s and early 1970s, however, labor shortages, growing rates of female workforce participation and the demands of new social movements helped propel the question of mothers' employment onto the political agenda. The response of governments to these new demands varied markedly. In Sweden, governments not only increased child care funding, but also adopted other policies that substantially eroded the financial viability of the male-breadwinner model. French policy makers also altered family policy to provide greater support for working mothers, although they were more cautious than in Sweden about encouraging mothers to work for pay. In the United States and the Netherlands, family policies hardly changed. The question of whether governments should encourage mothers to work outside the home either failed to become part of the political agenda or, if it did, reform efforts came to naught. At most, there were increases in part-day preschool programs, expanded day care subsidies for the poor, and, in the case of the United States, tax incentives for the use of private child care.

Why did these countries adopt such different policies? One precondition for policies to promote mothers' employment was widespread acceptance that the state should play a role in shaping the lives of a nation's families. As chapter 2 showed, patterns of religious cleavages and church-state relations affected beliefs about the appropriate relationship between the state and the family, creating an activist state tradition in both Swedish and French family policy and a more reticent state approach in the Netherlands and the United States. Although in Sweden and France the dominant question was *how* the state should act to affect family life, there was far less consensus on the state's role in the Netherlands and the United States, with particularly heated opposition to national family policies in the United States.

Policies affecting mothers' employment not only reflected institutionalized patterns of state-family relations, but also were driven by views on the acceptability of changing gender roles. The growth of women's workforce participation at a time of labor shortages helped put the issue of mothers' employment on the political agenda. Feminists and other activist women in trade unions and political parties also were critical agenda setters who helped draw attention to child care, parental leave, and other policies to support mothers' employment. However, the ability of these voices to have an impact hinged on the larger political environment within which they were operating. Where socially conservative forces were weak or constrained, governments were more likely to adopt programs that helped wage-earning mothers. Where conservative groups were dominant or highly mobilized, however, controversies about motherhood impeded state-supported programs for working parents.

Thus, Christian Democratic parties were politically dominant in the Netherlands and helped prevent much change in policies on mothers' employment, whereas the weakness of these parties in France moved center-right parties toward a more gender-egalitarian vision. Although pragmatic and at times limited in their policy stance, French center-right parties accepted the growth of mothers' employment and adopted measures to support this trend. In Sweden, the absence of a cross-cutting "values" or religious cleavage in the political system enabled the Swedish Social Democrats to forge a new, gender-egalitarian vision for public policy, one that would appeal to the growing strata of middle class, two-earner families. Finally, in the United States, a growing movement of social conservative forces—fueled in part by the political mobilization of conservative Christians—politicized gender and family questions, attacking policies such as federal child care as an undue interference in the market, an incursion into the family sphere, and discrimination against full-time homemakers.

Gender and the Welfare State's Golden Age

The pinnacle of the male-breadwinner model in Western societies came in the era after the Second World War, with both economic forces and public policies reinforcing the notion that men should be breadwinners and women should be full-time caregivers. Although the traditional family was a cultural ideal for many decades prior to the 1950s, economic realities precluded its realization for any but upper-class families. Many working-class families needed two incomes to survive, and mothers often remained in the workforce or were heavily involved in family-owned farms and businesses. However, the rapid economic growth of the 1950s and 1960s, coupled with greater levels of social protection and higher wages, enabled more working-class men to support their families on one income. The participation of married women in the workforce was extremely low (table 3.1).

Social policy in this period reflected and helped sustain the male-breadwinner model of social relations. This was evident in policies such as mandatory joint taxation of income, which discouraged mothers' employment; high male wages assured through negotiated wage agreements or

TABLE 3.1
Women's participation in the labor force by marital status,
early 1950s

	Married	Single
Austria	32.5	53.9
Belgium	15.4	45.8
Denmark	27.2	66.5
France	32.5	58.4
FRG	25.0	79.3
Great Britain	22.5	73.0
Netherlands	10.0	60.0
Norway	5.4	61.5
Sweden	14.5	63.0
USA	21.6	50.6

SOURCE: International Labour Office, *Women Workers in a Changing World* (Geneva: ILO, 1963), 35.

Figure is the percentage of economically active women among women aged 15 and older.

social conventions; eligibility for social security programs that reflected the assumption of female reliance on male incomes; and, in some countries, generous family allowance programs.[1] Day care policy also revealed the strength of these views, as few countries offered child care for any but very poor families. The dominant assumption was that children required full-time maternal care to develop properly, and that state-provided child care was appropriate only for children from abusive or "dysfunctional" homes. Such views were underpinned by the work of the psychiatrist John Bowlby, whose studies of psychologically damaged orphans from the Second World War inspired fears about the nefarious consequences of "maternal deprivation."[2]

All four countries shared these views, but there were differences in the degree to which social policy actively reinforced the male-breadwinner model. In Sweden, for example, joint taxation and the lack of child care strongly discouraged mothers' employment.[3] However, the right of married women to work was established in a 1939 law banning the dismissal of employees due to marriage, pregnancy, or childbirth.[4] In the Netherlands, by contrast, female civil servants and teachers lost their jobs when they got married; the practice was formally abolished in 1957 but continued for at least another decade in other sectors of the economy.[5] Another difference lay in the financial rewards provided to single-earner families. In the United States, joint taxation and a large personal exemption for dependents were the main financial supports for the male-breadwinner model, whereas France and the Netherlands offered both tax incentives and generous family benefits to one-earner families.[6] France, for example, had a specific benefit for single-earner, two-adult families.[7] Although there were similar male-breadwinner assumptions in the United States, they were less overtly enshrined in public policy.

The lack of subsidized and affordable day care also strongly discouraged mothers from working outside the home. In all four countries, publicly funded day care was limited to poor families. In Sweden, a series of parliamentary commissions in the 1930s and 1940s debated whether the state should subsidize child care for all, but the politically dominant Social Democratic Party (SAP) rejected the idea.[8] Throughout the 1950s and part of the 1960s, the official discourse on day care held that mothers should care for their children at home; there were only a small number of centers available for low-income families. In the Netherlands, many believed that child care was "immoral" in a developed country, and it was associated with totalitarian and communist regimes.[9]

Some preschool programs were available in all four countries, and parental demand for these services grew throughout the 1950s and 1960s. Table 3.2 shows that by 1970, access to programs was most widespread in France and the Netherlands. In many countries, these programs had a primarily educational function and were open for only part of the day or part of the week, rather than being organized around the schedules of working parents. In the Netherlands, schools ran from 9:00 A.M. to 12:00 P.M., had a two-hour lunch break during which children were expected to go home, and then had two more hours in the afternoon. The French *école maternelle* differed in that its schedule matched the long day of the primary school. In some areas, schools also would be open both before and after school hours, in order to better match parents' work schedules.[10] The *école maternelle* was unique in that it was free of charge, being seen as part of the regular public education system. Although the program was primarily valued for its educational content, some parents did see these services as a form of day care, putting children as young as two and a half in these programs.[11]

There were also some interesting differences in the availability of maternity leave and benefits. In both France and Sweden, paid maternity leaves were part of a larger set of state policies to protect maternal and child health. In Sweden, maternity leave was first created in 1937 and paid at a low flat rate. It expanded in 1954 and again in 1962 until it was a six-month leave paid at the same rate as sickness benefits.[12] The Netherlands also enacted a maternity

TABLE 3.2
Percentage of children in preschool, 1970–71

	AGE OF CHILD				
	2	3	4	5	6
France	15	55	84	100	School
Netherlands	0	0	80	94	School
Sweden	2	2	2	11	43
United States	Na	Na	20	62 (+11% in primary school)	School

SOURCES: Martin Woodhead, *Pre-School Education in Western Europe: Issues, Policies, and Trends* (London: Longman, 1979), 4; Bernard Trouillet, "L'education préscolaire: Quelques aspects et problèmes internationaux," *International Review of Education* 16 (1970–71): 12.

leave early in the twentieth century. The United States lacked even an unpaid leave, in part because the push for maternity leaves and benefits became intertwined with the drive for national health insurance. Opposition to greater national involvement in health care thus helped sink these proposals.[13]

At the very time that the male-breadwinner model seemed hegemonic across most Western countries, structural economic changes were gnawing at its foundations. Rapid economic growth in the 1950s and 1960s produced labor shortages in many countries, leading employers and governments to encourage mothers of older children to return to work. Expanding employment in either the private or the public sector also pulled women into paid work. In Sweden, the growth of the welfare state created a huge sector of white-collar jobs that were especially attractive to women.[14] Although many of these jobs were in the private sector in the United States, the tertiarization of the American economy also spurred the growth of women's employment.

By the early to mid-1970s, these structural changes had helped put the issues of child care and parental leave on the political agenda. It is important to note, however, that not all countries faced the same kinds of economic pressures. By the early 1970s, France, Sweden, and the United States were strikingly similar in their rates of women's employment (figure 3.1). Although employment rates would diverge in the 1970s and 1980s, owing in part to the policies they enacted during this period, when the question of mothers' employment first came on the agenda, these three countries were relatively similar in their rates of women's employment. In the Netherlands, by contrast, women's workforce participation was substantially lower and would remain so

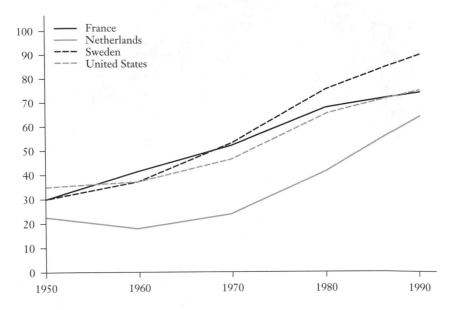

Figure 3.1   Percentage of women age 25–39 in paid employment, 1950–90
   SOURCE: International Labour Organization, Labour Statistics Database (Geneva, 1998–2004).

until the 1990s. The reasons for this will be discussed below, but here it is important to observe that the Netherlands experienced less pressure for policy change than the other three countries. Because of the low proportion of mothers in paid work, there was less demand for child care, parental leave, or other measures to help wage-earning mothers, although feminists did try to raise the issue.

How did these four countries respond to the rise of female employment and the pressures brought by the feminist movement? In tracing the actions of governments in this period, we can see the way new social pressures were filtered through distinct systems of partisan competition and existing repertoires of education and family policy.

Sweden: Statism, Secularism, and Gender Equality

Sweden made an abrupt shift in public policies toward working parents in the 1970s, creating a generous parental leave, allowing shorter work hours for parents, mandating individual taxation (which discourages one-earner families), and making massive investments in public child care. What is notable about Swedish policy in this period is that it was not simply a reactive effort to support women who worked outside the home. Rather, Swedish policy makers adopted transformative public policies that not only accepted the reality of changing gender roles and family forms, but also sought to remake society into one in which all women were in paid employment and men and women equally shared responsibilities for care and paid work.

Most explanations for these gender-egalitarian policies emphasize the political power of the Social Democratic Party (SAP), which was the dominant party in coalition governments from 1932 to 1976 and then returned to power in the early 1980s. Certainly, the SAP's enthusiasm for redistributive public policy was such that state-led solutions to social problems were favored over market-based approaches. As Jonas Hinnfors has argued, SAP leaders approached gender questions from the standpoint of the party's class-based egalitarianism, enabling it to incorporate a "new" social issue into its existing ideological framework.[15] Yet, the question remains: why did the SAP decide to support mothers' employment in the early 1970s when Social Democratic parties in much of Europe were slow to do the same? Ultimately, all Left parties in Europe have moved toward this orientation, yet the Swedish Social Democrats were on the vanguard of a new view of gender relations. In adopting this approach, party leaders ignored those within the party and labor movement who believed that public policy should favor male breadwinners and help mothers be at home. Finally, Social Democratic Party dominance alone did not assure a successful shift in public policy everywhere, for an equally powerful Left party in Norway did enact the same kinds of policies in this period.

Other accounts argue that the Social Democratic shift on maternal employment was due to labor shortages and/or the mobilization of women within trade unions and the SAP. It is true that labor shortages in the 1960s helped produce agreement among both labor unions and employers on the merits of female employment over immigration.[16] Nonetheless, the timing of labor shortages does not correspond with the shift in Swedish policy. The greatest labor shortages were in the 1960s, but major investments in child care only began in the 1970s, at which time a host of other measures were adopted to encourage women's employment. By that point, however, the economy had cooled, making industrialists less interested in promoting women's employment.[17] Business leaders were most concerned about labor shortages in the manufacturing sector, in which few women worked.[18]

Women's activism did contribute to the shift in the Social Democratic Party's orientation, without definitively moving the party toward a pro–women's employment stance. By the early 1960s, a wide-ranging debate about sex roles had begun that not only challenged the notion that motherhood should be a woman's main vocation in life, but also called upon fathers to increase their engagement in caring duties.[19] Women also played a central role in highlighting the issue of working motherhood, lobbying for child care and parental leave both inside and outside political parties and trade unions.[20] Of particular importance was the report of a commission chaired by Alva Myrdal, a powerful member of the Social Democratic Party who had long been at the forefront of debates about child care, women's rights, and family policy. The 1969 report, entitled *Towards Equality*, advocated reforms to ensure greater equality in Swedish society, including child care, parental leave, and tax reform.[21]

One direct consequence of the lobbying from within was the reform of the tax code from joint to mandatory individual taxation. Joint taxation generally favors one-earner families and discourages women's employment, especially in a context of steep marginal tax rates that "punish" the second income, which is piled on the first.[22] Mandatory individual taxation removes those benefits from single-earner families and encourages both members of a couple to work for pay. Individual taxation was discussed periodically through the 1960s but was not widely favored, particularly because it would impose a major tax increase on families with only one earner. Nonetheless, a small group of women pushed the issue and influenced the report of a 1969 government commission that called for the change.[23] Individual taxation was adopted in 1971, and it gave a large boost to women's employment by making full-time caregiving financially costly.[24]

In general, however, the lobbying of activists is not enough to drive a policy shift as profound as that which occurred in the early 1970s. Male party and union leaders would be unlikely to embrace such a major policy change unless they believed that it could yield electoral rewards. We must look at the larger political environment facing political leaders, including the parties with which they had to compete and the ideologies these parties espoused about gender roles and the relationship between the state and the family. This political environment reflected deeper structural forces—namely, the way in which religion had shaped the structure of partisan competition around questions of social values, and the legacies of past family policies.

One important dimension of Swedish politics was acceptance among the major political parties of the idea that the state should be engaged in family policy. As chapter 2 showed, the Swedish state had been active in child and family policy since the start of the twentieth century. The early fusion of church and state had facilitated the transfer of responsibility for the family from religious to secular authority and minimized the growth of a religiously based voluntary sector that would challenge the state's role in family life. This church-state fusion and the lack of a voluntary sector enabled the creation of a centralized system of primary education, reforms in family law that sought to remake domestic gender relations, and, by the 1940s, family support policies, when the dominant question was not whether the state should be engaged in assuring the well-being of the nation's families, but rather what form this intervention should take.[25] As two Swedish scholars of early education policy have argued, "The trust placed in the state to integrate the private domain into state policies has been far greater in Sweden than in any other western democracy."[26]

The other critical factor shaping debates about mothers' employment was the structuring of partisan competition along class lines without the cross-cutting values cleavage that is common in continental Europe. This feature of the Swedish party system reflected the historic weakness of religious cleavages in Swedish society and politics, which precluded the development of strong religiously based parties. A small Christian Democratic Party (KD), which was formed in 1964 in reaction to the pronounced secularization of Swedish society, has been the strongest advocate in the political system for the male-breadwinner model. Yet, the KD garnered less than 2 percent of the vote through the 1970s and failed to gain seats in parliament until 1991. Rapid secularization in the twentieth century further eroded the prevalence of conservative social values. By the 1970s, Sweden was one of the most secular countries in the world, with extremely low rates of regular church attendance (see figure 3.2). The conservative familialism prevalent in much of continental Europe evaporated early in Sweden, as the decline of religious belief produced more liberal attitudes about the family and support for feminist ideas.[27]

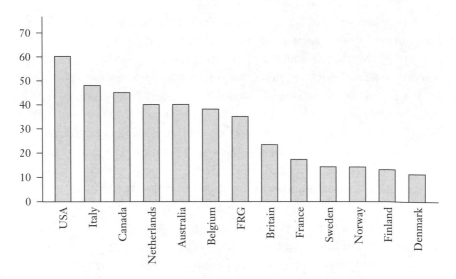

Figure 3.2   Percentage of the population that frequently attends church, 1981
SOURCE: World Values Survey, 1981.
Frequent church attendance is defined as once a month or more.

The secular nature of both society and politics enabled the SAP to reach out to a growing constituency of white-collar women while keeping the blue-collar voters that often held more traditional views of gender roles. Originally, the SAP was a working-class party with close ties to the unions that organize workers in the manufacturing sector. Since the late 1950s, however, the SAP had been making inroads into the middle class as the decline of the industrial sector made it imperative that the SAP widen its class basis. The future of Social Democratic power lay in its ability to maintain a cross-class coalition of voters.[28] Women were important to this strategy, because a significant source of Social Democratic support lay in the expanding stratum of female public-sector workers whose livelihoods were tied to the welfare state. By 1976, only 18 percent of women worked in manufacturing, while 28 percent were in tertiary employment and 50 percent worked for the public sector.[29]

Efforts to reach out to middle-class working women created tensions within the SAP: many party members viewed child care and other policies for working women as a bourgeois concern.[30] Many Social Democrats, including some female party activists, instead favored a home care allowance that would enable mothers to be at home for several years and care for their own children.[31] While this did not necessarily mean that these Social Democrats opposed policies that would help working mothers, it was indicative of the view that many working-class women would just as soon have the financial means to be at home, caring for their children, rather than working in difficult jobs.[32]

Given these tensions, the absence of a strong religious cleavage in Swedish politics was crucial to the ability of the SAP to knit together its cross-class coalition. The working class voted overwhelming for the SAP, rather than being divided by religion, as was the case in many continental European countries.[33] This solidarity left the SAP room to maneuver as it tried to draw in other groups, such as the growing middle class. Moreover, in competing for votes, the SAP did not have to tussle with a Christian Democratic party that might politicize family policy by tapping social conservative views in the public.

Of particular importance was the fact that the main competitors of the Social Democrats for centrist voters were the Liberals. This party drew much support from the educated women who were increasingly taking up paid work.[34] Reflecting the interests of this constituency, the Liberals were supportive of female employment and gender equality policies. Competition between Social Democrats and Liberals over this growing group of voters helped bring the Social Democrats around to a more supportive stance on this issue. Particularly because Social Democrats were able to frame child care and other social supports in class terms, they could simultaneously appeal to their blue-collar base and the growing stratum of white-collar workers.[35]

This is not to say that there were no advocates for the male-breadwinner family: both the center and conservative parties supported this model. However, although the center party came to advocate a home care allowance for mothers at home—a reflection of its rural constituency—conservatives were slow to embrace the idea because they opposed state intervention in family life. This division within the non-socialist bloc prevented advocates from unifying around a home care allowance.[36] There also was no clear Left-Right split among advocates for mothers' employment: both Liberals and Social Democrats came to favor child care and other supportive policies by the early 1970s. Thus, by 1972, the SAP party had made a major change in orientation, abandoning its earlier support for a home care allowance and embracing both expanded child care and a shorter, well-paid parental leave that both women and men could take.[37]

The influence of political secularization on these policies becomes especially apparent in comparing Swedish policy to that of Norway, where a strong Left party was unable to legislate a similar package of reforms despite similar labor shortages in the 1960s.[38] However, in contrast to Sweden, historic conflicts around religion helped produce the most significant Christian Democratic party in Scandinavia, the Christian People's Party (KrF). The secularization process had been more contested in Norway than in the rest of Scandinavia, and it generated religious and center-periphery cleavages that endured through much of the twentieth century. The result was the only Christian Democratic party of electoral significance among the Nordic states that represented both the rural parts of the country and religious voters, with considerable overlap between those two groups.[39] The success of the KrF also reflects the somewhat greater religiosity of Norwegian society.[40]

In the 1970s, the KrF influenced how political elites responded to the issue of mothers' employment, making conservative and center parties more vocal and successful in their opposition to shifting gender roles and the Social Democrats more cautious on this question. The KrF has not been politically dominant, but by the 1970s, its membership was rising rapidly, its vote share was increasing, and it was participating in bourgeois coalition governments. The conservative and center parties shared the KrF's conservatism on family issues to some extent, and the center party began emphasizing this dimension in its party platforms when there was a rapprochement between it and the KrF in the 1970s.[41] Because of the greater power of traditional values in Norwegian politics, the issue of mothers' employment became politicized in a way that it did not in Sweden. The center, conservative, and Christian Democratic parties all opposed the generalization of full-day child care, advocating part-day programs that would be dominated by pedagogical objectives and less oriented around parental employment.[42]

In the 1970s, the KrF attained its greatest electoral support since its formation—just when the Norwegian Parliament was discussing policies for working mothers.[43] Despite evident labor shortages, rising rates of women's labor force participation, and the development of a large public sector, the government developed fewer measures in the 1960s and 1970s to support women's paid work. Although a day care law was crafted under a Labor party government in 1975, it reflected the difficulties of reaching agreement on the controversial issue of publicly run full-day programs. Rather than follow the recommendations of a 1969 government commission in favor of central state control and expanded spending on public day care, the final law gave much responsibility to local governments, slowing the development of the public system.[44] Joint taxation of family income also was maintained, although spouses had the right to separate taxation.[45]

The development of the Norwegian child care system also reveals differences with Sweden in the balance between the state and civil society in education and family policy. Norwegian child care policy continued the long-standing practice of collaboration between the state and the voluntary sector, giving considerable latitude to local governments and voluntary organizations for the development of child care.[46] In this, Norwegian social services policy was closer to that of the Netherlands or West Germany, where voluntary organizations, many of them religious in origin, provide many educational and social services.[47] Allowing the voluntary sector an important role in the provision of child care services also has shaped the nature of these programs: many voluntary associations preferred part-day pedagogical programs over those oriented around parents' work schedules. Swedish child care policy reflected the statist orientation of education and family policy: the central government took responsibility for the provision of these public services rather than leaving responsibility to the voluntary sector. Private, nonprofit provision of child care was nearly nonexistent in Sweden until the 1980s, and these programs were barred from receiving public services until the early 1990s.

The form Swedish child care policy took also was shaped by the legacies of past policy. Most significant from the standpoint of working mothers was the move to eliminate part-day preschool programs. As chapter 2 showed, the lack of competition between the state and the religious voluntary sector prevented the growth of educational services for young children. This small preschool sector provided part-day programs with solely educational objectives and was staffed by teachers who did not want to encourage mothers to work full-time.[48] Starting in the mid-1960s, the state shunted these programs aside and began constructing a unified system of early childhood education and care for children under the age of seven. Thenceforth, public funds would subsidize programs that matched the working hours of many parents, although they also maintained a strong educational orientation.[49] This fusion of educational and care functions was to become one of the defining aspects of the Swedish child care system.

By the mid-1970s, the center of gravity in Swedish politics had moved away from the male-breadwinner to the universal-breadwinner model. The consensus around the new model was sufficiently broad that when a bourgeois coalition governed between 1976 and 1982, the public child care system continued to expand at a rapid pace. Although some of these parties still preferred paying mothers to care for their own children, there was no move to develop a care allowance at this time. Instead, parents of children under eight were given the choice of working a six-hour day—a policy that satisfied conservatives who wanted to preserve a greater degree of parental care. Otherwise, Swedish policy continued to underwrite the increase in working mothers, a social development that would shape the politics of mothers' employment for decades to come.

The Dutch Non-Debate about Working Mothers

While Swedish policy makers were fundamentally remaking family policy to support and promote women's employment, policies for working parents hardly came onto the political agenda in the Netherlands. As in Sweden, feminists tried to challenge the prevailing view about the importance of full-time maternal care for young children. Yet, because of the hegemony of Christian Democratic parties and the Netherlands' historically embedded reluctance to allow greater state involvement in the lives of children and families, Dutch policy makers rejected these demands. Although some other changes were made to the Dutch welfare state to remove some blatantly gender-discriminatory elements, the status quo continued with regard to policies for working parents.

The second wave of the feminist movement began to take shape in the late 1960s, with some feminists questioning whether women's aspirations should be limited to the home.[50] Feminist groups such as the Man-Woman Society and Dolle Mina ("Crazy Mina") began calling for child care and other supports that would help women work for pay. These efforts hardly made any

impact on the political class. A 1974 report commissioned by the government opposed full-time day care, favoring instead the part-day services that
could be justified on educational grounds.[51] The idea of supporting mothers'
employment gained little support from either the Christian Democratic or
the Social Democratic Party. Faced with such firm and widespread opposition, feminist organizations largely abandoned the push for public child care
and other such policies.[52]

What accounts for the failure of this issue to resonate in the wider polity?
The hegemony of Christian Democratic parties in the political system kept
the center of gravity on gender and family issues on the right, creating a broad
political consensus around the male-breadwinner model that was slow to
change. As chapter 2 showed, the religious cleavages and conflicts that were
central to Dutch political development produced a mobilization of Christian
parties around the schools struggle in the late nineteenth and early twentieth
centuries. Christian parties emerged victorious from these disputes and
would dominate Dutch politics thereafter. Catholics participated in nearly all
cabinets between 1917 and 1994, at times sharing power with Social Democrats, but more commonly with the Orthodox Protestants and liberals.[53] The
hegemony of the religious parties did begin to weaken after 1967, with the
emergence of new political parties in the late 1960s. Although they received a
lower percentage of the vote, religious parties continued to participate in government. Declining support also sparked a merger in 1980 of three religious
parties—two Orthodox Protestant and one Catholic—to form a rejuvenated
Christian Democratic Party that would govern in coalition governments
until 1994.[54]

The Dutch welfare state clearly reflects the influence of Christian—and
specifically Catholic—political parties. The major features of the Dutch welfare state were established in the decade following the Second World War, a
period of "Roman-Red" (Catholic–Social Democratic) governments.[55] One
goal was to bring about the "restoration of the family"—meaning, the traditional male-breadwinner family.[56] As a result, male breadwinners were
assured relatively high wages and generous benefits that could replace their
income if they became ill or disabled or when they reached retirement age.[57]
In addition, because the religious parties viewed the family, and not the
individual, as the core social unit, married women lacked an individual entitlement to social benefits and earned their social rights through marriage.

Married women had no right to a pension, and women who were not the main breadwinner in the family were not entitled to the minimum wage.[58] The system of joint taxation also discouraged two-earner families. Not surprisingly, married women's employment rates were extremely low.

The power of religious political forces also shaped the structure of social service provision. Catholics and Protestants shared a leeriness of state involvement in the lives of children and families, although their specific visions differed. The Catholic principle of subsidiarity held that responsibility for social affairs should be at the lowest possible level of society—such as families, churches, and local communities—but that state involvement was justified if those lower levels failed. This caveat left some room for policies to help families meet their responsibilities. The Protestant notion of "sovereignty in one's circle" informed an even more powerful rejection of any state involvement in family life.[59] A point of agreement was that religiously based voluntary associations should assume many of the responsibilities of the welfare state, and indeed they did. The system known as *particulier initiatief* gave public funding to private charitable organizations that provided many health, educational, and welfare services.[60] In the 1960s, more than 75 percent of Dutch preschoolers attended privately administered programs that received state funds. Most of these private programs were run by religious organizations.[61]

The previous century's religious conflicts shaped this preference for voluntary-sector control over social programs. As chapter 2 detailed, class and religious cleavages in the nineteenth century produced a far-reaching segmentation of Dutch society into four subcultural groupings: Catholics, Protestants, socialists, and, to a lesser degree, secular liberals. Each community developed a civil society of its own, including newspapers, radio and television stations, sports clubs, and other voluntary associations. To accommodate the demands of these communities for schools that reflected their own views, the compromise of 1917 allowed them to run their own publicly funded schools along religious or secular lines. This became the basis for the wider Dutch welfare state model of publicly funded, yet privately administered, educational and welfare programs. Such an arrangement contrasts strongly with the Swedish and French models of central state control over education and social welfare services.

The strong and widely held view that families should be responsible for the care of their own members meant that the expansion of Dutch social services was slow. In the 1950s, Catholics removed social services policy from the Social Democratic–run Ministry of Social Affairs, placing them in a new social services ministry that they controlled.[62] Because Catholic ministers sought to reinforce and support the traditional family, the development of services such as child care was extremely limited. Voluntary associations ran the few available centers, and these were aimed at single mothers and children from otherwise troubled families.[63]

The availability of preschools did continue to expand owing to their place within the education system. By 1970, 90 percent of four- and five-year-olds were attending kindergarten—a far higher percentage than in Sweden, and close to French levels of preschool education (table 3.2).[64] This expansion was due in part to a requirement in Dutch education policy that the central state had to provide a pre-primary or primary school if a certain number of parents requested it so that children would not be forced to attend a program not in line with their parents' religious orientation. However, although a law in the mid-1950s guaranteed subsidies for these kindergartens, it also removed the caregiving elements of these programs. The entrance age increased from three to four, children could no longer stay for lunch, and the school hours were shortened.[65] The purely educational function of these programs was thus clearly established, diminishing the ability of these services to help mothers in paid work.

Although the confessional parties clearly shaped the welfare state to reinforce the male-breadwinner model, there was wide agreement across the political spectrum on these goals. In the 1950s, only the Dutch women's movement called for public child care for working mothers. The rest of the Left, including the Social Democratic and Communist parties, accepted that mothers should devote themselves full-time to the care of their children. These views hardly changed in the 1970s, a time when Left parties in France and the Nordic countries shifted toward supporting mothers' employment. In 1969, some women within the Social Democratic Party, the PvdA, noted that perhaps separation between mothers and young children was not "sinful"—hardly a ringing endorsement of nonmaternal care.[66] Moreover, a Nobel prize–winning Social Democratic economist, Jan Tinbergen, declared that state-funded day care was symptomatic of social and cultural crisis. In 1975, a left-wing coalition government came to power and published the first paper on women's equality policy in 1977. However, this paper did not offer any discussion of women's participation in the labor force and described day care as appropriate only for single mothers.[67]

Why was the Left so uninterested in supporting mothers' employment? One reason was the impact of widespread religiosity on the strategies and behavior of Left parties. The Dutch Social Democrats did not have the monopoly over the working class that the Swedish Left had; instead, the class cleavage was cross-cut by religion. This meant that the Dutch PvdA had to compete with Christian parties for the working-class vote, which brought them toward a more traditional line on family policy and other social questions. After the Second World War, Social Democrats adopted what van Kersbergen describes as a "personalist socialism" that mixed Christian values, socialism, and humanism.[68] The move also enabled the PvdA to participate in coalition governments with Catholics in the postwar period. One important source of agreement was family policy: that women would be full-time caregivers and men full-time breadwinners was hardly in dispute.

Another element of Dutch politics that arose out of the religious conflicts earlier in the century was the tradition of elite accommodation. With Dutch society deeply divided between religious, secular, and socialist blocs, stability in political life was assured by elite bargaining that smoothed over these cleavages. To stabilize what could quickly degenerate into vituperative conflict, political elites negotiated controversial issues between them and crafted public policies that reflected a consensus.[69] The consequence of this accommodationist style was to narrow the range of policy options. Although Catholics, Protestants, liberals, and socialists were able to agree upon the need to build an encompassing set of social policies that would stabilize social relations and foster the prosperity of the nation, all four parties also agreed on the importance of the traditional family model, with a male breadwinner and female caregiver, as the foundation of Dutch society.[70] Bussemaker argues that this ideology of the family was a consensus position in an otherwise deeply divided society and perhaps even gained strength because it was one issue that bound the polity together in agreement.[71]

Finally, the stance of the PvdA also reflected the effects of the economic and welfare state model, which assured that few women were in paid employment and thus limited the constituency for expanded child care and other supports for working mothers. Swedish policy had inadvertently mobilized a high level of women's employment through the welfare state and thus created new

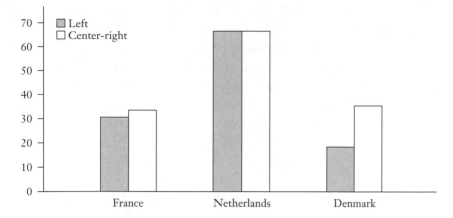

Figure 3.3   Percentage of left-wing and center-right female voters who are
housewives, 1975–79
SOURCE: Eurobarometer.
Question asks about vote intention in national elections.

social demands; the opposite occurred in the Netherlands. Not only did the
welfare state assure a high wage level for the male breadwinner, but very high
productivity rates created widespread prosperity. Many other European
countries shared the Dutch belief in the male-breadwinner model, but more
Dutch families could afford to live it.[72] The underdevelopment of social services also removed a potential lure for female workers. Although the expansion of the welfare state in the 1960s and 1970s did draw more mothers into
paid employment, they usually went to work part-time, after their children
were at least in primary school.[73]

The potential political consequences are shown in figure 3.3, which dis-
plays the percentage of leftist and center-right female voters who are housewives in France, the Netherlands, and Denmark (comparable Swedish data
was unavailable for this period). The figure shows that the proportion of self-
identifying housewives remained quite high in the Netherlands throughout
the 1970s and was just as high among leftist voters as it was for the constitu-
ents of center-right parties. As a result, there was little pressure from within
the Social Democratic voting constituency for a changed stance on mothers'
employment. It is not surprising, then, that child care or parental leave was
not a high priority of the Social Democratic Party in this period: such policies
were contrary to the needs and values of its own constituency.

There were some policy changes in the 1970s that sought to remove some of the more discriminatory elements in law and social policy. The possibility of separate taxation was introduced in the 1970s, and explicit discrimination against married women was reduced or eliminated in some benefit programs.[74] Another significant development in the 1970s was that parents began creating educational programs for children before they entered kindergarten, known as "playgroups." But playgroups usually were available for only part of the day a few days a week. The aim of these programs was not to support women's employment, but rather to offer developmental stimulation to young children. Other than this, the only publicly subsidized child care was limited to poor or disadvantaged families. There were few private alternatives and no tax subsidies to encourage the development of a private market.[75]

In short, during the key period of welfare state expansion, there was little change in Dutch policies for working parents. Not only did socially conservative Christian parties dominate politics and shape policies in support of the male-breadwinner family, but the Social Democratic Party offered little criticism of this model. The slow change in the numbers of employed women also limited the possibilities for change. It was to be several decades before many more women entered the labor market and the power of Christian Democrats had eroded, opening the door to new kinds of family policies.

France: Statist Pragmatism toward Working Mothers

The French case lies between the Dutch and the Swedish ones in the extent of policy change. French policy makers accepted the reality of mothers' employment and sought to support it. The shift to a more widely available day care system began under center-right governments, which increased the supply of public day care and opened up eligibility for these programs to non-poor families. There also was a rapid expansion of the preschool system for children aged three to six, such that these programs were universally available by the end of the 1970s. Although a significant boon to working mothers, these measures were not accompanied by a wider array of policies—such as a gender-egalitarian parental leave or reform of the tax code—that would fundamentally challenge the male-breadwinner model. French policies for working mothers were often supportive but lacked the transformative vision embodied by Swedish policy.

How can we make sense of this mixed French model? One difference between France and Sweden is the comparative weakness of leftist political power. During the first two decades of the Fifth Republic, Gaullist and other center-right parties dominated French politics. The French Socialist Party gained power only in 1981, a time when economic fortunes had shifted and expansionary welfare state measures became more difficult. Given that the leftist vision of universal publicly run *crèches* and generous parental leave was not espoused by the center-right parties in power, such policies had little chance of being enacted during the 1970s. Even so, the center right accepted the reality of mothers' employment and did not seek to reinforce the male-breadwinner model once feminists and Left parties began contesting it, a stance that distinguished these parties from the Christian Democrats that dominated politics in neighboring countries. In addition, even though they were excluded from power, French Left parties advocated parental leave, child care, and other policies to support mothers in paid work. Compared to the Netherlands, the entire spectrum of political opinion tilted more favorably toward mothers' employment.

Party ideologies on this issue were shaped by the legacy of an active state role in the lives of children and families. As chapter 2 argued, conflicts and competition between clerical and anticlerical forces resulted in an expanded role of the state in the lives of children and families. The groundwork for this was laid by family benefits policies and the national preschool system. By the 1930s, there was a wide political consensus that it was the state's responsibility to take care of family needs, whatever those needs may be. Agreement on this continued after the Second World War, when the family became a central category of analysis in the social security system.[76] While Christian Democratic parties in other countries hewed to the principle of subsidiarity, a "reverse principle of subsidiarity" prevailed in France, with the central state directly involved in providing children's education and assuring family well-being.[77] All political parties in France agreed that the well-being of French families was too important to leave to lower levels of government and society.[78]

Thus, after the end of the Second World War, policy makers constructed a set of institutions that would guide family policy thereafter. In 1945, a new national agency was created, the Protection maternelle et infantile (PMI), to provide maternal and child health services to all families. Public day care for under-threes—the *crèches*—came under the PMI's regulatory purview. Policy makers also built on the system of employer-provided family allowances to create a national family allowance fund (Caisse Nationale d'Allocations Familiales [CNAF]) that provides cash allowances and family-related services.[79] The structure of the fund is complex: it is managed by the representatives of labor unions, business, and family associations, but also has over one hundred local branches that distribute benefits. Although the CNAF has some independence from the state, its priorities often are shaped by those of the current government.[80] The centralized public preschool system also revealed the acceptability of a direct state role in the education of young children. As chapter 2 showed, the incorporation of preschool programs into the French national education bureaucracy in the late nineteenth century established central state responsibility for these services, putting early childhood education under the aegis of a powerful centralized ministry.[81]

The structure of partisan competition also shaped political perspectives on working mothers. In contrast to virtually all continental European countries, Christian Democracy never became a powerful political movement in France. The weakness of French Christian Democracy has its roots in the historic conflicts described in chapter 2: the clashes between secular republicanism and Catholics poisoned relations on both sides. The antidemocratic orientation of many Catholics impeded the reconciliation between Christians and democrats, while the anticlericalism of radicals, socialists, and communists made it difficult for Christian Democrats to expand their constituency on the left.[82] In the years following the Second World War, efforts to build a larger political following foundered over the issue of whether the state should offer financial support to private Catholic schools.[83] Christian Democrats in France, unlike those in other Western European countries, repeatedly failed to widen their base on either the left or the right.[84]

With the exception of the Mouvement républicain populaire (MRP), Christian Democratic parties have played a minor role in French political life. The MRP rose to political prominence after the Second World War and was a pivotal coalition partner in the Fourth Republic (1946–58). The MRP's political fortunes rapidly deteriorated over the 1950s, and its share of the electoral vote declined from 26 percent in 1946 to a mere 11 percent by

1956. With only weak support by the Catholic church, and thanks to its own hesitancy to embrace the church as an ally in a climate of hostile anticlericalism, the MRP failed to extend its base across the conservative electorate.[85] By 1962, MRP voters had abandoned the party in droves.[86]

The weakness of Christian Democracy would shape the views of both the Left and the Right on women's employment. On the left, the Socialist Party did not have to compete with Christian parties for the working-class vote. The party also maintained its traditional anticlericalism, although some religious activists had influence within the Left.[87] In general, however, the anticlericalism of the French socialists distinguished them from the Dutch or German Social Democratic parties, which achieved a rapprochement with religious parties in the postwar period. Instead of competing with a religious party for the working-class vote, the socialists faced a strong Communist party on their left flank that often favored women's employment. Although not always a reliable friend of feminist causes, the French socialists often challenged the gendered status quo, questioning traditional gender roles in a way that Left parties in many other continental European countries would not.[88]

On the right, the French Gaullist party is a distinctive force; it is no mere substitute for Christian Democracy. Charles de Gaulle was a practicing Catholic, yet Christianity played little or no role in the party's discourse. In addition, the Gaullist political movement departed from conventional conservative or Christian Democratic parties in many ways, not least of which was de Gaulle's embrace of state-led social and economic modernization as a preeminent objective of state policy.[89] While Christian Democrats in the rest of Europe embraced the principle of subsidiarity, the Gaullist party sought to develop a powerful state apparatus that would remain independent of social forces.[90] De Gaulle's commitment to French national greatness justified pragmatism in public policy in the belief that leaders should pursue the course that best serves the French nation regardless of received ideologies, leading de Gaulle and his successors to adopt public policies that often defied traditional definitions of Left and Right and to display flexibility on some moral issues.[91] The lack of fidelity to Catholic doctrine also reflected the shrinking influence of Catholicism in society in politics. As early as the 1970s, rates of religious practice were nearly as low as those in the highly secularized Scandinavian countries (see figure 3.2).

Nonetheless, one should not neglect the influence of familialism over French family policy. Familialism—a view that values the traditional family and the policies that support it—has been an important strand of thought in French family policy that has its roots in Catholic political movements to defend large families.[92] These views have had influence through the conservative family groups in the Union Nationale des Associations Familiales (UNAF), an umbrella organization that includes most of the major family associations. Representatives of UNAF have seats on nearly every state council or commission that deals with questions pertaining to the family, including the national family benefits fund.[93] The MRP also espoused familialist views during the Fourth Republic and helped engineer public policies that supported the male-breadwinner model.[94] French family policy in the 1950s created what historian Antoine Prost has called the "golden age of familialism."[95]

Already in the Fourth Republic, however, there were signs that the MRP and conservative family associations would not become the hegemonic force in constructing family policy. While the incorporation of the family movement into state policy making gave them a voice in matters of public affairs, it also contained their influence. Generally, even if UNAF has opposed a particular policy, once a decision by state officials is taken, UNAF accepts the decision.[96] In the 1950s, a number of important political figures, such as Pierre Mendes-France, Jacques Chaban-Delmas, and Edgar Faure, were already resisting the lobbying of the family movement and opposed housewife allowances and other benefits that encouraged women's exit from the labor market at a time of labor shortages.[97] More important, the demise of the MRP brought the golden age of familialism to a close. Mirroring the decline in the MRP's vote share, the value of family allowances reached their highest level in 1955 and declined thereafter. The benefit for housewives was only weakly revalued and became more of a symbolic policy than a lure to keep mothers out of paid employment.[98]

By the mid to late 1960s, France had a long tradition of an active state in family matters and children's education, and the political scene was dominated by a secular center-right party. It was in this context that governments accepted the reality of working mothers and tried to address their needs. Some of the first demands came for expanded access to preschool education. Gaullist government officials hastened to meet the demand, with little hand-wringing over the potential consequences for mothers' employment and the mother-child bond. Increased demand for nursery school education was viewed as a social fact, created by urbanization and increasing participation of women in the labor force, that must be recognized and satisfied by expanded services.[99] While in neighboring West Germany publicly run preschools were viewed as a worrisome intrusion of the state in the lives of families, in France the Gaullist government assumed that the state should provide these programs.[100]

The rapid expansion of early childhood education in the 1960s and 1970s also was due to the institutionalization of preschools in the national education system that chapter 2 described. The Ministry of National Education oversaw the expansion of these programs, marshalling scarce resources to respond to parents clamoring for these schools. Ministry officials also were pushed by highly organized teachers' unions, whose members staffed both the primary and pre-primary schools.[101] By the mid-1970s, 80 percent of three-year-olds, 97 percent of four-year-olds, and 100 percent of five-year-olds were attending these noncompulsory schools.

Government officials also were pragmatic and nonmoralizing about mothers' employment. Since the 1950s, government planners had seen women's employment as a way to redress labor shortages, yet these needs were often met by foreign labor.[102] The issue arose again in the late 1960s and early 1970s when officials began to discuss the potential costs of immigration. Women's participation in the labor force was again favored as a way to cope with tight labor markets.[103] Moreover, as figure 3.1 shows, the percentage of women in paid employment who were in their prime child-raising years (25–39) increased steadily through the 1960s and reached the Swedish level in 1970.

The student and worker revolts of May 1968 put gender equality and child development on the agenda.[104] The revolts had a major impact on French politics and public policy, sparking reforms and new thinking about many social problems.[105] Women were one of the many groups mobilized by the May events, and one of the issues that arose during the 1968 revolt was day care. Because many mothers realized that the lack of such services would hamper their political activism, they set up twenty-four-hour *crèches* in the Sorbonne.[106] Renewed attention to child care also reflected the utopian visions of the day, which saw children as the foundation of transformative social projects. At a number of Paris universities, students founded *crèches sauvages* (unregulated centers) that were outside official government control and sought to break free of the older, "medicalized" model of child care.[107] The spread of these new values and ideas produced a major shift in the public *crèches* as they shed their hospital-like environment and became colorful centers for child development and creativity.[108] This change improved the image of the *crèches* in the eyes of the middle-class parents, many of whom began seeking out these services in 1970s.[109]

Center-right governments in the 1970s responded to these demands by increasing spending on the public day care system at a time when conservative welfare regimes elsewhere on the Continent maintained policies to shore up the traditional family. Prime Minister Jacques Chaban-Delmas, a Gaullist, made some of the first major investments in day care while opening up these services to non-poor parents. Electoral pressures then pushed conservative and centrist politicians to repeatedly voice their support for public child care, particularly with the intensifying pressure from the Left after the Socialist and Communist parties reached an electoral pact in 1972. The Left's common program promised to create 1,000 more *crèches* if elected, and the Communist Party in particular was a strong advocate for improved access to day care and preschools.[110] The response of many on the right was to avow their support for more child care. During the 1973 legislative elections, Prime Minister Pierre Messmer promised to create 2,000 *crèches* or 100,000 more places between 1973 and 1978. It was later revealed that he had accidentally added a zero and that the real plan was to create 200 more *crèches*. Messmer continued to maintain that he intended to build 2,000 new centers, although such a massive investment was never implemented.[111] The episode is revealing of how politicians across the political spectrum hastened to voice support for child care and wage-earning mothers.

These electoral pressures also were evident under President Valéry Giscard d'Estaing, who sought to attract female voters in the 1970s with gender egalitarian reforms.[112] Unlike Christian Democratic parties in other European countries at the time, Giscard d'Estaing embraced a program that included expanded access to contraception, liberalization of abortion and divorce laws, greater assistance to single mothers, and support for mothers' employment.[113] He appointed Françoise Giroud Secrétaire d'Etat à la condition féminine, and she advocated women's work outside the home and the construction of more day care centers.[114] Simone Veil, the minister of health who penned the abortion liberalization law, also was committed to expanding the supply of day care. As a result, substantially more resources were devoted to *crèches*. In 1974, the government invested more public resources in day care, and the number of places in public centers increased by 72 percent between 1974 and 1980.[115]

By the 1970s, the national family benefits fund (CNAF) began emerging as an important player in the development of child care policy.[116] The CNAF manages the contributions paid by workers and their employers that entitle them to family benefits. Because the CNAF's mission is to be responsive to the families that are its contributors, it is attuned to the changing needs of families. The CNAF does not have much control over family benefits policy, which is decided by the Ministry of Social Affairs; but the one area over which the CNAF does have power is *action sociale*, or family-related social services.[117] One key decision was in 1970, when the administrative council agreed to direct subsidies to the operating costs of a range of social services, including day care. This created a steady funding source for family-related services on which local governments could rely when planning these programs.[118] Throughout the 1970s, the fund became more active in promoting the development of social services, and most subsidies for these services have gone toward day care centers.

Even with these developments, there were limits to how much change French governments would embrace in the area of mothers' employment. Policies toward working mothers were essentially reactive and limited. To the extent that mothers began working in higher numbers and began seeking child care and other services, government and CNAF officials felt pressure to respond; however, they did not embrace a transformative vision to remake French society along the lines of the universal-breadwinner model emerging in Sweden.

There were several reasons for this more limited approach. First, the most gender-egalitarian visions were espoused by Left parties that were out of political power. In addition, although conservative familialist forces in no way dominated the French debates about child care, these forces were better organized and more influential than in Sweden. The CNAF has offered a platform of influence for conservative family associations that they used to promote generous family allowances and a tax system that favors large families. Both created incentives for mothers to be at home with young children.

Although family associations were willing to countenance some diversion of family fund resources to day care, they continued to defend the male-breadwinner model and the policies that support it. Thus, a Swedish-style tax reform that effectively eliminated the male-breadwinner model was impossible in France.

As a result, though government policy often was supportive of working mothers, there was no attempt to push a larger transformation of French society. As figure 3.1 shows, the percentage of working women in France was high relative to that in the Netherlands by the mid-1970s but stayed relatively constant thereafter. Public policy in Sweden was reinforcing a social revolution in the behavior of women and nature of family life, but in France the pace of change stagnated. As we shall see in the next chapter, this had important implications for the politics of mothers' employment in succeeding decades.

The United States: Antistatism and Social Conservatism

Given the traditional discomfort with family policy in the United States and the generally low degree of state intervention in the marketplace, the fact that the United States adopted only limited policies to support mothers' employment in the 1960s and 1970s is perhaps not surprising. Nonetheless, there were serious attempts to improve the situation for working mothers, and such measures initially met with wide support. These efforts ran into a resurgent conservative movement that not only opposed expansions of federal power, but also drew strength from newly mobilized religious conservatives and the backlash against civil rights policy. Disparate strands of conservative thought unified around antipathy toward feminism, family change, and federal intervention in local affairs. Faced with the growing politicization of gender and family issues, policy makers responded to ever growing numbers of working mothers by encouraging private market solutions, rather than by trying to devise federal family policies.

As in France and Sweden, social-structural change helped bring the issue of working mothers onto the political stage. By the 1970s, roughly the same percentages of women aged twenty-five to thirty-nine were in paid employment in the United States, Sweden, and France (see figure 3.1). A widely

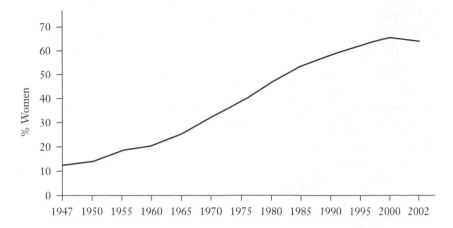

Figure 3.4   Percentage of American mothers with children under 6 in paid employment

SOURCE: U.S. House of Representatives, Committee on Ways and Means, *2004 Green Book*.

noted trend at the time was the rapid increase in paid work among mothers with children under six (figure 3.4). The growth of single-parent households and rising divorce rates also garnered increasing attention, particularly in the context of debates about poverty and welfare. These trends contributed to wider discussions about family change and the needs of parents. What remained to be seen was how the dominant political forces would respond to these social changes.

On the one hand, the weakness of leftist political forces would lead us to expect, at most, policies targeted to very-low-income parents. The United States has never had a true Social Democratic party, and the Democratic Party has always contained forces both for and against expansionary federal policies. Southern Democrats were some of the most powerful actors shaping the politics of the welfare state in the decades following the Second World War, but they were fiscal conservatives committed to restraining the growth of government.[119] The power of unions has varied but generally waned since the 1960s, and unions have never enjoyed the regularized access to policy making enjoyed by unions in many European countries.[120] With the exception of programs for the elderly, the American welfare state has largely been a residual one that leaves most people to satisfy their welfare needs in the private market.[121]

Although it seems unlikely that the United States ever would have adopted either Swedish-style universal day care or the centralized preschool system found in France, if there was any time for an expanded role in early education and care policy it was in the late 1960s and early 1970s. Some have characterized this period as one of the "big bangs" in American social policy, a time when grand visions of social transformation were possible.[122] Social spending dramatically increased in this period, and the determination of Lyndon B. Johnson and his administration to wage a War on Poverty signaled a new federal commitment to social welfare policy, with a particular interest in the lives of young children. The Johnson administration created Head Start, a federally funded program that offered early education, nutrition, and health services to disadvantaged children. The Nixon administration was hostile to Johnson's War on Poverty, but Nixon was not reflexively opposed to the welfare state and often backed more progressive social policy initiatives than his Democratic predecessors and followers.[123] Nixon's pre-inaugural Task Force on Education reported that the most important issue in American education was that two-thirds of American children lacked access to pre-elementary education services, and the Task Force on Welfare called for federally funded construction of day care centers.[124] Nixon's February 1969 message to Congress on poverty called for increased spending on child care, declaring, "So crucial is the matter of early growth that we must make a national commitment to providing all American children an opportunity for healthful and stimulating development during the first five years of life."[125]

Many of the most significant political actors at the time were relatively moderate on gender equality issues. Although the Democratic Party was more centrist than the typical European Left party, the Republican Party was not equivalent to a European Christian Democratic party either. In fact, the Republican Party had been the stronger champion for women's equality in the decades immediately following the Second World War, and both parties supported the Equal Rights Amendment by the end of the 1960s.[126] This moderate stance on gender equality was reflected in public policy. Aspects of tax and Social Security policy discouraged married women's employment, but because there were fewer social benefits to start with, there were fewer measures that actively discouraged mothers' employment than in a country such as the Netherlands.[127] Even though the lack of redistributive measures and labor market regulation offered minimal assistance to wage-earning mothers, there were fewer legal and policy constraints on women's employment than were found in many continental European countries.

The 1960s and 1970s also was a time of extraordinary ferment around women's equality policy. Since the 1964 Civil Rights Act included sex as a category protected from discrimination, policies to promote women's employment and educational opportunities had steadily expanded. A series of measures passed in the 1970s shored up antidiscrimination measures for women and mandated equal treatment in federally funded education. The mobilization of the second wave of the women's movement played a critical role in spurring these policy changes.[128] Although feminists would not be the main actors in the debates over federal child care policy, feminist activism helped put the issue of child care on the political agenda and would later prove key in pushing the Pregnancy Discrimination Act—a precursor to the unpaid parental leave created in the 1990s.[129]

Other forces at work in American politics pushed against expanding the welfare state on behalf of working parents. Many people assumed that family matters belonged to states, local governments, or families themselves and that federal involvement in family policy was an intrusion into a protected, private sphere. As chapter 2 noted, efforts earlier in the century to develop universal child health and family allowances came to naught. Campaigns to create a system of child allowances in the 1950s and 1960s also failed: opponents argued that these allowances were either the product of papal or communist machinations, or a pro-natalist policy that would encourage low-income people to bear more children. More broadly, many were concerned that such a policy would increase the involvement of the government in the lives of families.[130]

Chapter 2 showed that antistatism in the United States has its roots in the country's tremendous religious diversity. Antistatism was reinforced in this period by racial tensions and the backlash against civil rights and welfare. Efforts to expand civil rights policy into new domains sparked outrage. Court-enforced busing drew particular animus as an example of federal intervention in state and local education policy. It was also in this period that Aid to Families with Dependent Children (AFDC) and other income support policies became increasingly associated with African Americans.[131] Although these programs had never been particularly popular in the past, blacks had largely been excluded from them. By the late 1960s, efforts to promote equal access to government programs expanded the numbers of blacks receiving income support. A racialization of welfare policy ensued, with popular stereotypes fed by politicians' claims that African American "welfare queens" were living it up on public assistance. Such claims spurred a larger attack on the welfare state throughout the 1970s and reinforced the antistatist views of many in politics and in the population.[132]

These conflicting trends and pressures collided in the early 1970s in the first effort at a federal policy for working mothers—the attempt to create a federally funded child care program for non-poor families. At first, the prospects for such legislation appeared bright, for Democrats and moderate Republicans in Congress agreed that working mothers needed more assistance. A bill to create a system of federally funded, locally run child care centers, the Child Development Act (CDA), passed both the House and the Senate in 1971 with bipartisan support.[133] One of the most striking features of the legislation was its aspirations to universalism: the CDA would have allowed non-poor families to use subsidized child care programs, paying for them on an income-based sliding scale. These aspirations were not entirely realized in the version of the bill that passed in 1971, but many had high hopes that once a federal role was established in this area, further expansion would come later.

Aspects of the CDA quickly embroiled it in some of the larger conflicts of the time. First, civil rights and antipoverty activists were the key drivers behind the legislation, and they pushed a version of the bill that looked very much like the War on Poverty's community action programs of the 1960s.[134] These programs gave a good deal of control to local nonprofit organizations, bypassing state and local governments that wanted to maintain power over federal dollars. As a result, community action programs were extremely controversial and hotly opposed by many in both Congress and the Nixon White House.[135] Employing this model for the CDA thus eroded support for the bill among moderates otherwise disposed to support it. Most significantly, Nixon despised the War on Poverty and, since the start of his administration, had attempted to dismantle its remaining programs. Not surprisingly, then, Nixon regarded the initiative with a good deal of suspicion.[136]

What definitively sank this and future child care proposals was the mobilization of conservatives against what they viewed as a harmful expansion of federal power into the lives of children and families. Advocates for the CDA put great emphasis on the importance of good quality child care for child *development*. Such language incensed conservatives, who viewed this as government interference in child rearing. Some asserted that an elitist corps of behavioral scientists would attempt to shape children's minds through these federally funded centers. "This was not a day care bill, it was about child development," recalled one opponent of the CDA in the administration, drawing a distinction between services that merely help working parents and more interventionist social programs.[137] Some of the strongest rhetoric came from conservative columnists and the newspaper *Human Events*. One editorial proclaimed that the child care legislation aimed to "Sovietize Our Youth" and contained "the seeds for destruction of Middle America."[138]

Although these views did not predominate in the Republican Party at the time, the conservative campaign successfully politicized the notion of federally funded child care and was the first stage of a larger conservative mobilization against family policies. The first success came in convincing Nixon to not only veto the legislation, but to do so in a way that reflected conservative concerns. Nixon apparently acceded to their demands because he was already unsympathetic to the bill and also because he was seeking to mollify conservatives angered by his proposed welfare reform and opening up of relations with China.[139] In his veto message, Nixon emphasized the unacceptability of federal involvement in the lives of children, asserting that direct federal provision of day care services "would commit the vast moral authority of the National Government to the side of communal approaches to child-rearing over the family centered approach." Government policy, Nixon said, should instead "cement the family in its rightful position as the keystone of our civilization," and he assailed the "army of bureaucrats" the CDA would create.[140]

The hard-line veto dashed immediate efforts to revive federally supported, broadly available child care services. The notion of federal involvement in anything but residual services for the very poor became politically toxic.[141] Within the Nixon administration, supporters of a day care bill either changed their minds or left, while the moderate Republicans in the House that had been crucial to the effort balked at the prospect of a second day care bill in 1972. Even Democrats were wary, fearing that similar legislation would arouse too much controversy in an election year.[142] The veto blocked what was probably the most significant chance for an expanded federal child care policy in this period.

The successful campaign against the CDA also was the first strike of a growing social and political movement—later termed the New Right—that emerged out of the religious and racial conflicts of the time. The New Right brought together economic libertarians, cold-war hawks, and social conservatives. These last were the new ingredient in conservative politics, and they brought with them a particular focus on gender- and family-related questions.[143] Strategists for the movement emphasized these moral issues to appeal to conservative Protestants and Catholics angered by feminism, liberalized sexual mores, and family change. In this, the New Right represented a resurgence of religious politics in America, evidenced by the creation of the Christian Coalition and growing national prominence of evangelical leaders.[144] The New Right also capitalized on resentment toward federal civil rights policies and the shift of southern white voters from the Democratic to the Republican Party. Exemplifying these two sources of antistatism was an attempt by the IRS to shut down some Christian schools for discriminating against minorities. Although initially few Republicans were sympathetic to the complaints of these schools, key figures in the New Right saw this as the kind of issue around which they could mobilize groups currently outside the political process.[145] Antipathy to federal government expansion was the common denominator between diverse strands of thought in the new conservative movement.

Energized by the Nixon veto, conservative groups mounted opposition to child care legislation throughout the 1970s. In 1973, they founded the National Coalition for Children, an organization dedicated to "preserving the family as the fundamental unit in society." In 1975, they allied with the American Conservative Union to fight efforts to re-launch child development legislation.[146] An anonymous flier that was circulated in a number of communities claimed members of Congress believed government should displace parents from their responsibility for raising children. The flier spread like wildfire, allegedly through local conservative and fundamentalist Christian organizations. Its claims became the basis of radio shows, editorials, and television broadcasts, all of which fanned the flames of opposition. Tens of thousands of angry letters poured into the offices of the Department of Health, Education, and Welfare and of representatives or senators who had favored the child care legislation.[147]

Opposition to federal child care initially highlighted fears about government interference in the family, but the growing influence of social conservatives in the movement put greater emphasis on the male-breadwinner model. These conservatives, who had been mobilized by a number of issues concerning sexuality and the family, criticized policies that contravened traditional gender roles and encouraged mothers to work outside the home.[148] Two of the major figures in the movement were the anti-ERA activist Phyllis Schlafly, who argued that government help for working mothers discriminated against housewives, and Paul Weyrich, one of the architects of the New Right in the 1970s. These conservatives argued that day care was bad for children and that mothers for the most part wanted to be home with their children, not in paid employment. Others argued that public subsidies were unnecessary—most families were able to arrange day care through informal or familial arrangements.[149]

With the politicization of child care and other policies for working mothers, policy makers turned to the tax code as a way to subsidize private alternatives. The first tax break for child care expenses had been created in 1954 and was repeatedly expanded in the 1970s.[150] The first major increase in the tax break came the day after Nixon vetoed the Child Development Act, when he signed a Revenue Act that substantially raised the income ceiling on eligibility for the tax deduction. In 1975, the income threshold was further expanded, and in 1976, the tax break became a non-refundable tax credit. The largest expansion would come in 1981 under President Ronald Reagan, who delivered substantially larger tax subsidies to parents using child care.

These tax credits helped propel the growth of a private child care market and thus reinforced the public-private divide in the provision of social welfare.[151] Non-poor families were expected to rely on private child care; only very poor parents—especially single mothers receiving welfare—could receive any public child care assistance. As one conservative opponent to the CDA wrote at the time, "No one questions the basic proposition, that more mothers can be put to work, gaining self-respect and paying taxes, if day care facilities can be provided for their children."[152] In the 1970s, child care assistance programs faced cuts owing to the deteriorating fiscal environment, but in the long run federal spending for welfare-related child care would increase. The same was true for Head Start, the child development program that was the model for the CDA. According to conservatives, Head Start was targeted to the poor families who really needed this kind of intervention with children, whereas the CDA would have imposed this on the middle class.[153] Head Start was to face other political challenges over the years, but the program gained champions on both the left and the right.

In short, federal spending on child care was acceptable as long as it was targeted to the poorest and most disadvantaged members of society. For everyone else, private markets were to supply the needed services. As the succeeding chapters will show, this public-private divide for family-related policies was to have important political and social consequences.

Conclusion

In most countries, the period of welfare state expansion came at a time when the male-breadwinner model was the norm, or at least the ideal, for most families. This ideal was reflected in both social arrangements and the public policies of the day, which assumed that most married women were at home full-time during their child-raising years. By the mid-1960s, however, the situation began to change as labor shortages, rising rates of female education, and value changes began to propel more women into paid work who expected to stay there upon having children. In many countries, the question of mothers' employment had come onto the political agenda by the early 1970s. However, the four countries studied here responded in very different ways to these political pressures.

The types of policies that were adopted not only represented different immediate answers to the difficulties faced by working mothers, but also helped put welfare states on distinct trajectories. In the decades ahead, these varying policy approaches would shape the politics of mothers' employment by influencing public expectations and constituencies for different sorts of programs. Sweden moved toward a universal-breadwinner model, with strong public demand for increasing access to day care and other policies that facilitated mothers' employment. The Netherlands maintained its male-breadwinner approach until well into the 1990s, when autonomous political and social change finally began to create pressures for reform. French policies would generate a mixed constituency—one favoring both support for mothers' employment and support to mothers at home. The United States would take its own unique path by "privatizing" the issue of work and family. The growth of private market alternatives would stifle political movements for a broader set of policies to help working parents.

CHAPTER FOUR

The Politics of Child Care and Parental "Choice"
in Sweden and France, 1975–2005

By the mid-1970s, the golden age of the welfare state had come to an end. Decades of economic expansion were replaced by stagnant growth and chronic unemployment. In some countries, these economic changes were matched by ideological shifts as tax revolts, the spread of free market ideologies, and attacks on Keynesian economic policy all challenged the foundations of postwar economic and social policy. At the same time, family change continued unabated, as evidenced by the growth of women's employment and rising rates of divorce and single motherhood. With the emergence of new social risks and needs—such as the poverty risks of single motherhood or the needs of working parents for child care—the mismatch between social realities and the structures of the welfare state became increasingly evident. Although many years of social policy expansion took place when the male-breadwinner model reigned hegemonic, in recent decades there have been dramatic changes in gender relations at a time of greater restrictions on the state's capacity or willingness to address social problems.[1]

This chapter traces the evolution of work-family policies since the mid-1970s in France and Sweden—two countries in which there was a clear consensus on the active role of the state in family policy, and whose governments had already taken steps in the 1970s to support mothers' employment. Both faced economic challenges that could undermine their existing policies for working parents, as well as debates about whether public policy should prioritize day care spending or offer subsidies for lengthy periods of parental care at home. In Sweden, the continuous expansion of the public day care system since the mid-1970s revealed a willingness to prioritize mothers' employment policies in a time of welfare state constraints. The length of parental leave also increased, but in a way that altered women's position in employment without fundamentally undermining the attachment of women to the labor market. In France, government policy in the late 1980s and 1990s encouraged women to withdraw from paid work for a longer period of time. Public day care also expanded slowly, while new policies subsidized less regulated forms of day care that were cheaper for the state. In short, while Swedish policy maintained its commitment to universal public services for families, France developed a more mixed model—both in the kinds of services developed and in offering subsidies to mothers at home and at work.

To account for these distinct trajectories, this chapter traces the institutionalization of different approaches to work and family issues in each country. In Sweden, the dramatic shift in public policy in the 1970s quickly transformed Swedish society into one of universal breadwinners, in which nearly all parents were in paid employment. This muted potential conflicts between male-breadwinner and two-earner families, shifting the political spectrum away from the traditional family model while creating a large, unified constituency in favor of expanded public child care. In France, the less ambitious policy changes of the 1970s reinforced divisions on work-family questions, creating constituencies for both feminist and traditional policy approaches. Because of economic slowdown and high unemployment in France, policies to promote women's retreat from paid work gained currency among policy elites, as did cheaper forms of child care that would both save the government money and create low-wage jobs.

Tracing the evolution of French and Swedish policy over this time period enables us to investigate the mechanisms of path dependency that shaped the politics of family policy. In both France and Sweden, the key mechanism was how different sets of policies affected identities and constituencies for social programs. Day care programs were relatively new and did not immediately generate such constituencies, leaving them vulnerable to government austerity measures. In Sweden, however, other policy changes in the 1970s produced a massive increase in women's employment, creating a huge demand for services that both leftist and rightist governments would struggle to meet. In an already highly secularized society, this reinforced support for the idea that mothers should work outside the home and that the Swedish state should help them do so. In France, more moderate policy changes did not effect a similar transformation of French society into universal breadwinners. This played into existing societal divisions between advocates for working mothers and defenders of mothers at home.

Interestingly, the declining prevalence of the male-breadwinner model did not lead to a full embrace of the two-earner model in either country in the immediate term. In both, public sentiment increasingly embraced gender equality goals and the acceptability of mothers' employment, and this was especially true in Sweden. However, when it came to people's own situations, the difficulties of combining full-time work with caring responsibilities led many to seek a middle road—one in which women combined reduced time in paid work with significant caring time at home. This created an opening for conservative parties that advocated providing benefits to parents who care for their children at home, rather than spending more on public day care. Such claims had greater resonance in France than in Sweden, but they would leave their mark on public policy in both countries.

Path Dependency and the Welfare State

Many studies of the welfare state rely to some degree on the notion of path dependency. Social policies and programs often have deep historical roots, and in many countries these programs have endured through decades of social and political changes. Given the political popularity of the welfare state, it can be very difficult for politicians to cut or reform social programs. As Paul Pierson showed in his study of Britain and the United States, even Margaret Thatcher and Ronald Reagan failed to make a meaningful dent in the size of the welfare state during the 1980s, although Thatcher had somewhat greater success in this regard.[2]

This view of institutional stability has been criticized as unduly static and incapable of explaining change outside of random or sudden events.[3] The empirical record shows that the welfare state and other institutions are not frozen in place; we can find examples of either significant reform or a slower accumulation of smaller adjustments that add up to meaningful change. To make sense of this complex mix of stability and change, Kathleen Thelen advocates greater attention to the precise mechanisms that lead to the reproduction of institutional arrangements.[4] Changes in these mechanisms can help us understand the forces driving changes in institutions, allowing scholars to develop a more nuanced account of path dependency—one that does not assume that welfare states are forever locked in their current shape and that can account for both stability and periods of change.

A major source of continuity in the welfare state is the way social programs create or reinforce supportive constituencies. Universalistic social programs often spawn broad-based groups of backers that will lobby to preserve and expand benefits or services. As Andrea Campbell shows in the case of the elderly, American social programs for seniors helped generate a sense of political consciousness among them, spurring activism in defense of these programs.[5] Moreover, the political consciousness of political groups need not be wholly generated by the welfare state; rather, the power and influence of existing groups can be reinforced by the social programs they helped engineer. Although unions and Left parties require some amount of political power to create broad-based social programs, these programs then become part of their "power resources," reproducing the unions' and parties' position in power while solidifying political support for these programs.[6] Finally, social policies shape people's expectations about what the state will provide and how to organize their lives. With pensions, for example, people work and save around particular assumptions about the pension available to them later on. This gives beneficiaries a strong stake in the status quo, making it politically difficult to alter the system later on.[7]

The same is true for the child care arrangements of working parents. Public policies influence people's decisions about work and family and their expectations about state support. To the extent that policy changes eliminate the possibility of mothers being at home full-time—as occurred in Sweden during the 1970s—the demand for child care and other policies for working mothers is likely to be extremely high. Policies that reinforce the male-breadwinner model or adapt it to maintain extensive maternal care fragment the constituency for a service such as public day care. More fundamentally, the choices parents make in this area help constitute their own identities and beliefs about what mothers of young children ought to do—work for pay or care for their children at home. The societal reproduction of these views is suggested by studies showing that beliefs about mothers' employment are shaped by what one's own mother did.[8] Societies in which high percentages of people experienced their own mothers working show higher overall rates of support for mothers' employment. Thus, to the extent that social policy preserves the male-breadwinner family, support for this model is likely to endure.

Although the social embeddedness of the welfare state can be a source of stability, it also can be a force for change. Societies are shaped not only by a particular set of social programs, but also by other public policies, economic structures, social institutions, and cultural patterns that may embody alternative logics. Even during the heyday of the male-breadwinner model, the realities on the ground often looked quite different. Women worked outside the home either because they wanted to or because they had to, and families failed to conform to the images propagated by both public policy and mass culture.[9] Moreover, despite continuities in public policies, shifts in these other structures are likely to occur. Thus, even though many Western countries lack supportive policies and programs for wage-earning mothers, mothers' participation in the workforce has risen in all of them since the 1970s. The male-breadwinner model is in decline everywhere.[10] In the face of social change, rigid policies create contradictions and tensions that can open up space for political competition around new kinds of issues. There is never a direct line between social need and policy response, but in a competitive political environment, unmet needs can be grist for the partisan mill and put new questions on the political agenda.

Since the 1970s, not only has there been a rise in women's employment, but also other social structural changes have shaped partisan responsiveness to the work-family issue. In most countries, the historic cleavages underpinning the party systems have continually eroded, resulting in the shrinking of the working class and, in most places, growing secularization. Feminism, environmentalism, and other post-materialist values have become increasingly significant, challenging both the traditional workerist approach of the Left and conservative social values of the Right.[11] The United States is exceptional in this regard: rates of religiosity continue to be high and conservative religious forces became increasingly mobilized since the 1970s. However, in all countries the dominant political forces have faced changes in their traditional bases of support and sought to reach out to new social groups. These sorts of social developments create openings for new issues on the political agenda.

In evaluating the extent to which significant policy shifts have occurred, it is important to first define what is meant by policy change. Small-scale policy changes are always taking place in any country as programs are tweaked to fit evolving circumstances. These are incidents of what Peter Hall labels "normal policymaking," in which policy settings or instruments are altered.[12] To the extent that these minor alterations remain within the overall logic of a policy, they are an example of policy continuity rather than a significant change. However, policies that challenge the basic principles that had hitherto shaped public action represent a fundamental departure from the status quo. Sweden's decision to abandon the male-breadwinner model in the 1970s was a paradigm shift in the assumptions informing Swedish family policy. It put Sweden on a substantially different path with regard to mothers' employment than it had been on before. The Swedish example is one of change through a dramatic reversal of past policy, but important shifts may also emerge from the slow accumulation of smaller-scale changes.[13] This and succeeding chapters will follow a multitude of policy developments and analyze their cumulative consequences for the overall policy paradigm in each country with regard to work and family.

In Sweden and France, two different models of public policy have become institutionalized through their connection to particular social constituencies. In Sweden, there has been overall policy continuity since the 1970s in that the basic principles of the Swedish model have not been substantially challenged. This is less true in France, in part because the French had adopted a less coherent set of policies in the 1970s. Since about the mid-1980s, however, French policy makers have moved toward a mixed strategy of supporting a diverse range of options for working parents. Since that time, smaller policy shifts have not fundamentally challenged the overall model of French work-family policy.

Sweden: Family Politics in a Universal-Breadwinner Society

By the mid-1970s, many Western countries were in the throes of an economic downturn that has continued to the present day. Annual economic
growth slowed dramatically from the previous decades, as did growth in productivity rates. Perhaps most significant for women's employment policy has
been the rise in joblessness, which has climbed to double-digit figures in
many European countries. Gone are the days of labor shortages and calls for
measures to increase women's employment. Fiscal shortfalls have also undermined efforts to expand the welfare state in new directions. As Huber and
Stephens have shown, by the mid-1970s the golden age of the welfare state
effectively was over. Although they find only a few examples of outright social policy retrenchment among advanced industrialized states, spending
growth has slowed and many states have trimmed social programs.[14] In general, expansive new social policy initiatives have been taken off the table.

The economic slowdown has also affected Sweden, although unemployment remained comparatively low through the 1970s and 1980s. Nonetheless, governments of the Left and the Right alike made cuts to social spending in the late 1970s and 1980s, signaling some agreement that the size of the
welfare state had reached its limits.[15] The real economic crisis hit Sweden in
the 1990s, when a series of policy missteps exacerbated the recession and
produced a sharp rise in unemployment.[16] The result was significant cuts to
the welfare state, including family policy. Spending per child on child care
dropped and did not increase again until the late 1990s.[17] Rather than reduce
access to services, the child-to-staff ratio in these programs increased, fees
charged to parents went up, and wage increases for workers were curbed.[18]
There also were cuts to parental leave payments (parental insurance) as wage
replacement rates dropped to 75 percent of wages in 1996. Although insurance benefits increased again in 1998 to 80 percent, these benefits have never
returned to the 90 percent replacement rate of previous years, nor has the
ceiling increased to keep up with rising wages.[19] As a result, a growing proportion of workers, most of them men, have had annual earnings above this
ceiling, thereby reducing the percentage of income replaced by the benefit.[20]

Despite these economic challenges to the welfare state, the essential elements of the Swedish family policy model have remained and been reinforced. Since the mid-1970s, access to public child care has continually in-

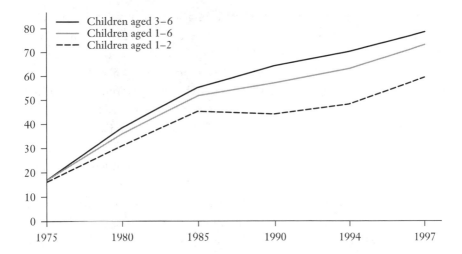

Figure 4.1   Percentage of Swedish children in child care, 1975–97
    SOURCE: Christina Bergqvist and Anita Nyberg, "Welfare State Restructuring and Child Care in Sweden," in *Child Care Policy at the Crossroads: Gender and Welfare State Restructuring*, ed. Sonya Michel and Rianne Mahon (New York: Routledge, 2002), 289, 293.

creased (figure 4.1), and there has been a substantial increase in after-school programs.[21] Despite a deep recession in the early 1990s, the number of places in these services increased threefold, so that about 40 percent of all seven- to nine-year-old children attend after-school programs today.[22] Running parallel to the expanding child care system has been a continual increase in the amount of caring time for parents. Since the late 1970s, parents have had the right to work a six-hour day until their child turns eight. In addition, parental leave time has increased, going from the six-month leave created in 1974 to sixteen months today. The parental leave benefit is generous by comparative standards: parents receive 80 percent of their previous wages, up to a ceiling, for thirteen months, and then a low flat-rate benefit during the remaining three months. Parents also can be absent from work for an additional three months without pay and are entitled to 120 days a year to care for a sick child (paid at 80 percent of wages up to a ceiling).[23]

These measures have aroused some criticism, given that women take the vast majority of parental leave days and then are far more likely than men to work reduced hours for several years thereafter. In response, policy makers have worked to increase the amount of parental leave taken by fathers. Currently, two "daddy only" months of leave are set aside for fathers or are otherwise lost to the couple, and debate is ongoing about whether to expand the father's proportion of parental leave. There also have been government campaigns to encourage fathers to take more leave days, and fathers receive information from the Swedish Social Insurance Agency about the importance of fathers having close relationships with their children.[24] In addition, although the parental leave is long, Sweden has not adopted a long care leave of the kind found in France, Norway, or Finland, in which parents receive a low flat-rate payment for two or three years if they care for their children at home. Sweden briefly adopted such a leave but soon rescinded it (discussed below).

In short, though there have been challenges to the "parent worker" model over the past three decades and some notable policy shifts, the policy paradigm of universal, high-quality day care and generous parental leave remains in place. Why have Sweden's generous family policies and commitment to gender equality been relatively unaffected by economic difficulties? The answer lies in the effects of policy on social identities. As chapter 3 described, Swedish policy makers effectively legislated the demise of the male-breadwinner family in the late 1960s and early 1970s, making it financially onerous for one parent to be home full-time. Of particular importance was a tax reform that essentially eliminated the full-time homemaker from Swedish society. Between 1970 and 1980, the percentage of employed mothers with children under the age of six went from 48.6 percent to nearly 74 percent. By 1985, that figure had reached 81 percent.[25] This created strong demand for the continued expansion of the Swedish day care system while softening divisions between advocates of working mothers and defenders of the male-breadwinner model. We can see this in comparative studies of public opinion, which show Swedes to be less sympathetic than people in most countries to the idea that mothers should stay home full-time when their children are young (table 4.1). Notably, many Swedes say they prefer that women work part-time when they have young children, which reflects the experience that many people have of one parent (usually the mother) reducing their working time while children are young.[26] Nonetheless, support for full-time caregiving at home is extremely low.

Because of broad agreement on the acceptability of mothers' employment and the very real needs of most parents for child care, when the non-Socialist parties have been in power they also have expanded the public day care

TABLE 4.1
Views on whether mothers should work when they have a child under the school age, 1994

	Work full-time	Work part-time	Stay home
Austria	2.8	36.7	60.5
Germany (East)	14.8	64.5	20.7
Germany (West)	1.3	30.2	68.5
Great Britain	5.7	31.5	62.7
Italy	5.1	55.9	39.1
Netherlands	15.1	44.8	40.1
Norway	7.7	47.5	44.8
Sweden	8.6	61.9	29.5
USA	11.1	34.2	54.7

SOURCE: International Social Survey Program, Family and Changing Gender Roles II (1994).

system. This was first evident when a bourgeois coalition government came to power in Sweden in 1976. Although some of the parties in the coalition had campaigned in favor of long care leaves for mothers, once in office the coalition government dropped this idea and instead devoted greater resources to child care to meet strong public demand.[27] Thus, at a time of other cutbacks in social spending, access to public child care rapidly increased (figure 4.1). Similarly, though Social Democratic governments made other cuts in social spending during the 1980s, the public day care system continued to grow.

In addition to expanding public subsidies, the development of the system increasingly has been through municipal day care centers staffed by public-sector employees. This was the most expensive route for public authorities, requiring a substantial investment in day care facilities and a well-paid, unionized staff. Initially, local governments were unable to meet the demand for day care and instead turned to family day care—women caring for children in their own homes—which was both quick to set up and cheaper for public authorities. Since about the mid-1980s, however, the proportion of children in family day care has declined dramatically, and today only about 10 percent of children are in family day care programs.[28]

The demise of the male-breadwinner model in Swedish society did not eliminate political divisions on the question of working mothers, but it shifted them to a new consensus point around which parties have carved out their own agenda. Specifically, the non-Socialist parties have pushed alternative forms of policy that are consistent with the general agreement on the acceptability of mothers' employment. One common theme of their policy proposals has been the promotion of "parental choice" in matters of child care. Challenging the state monopoly in the provision of services, these parties have advocated both more private provision and giving more responsibility to local governments.[29] Family day care is another form of child care favored by these parties, which some policy makers have touted as cheaper, more homelike, and offering parents a greater array of services.[30]

Another aspect of parental choice policy is to provide parents financial support so that they can care for their own children at home for two or three years. This policy potentially appeals to a number of the main constituencies of the non-Socialist parties, such as the Center (Agrarian) Party's constituency of rural voters, who often live far from child care centers. The conservatives (Moderate Party) also came to support it after abandoning their opposition to state involvement in family policy.[31] One of the care allowance's strongest champions was (and remains) the Christian Democratic (KD) Party, which appeared in the mid-1960s but lacked sufficient electoral support to enter the parliament until the late 1980s. Though it represents only a small percentage of the population, the KD was to be an important partner in a bourgeois coalition government between 1991 and 1994.[32]

Although the care allowance could potentially appeal to the constituencies of the non-Socialist parties, it also could damage the SAP by tapping the preferences of many in its own blue-collar constituency for maternal care at home. As chapter 3 argued, the issue of mothers' employment posed a dilemma for the SAP given the preferences of some within its blue-collar base for subsidies to mothers at home. Because of the predominance of class-based voting and the weakness of the Christian Democrats at that time, the SAP was able to reach out to an emerging sector of white-collar workers through gender-egalitarian family policies. Still, tensions within the SAP remained. As figure 4.2 shows, from the early 1990s people with lower levels of education were a significant SAP constituency and were more likely to support mothers being home while their children are young than those at higher levels of education. Working-class families also were long underrepresented in the public child care system, which was filled disproportionately with the children of white-collar workers (although the balance has improved in recent years).[33] Men in these families also have been the least likely to take much paid parental leave.[34] Ambivalence about mothers'

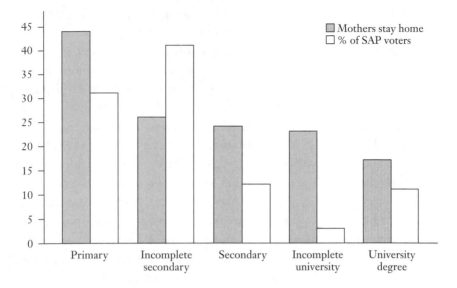

Figure 4.2   Beliefs about mothers' employment by education and percentage of SAP voters from each education group
    SOURCE: ISSP, Family and Changing Gender Roles II (1994).
    Question asks whether respondent believes mothers of preschool-aged children should work or remain at home.

employment among some of the SAP's blue-collar voting base is reflected in the way these voters have used the services and benefits of the welfare state.

At the same time, however, women within the SAP have strongly opposed a lengthy care allowance for parents, which they view as a trap for women that would exacerbate gender inequalities in paid and unpaid work.[35] It is important to note that family policy changes in the 1970s were matched by wider changes in women's place in politics, with women increasingly entering the corridors of political power. A number of the political parties, including the SAP, mandate a certain percentage of women candidates in every election, which has led to some of the highest percentages of women in parliament in the world. In the SAP, the women's federation has been a significant and growing force, pushing strongly for public child care and other family policies to promote gender equality that often go beyond the party's mainstream.[36] The Social Democratic women's federation strongly opposed care leave in the 1990s as contrary to women's equality and a threat to the public child care system.[37]

Thanks to these varied perspectives on mothers' employment, electoral competition between the Social Democratic and bourgeois parties led to continual expansions in parental leave but also a growing emphasis on paternal caring time. From the beginning, the well-paid six-month parental leave was the Social Democratic response to calls for a three-year care allowance.[38] In making the parental leave generously paid and open to both men and women, the SAP satisfied those clamoring for a gender-egalitarian vision of public policy as well as parents seeking more time at home. The expansion of parental leave over the succeeding decades reflected not only the continuing shortages in the public child care system, but also the pressures of the bourgeois parties. Parental leave was expanded to seven months in 1975 and then, under a bourgeois coalition government (1976–82), increased first to nine months and then to twelve.[39] There were additional extensions of leave time to care for a sick child such that, by 1980, parents were entitled to sixty days of paid leave per child, per year.

The next major expansion of parental leave came in 1989, when a Social Democratic government increased the leave time to fifteen months, twelve of which were paid at 90 percent of previous wages. This move was a response to the calls of the bourgeois parties during the 1988 election for a long care leave. Particularly given the appeal this held for working-class voters, the SAP could not simply call for more day care, but responded with plans for a well-paid eighteen-month leave and a guarantee of a day care place for every child above the age of eighteen months.[40] The expansion of the leave to fifteen months in 1989 represented a first installment of this promise.

While parents were gaining more paid leave, they also secured the right to reduce their work time. In 1978, a bourgeois coalition government created a formal guarantee that parents of children under eight could work a six-hour day. Unions and the Social Democrats long had opposed part-time work, yet employment data show that the increase in women's workforce participation since the 1960s had been largely in part-time positions.[41] Clearly, unions already had been tolerating the growing prevalence of part-time work. The establishment of mandatory individual taxation early in the 1970s, coupled with high marginal tax rates, created incentives for married women to work at least part-time.[42] By the 1980s, the SAP dropped its opposition to reduced work time, and the proportion of women in part-time employment continually increased. Since the mid-1980s, that proportion has declined again, although it remains high by comparative standards.[43]

Debates over the care allowance intensified in the 1990s after a bourgeois government came to power in 1991.[44] Most of the parties in the coalition favored the care allowance idea, and the coalition included a particularly enthusiastic champion of this policy—the Christian Democrats. However, one coalition member, the Liberal Party, worried about the potentially negative effects on women's employment. The outcome of bargaining between these factions of the government produced a mixed policy. On the one hand, a law was passed in 1993 that gave parents the right to three years of paid leave, one year of which would be paid at a 90 percent wage replacement level (up to a ceiling), while the rest would be covered by a low flat-rate amount (around €450 per month). The latter amount also could be used to purchase child care services. The Liberal Party insisted on allocating one month of the well-paid parental leave to fathers only so that men would be induced to take more leave. This ensured that some gender equality goals would be inserted in a policy that was otherwise expected to depress the participation of mothers in the workforce.

The government made other changes that reflected the center-right parties' views on parental "choice."[45] In 1992, block grants replaced the system of earmarked grants to municipalities for the provision of child care and other services. This gave more responsibility to local governments to determine how to allocate public monies. Another important change was the development of for-profit child care. Initially, the Social Democrats held firm in opposing private providers, passing a law in 1982 that banned for-profit private providers and regulated other private services. The bourgeois government rescinded the law in the 1990s, allowing for-profit child care to receive public funds.

Since the Social Democrats' return to power in 1994, they have sought to reinforce the public child care system while maintaining other elements of the bourgeois parties' approach. The Social Democrats did not reverse the law allowing for-profit private providers to exist and receive public funding; as a result, the percentages of children in privately run services grew from 5 percent in 1990 to 17 percent in 2002.[46] They also maintained the previous government's decentralization of responsibility for many social services. At the same time, however, the Social Democrats have sought to shore up the public system. A 1995 law required that municipalities provide child care without unreasonable delay for all children between the ages of one and twelve whose parents were working or in school. Since 2001 there have been additional reforms, such as requiring all cities to provide a day care place for at least three hours a day to all children aged one to five whose parents seek it.[47] More recently, government policy has sought to reduce the cost of these programs to parents. All children aged three and four currently are entitled to three hours a day of free child care. In 2002, the Social Democratic government enacted a *maxtaxa*, setting fees for child care services at 1–3 percent of parental income below a fixed maximum.

The Social Democrats also have increasingly emphasized the educational dimensions of the child care system. Since the 1970s, the Swedish child care system has followed the "educare" model, in which educational and care-giving tasks are intertwined.[48] In the 1990s, the educational dimension of these programs was highlighted as responsibility for child care was shifted from the Ministry of Social Affairs to that of education and a national curriculum for these programs was adopted.[49] This was important in further squeezing out family day care programs because the creation of an official pedagogy for the preschool sector—one that does not apply to family care—gives municipal day care the imprimatur of the educational system that family day care lacks. Since the mid-1980s there has been a constant decline in the proportion of children in family day care while access to municipal day care centers has expanded.[50]

On the question of parenting time, the Social Democrats have supported a lengthy, well-paid parental leave while also pushing fathers to take more leave days. Upon their return to power in 1994, the SAP immediately rescinded the bourgeois government's extended care allowance. This was done in the name of gender equality, but few criticized the already lengthy parental leave that drew women out of the labor force for extended periods. If anything, many Social Democrats would now like to improve the leave by lengthening it and/or increasing its remuneration. To mitigate the potentially gender-inegalitarian consequences of this, the Social Democrats have focused on turning men into more active caregivers. In 2002, a second month of fathers-only leave was created. As figure 4.3 shows, the proportion of parental leave days taken by men has climbed continuously since the 1970s, reflecting both the creation of daddy-only days and government efforts to promote paternal

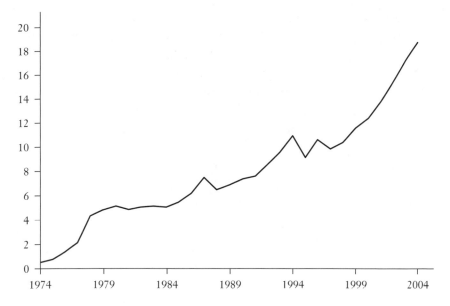

Figure 4.3 Percentage of parental benefit days used by Swedish fathers, 1974–2004
SOURCE: Swedish Social Insurance Board, courtesy of Livia Oláh.

care. However, a disproportionate share of these men are unemployed or weakly attached to the labor market, receiving social assistance, or earning very low wages.[51]

Currently, there are discussions within the political parties, trade unions, and in the media about whether to expand the amount of time that cannot be transferred between parents, effectively increasing the quota of daddy days.[52] Different factions within the labor movement and the SAP are debating this issue, with some advocating as much as a fifty-fifty split in the use of parental leave by mothers and fathers and others arguing that this is too coercive and will reduce the total time of leave available when men do not take up their share. This could force younger children into the day care system—something few people want to do.[53] Others argue in favor of a parental leave bonus that would pay 90 percent of wages (rather than the current 80 percent) to parents who split the leave time evenly. Whatever is finally enacted, it seems likely that future parental leave policy will try to encourage men to take more leave.[54]

Overall, the Swedish model of work-family policy has shown remarkable continuity, despite economic challenges to the welfare state. It appears that most political parties now accept the mix of extensive public child care and well-paid parental leave.[55] Support for a lengthier flat-rate care allowance has dissipated among the political parties, with the exception of the Christian Democratic Party and some within the Conservative Party. Most have abandoned the idea of such an allowance, finding that there is little public support for this policy.[56] At the same time, there is wide support for the publicly funded child care system. Sweden appears to have settled at an equilibrium in which universal child care and extensive parental leave serve the needs of most parents and are politically secure public policies.

France: The Reproduction of an Electorate Divided on Gender and Family

The French commitment to mothers' employment was more tentative from the beginning and thus more strongly affected by the economic downturn. French governments in the 1970s enacted policies to help working women, but they did not attempt a wholesale transformation of French society into one of parent workers, as had occurred in Sweden. Without reforms to parental leave, the tax code, or working time—and given the still inadequate supply of child care for children under three—some incentives remained for women to leave the labor force upon having children. Mothers' employment continually increased since the 1970s, yet larger changes in the structure of work and family life did not come about. Given that public policy has effectively reinforced constituencies for both public child care and support for mothers at home, French policy makers continually try to deliver something to each. This reflects both the political calculations of the parties and the adverse economic circumstances.

Compared to Sweden, France has been harder hit, and for longer, by the economic crisis that beset the European continent in the 1970s. After decades of high growth rates and full (male) employment, economic growth plummeted in the 1970s. Joblessness began to climb by the mid-1970s, reaching 9 percent in 1980. Since then, unemployment rates have rarely dipped below double digits, with some regions of France and particular categories of workers, such as youths, experiencing unemployment at rates double that of the nation as a whole. The economic slowdown also brought fiscal imbalances and a resulting need for budgetary restraint. This only intensified in the 1990s with the move toward a common currency, as the Maastricht criteria specified maximum deficit and public debt requirements for those countries entering the Economic and Monetary Union. To this day, stubbornly high unemployment and fiscal austerity cast a shadow over all social and economic policy debates.

Despite the economic downturn, aspects of the French child care system that were well institutionalized by the 1970s have been secure, and there have been no efforts to restrict access to the system. As chapters 2 and 3 detailed, the national preschool system, which originated in the nineteenth century, offered almost universal provision by the time the economic crisis set in. This created a unified constituency of parents behind these programs, who viewed the *école maternelle* as a right for all children and the first stage in their educational trajectory. These programs are overseen by the powerful Ministry of National Education and are staffed by unionized teachers who fight to preserve their piece of the budgetary pie.

Not surprisingly, then, access to the *école maternelle* has only improved. By the end of the 1980s, all three-year-olds were guaranteed a place in a public preschool.[57] An increasing proportion of two-and-a-half-year-olds were in these programs as well, spurring debates about the appropriateness of these structures for younger children.[58] Although the dominant orientation of these schools is educational and children attend them whether their parents are working or not, for some parents these programs are a form of free child care—at least between 8:30 A.M. and 4:30 P.M. Municipalities also may find them cheaper than creating public *crèches*. While city governments cover the building and maintenance costs of preschools, the national education ministry pays teacher salaries, which is often the most expensive aspect of public services. In recent years, some municipalities have created after-school programs that extend coverage to a full day, and around 14 percent of children aged three to six are currently in such programs.[59] Even where after-school services are lacking, the *école maternelle* has already covered much of the day, at little cost to parents.

The commitment to public child care for children below the age of three has been more fragile. The initial commitment to the *crèches*—formal day care centers staffed by highly trained personnel—waned by the mid-1980s. Instead, governments of the Left and the Right alike began privileging family day care (*assistantes maternelles*)—programs that are cheaper because women run these programs out of their own homes, lack much specific training, and are paid less. French governments also have favored providing a low flat-rate payment to parents that helps one of them be at home during the first three years of a child's life. The initial benefit, the *allocation parentale d'éducation*, was created in the mid-1980s and subsequently expanded. Unlike Sweden, France has not established a longer, well-paid parental leave, but it has a maternity leave of sixteen weeks that covers about 84 percent of an employed parent's previous salary.[60]

The evolution of French work-family policy has been driven in part by the economic climate. Many scholars have argued that child care policy has been subordinated to one goal since the 1980s—the fight against unemployment.[61] Policy makers therefore have sought to encourage mothers to withdraw from the labor market, at least for a few years, and more recently have promoted part-time work. Similarly, encouraging parents to hire nannies and other home help is part of a strategy centered on creating *emplois de proximité*—personal service jobs such as child care, home health assistance, housecleaning, and so on that create work for the less skilled.[62] The emphasis on family day care over the public *crèches* similarly reflects the economic environment. In a time of tight budgets, EU-imposed debt limits, and ever rising demand for child care, family day care has been a cheaper and more flexible way to deliver services while also creating jobs for less educated workers. Instead of constructing new facilities and hiring expensive, well-trained staff, family day care is run by women out of their own homes who cycle in and out of this form of employment according to prevailing demand and their own family situation.

However, economic circumstances alone cannot explain these trends in family policy. After all, the public preschools have not suffered as much in this adverse fiscal and economic environment. French family policy also has not sought to return all women to the home, because subsidies for family day care have continually increased. Finally, despite the adverse circumstances, the French state devotes substantial resources to the family, and this has not declined since the 1980s.[63] What has shifted over time is the orientation of this spending.

TABLE 4.2
Work time arrangements in couple households with children,
2000 (%)

	One-earner couple	Male full-time Female part-time	Male full-time Female full-time
Austria	32.6	27.7	38.8
Belgium	27.3	28.3	40.8
France	36.0	16.3	45.4
Germany	39.7	32.9	26.1
Italy	53.6	13.0	31.2
Netherlands	32.7	52.9	10.8
UK	29.8	40.0	28.6

SOURCE: Eurostat, *Statistics in Focus* 3-9/2000.

French work-family policies also reflect the bifurcated public that has developed on these questions since the 1970s. Here, the contrast with Sweden is instructive. As chapter 3 showed, French governments approached mothers' employment from a pragmatic standpoint—one that was less conservative than the views of elites in other continental European countries but that lacked a commitment to gender equality and women's employment per se. Although French governments adopted policies to support wage-earning mothers, they did not embark on a wider transformation of society and gender relations that would eliminate the male-breadwinner model and shift all mothers into paid work. The full-time housewife in Sweden has largely disappeared, but France has maintained a constituency supportive of the male-breadwinner model, or at least some version of it during the early years of children's lives.

Thus, although France and Sweden started from very similar levels of women's employment in early 1970s, Swedish women's employment rate rose rapidly thereafter while that of French women increased at a slower pace. This divergence reflects the limited options for part-time work in France during the 1970s and 1980s as well as the short maternity leave and limited child care options during the first three years of a child's life. As a result, many women face a stark choice between full-time work and full-time child care at home. France has some of the highest percentages of women working full-time in Western Europe, yet it also has high percentages of women at home full-time (table 4.2). By contrast, the percentage of women working part-time is comparatively low.

TABLE 4.3
Stated preferences of parents for child care arrangements, 1990 (percentages)

	France	Netherlands	West Germany	Denmark	Great Britain
Stay full-time with the child	37.6	54.1	44.4	21.7	54.7
Part-time work, use child care	20.2	23.2	21.1	43.8	20.4
Full-time work, use child care	42.3	22.6	34.0	34.5	24.8

Eurobarometer 34.0, 1990.

Response to the question: "Supposing you could have a completely free choice, which one of these arrangements would you have preferred when your child was, or your children were, too young to go to school?"

The resulting bifurcation of French families can be seen in the stated preferences of parents with regard to work and care. In 1990, French parents were almost evenly divided between the notion that parents of young children should work full-time and the idea that one parent should be home full-time (table 4.3). A comparatively small percentage favored part-time work. More generally, there is support for mothers to work, if they wish, but they should also have the possibility of being at home with their children.[64] A recent study of parents with young children found that 62 percent of those surveyed favored benefits for one parent's full- or part-time withdrawal from paid employment. Only 15 percent wanted increased spending on public child care (*crèches*), while an additional 24 percent favored more financial support for nannies or family care.[65] Surveys consistently have shown high proportions of people favoring one parent's interrupting his or her work to care for a child at home.[66]

These views are represented in the family benefits policy-making system by the conservative family associations that have long defended the interests of full-time homemakers.[67] These organizations are careful in making their claims, couching them in the language of "free choice" or the ability of men and women to "reconcile work and family life." Few will directly argue that all mothers of young children should be at home. Still, advocates for home care allowances are well placed in the policy-making system, and they also favor subsidies for more individualized services, such as family day care or nannies.[68]

One of the traditional leftist constituencies—people with lower levels of education—is also more likely to favor policies that help mothers stay home with their children. University-educated women show the strongest support for mothers' employment and the public *crèches*, and their children have long been overrepresented in the public day care system. Less educated and lower-income parents often prefer that a mother be at home but lack the financial means to do so themselves.[69] Either because they find the highly professionalized *crèches* alienating, or because it is so difficult to get a place in these programs, lower-income parents tend to use family day care, the form of care these parents say they prefer, rather than the public *crèches*.[70]

This is not to say that support is lacking for the public *crèches* or mothers' employment. There are many strong supporters of the two-earner model among unions and the political parties, particularly the Communist Party and its affiliated union, the Confédération générale du travail.[71] In addition, family associations are not a unified force: some strongly favor services that help wage-earning mothers. This diminishes the extent to which the UNAF can push a traditional family policy agenda.[72] The public *crèches* also benefit from a favorable image; for many years, parents have reported these as the most beneficial form of care for young children, although some parents see *crèches* as less flexible than family day care or hiring a baby-sitter in one's home.[73] In addition, many parents have expressed unhappiness at their inability to access or afford the kind of care services they prefer, be it formal day care centers, family care, or hiring a nanny at home. For all these reasons, both the socialist and center-right parties have favored increased day care subsidies for many years.

In short, more limited policy changes in the 1970s contributed to a divided public on the question of mothers' employment that would be reflected in the behavior of the political parties. The center of gravity in the political system clearly moved away from a conservative view of mothers' participation in the workforce but did not go as far in this regard as in Sweden. Since the mid-1980s, government policy has sought to appeal to these diverse views, crafting policies that would meet the economic objectives of fighting unemployment and containing government spending while also resonating with the families' preferences. The resulting mix of policies and programs often has been couched in the rhetoric of maximizing "parental choice."

This marriage of economic and political interests is reflected in efforts by both center-right and leftist governments to develop flexible, less regulated forms of child care such as family day care. The practice of women caring for other people's children in their own homes had long been a major form of child care in France but was done entirely in the black market. The regulation and promotion of family day care first began in the late 1970s, during the presidency of Valéry Giscard d'Estaing. In 1977, the government officially labeled these caregivers *assistantes maternelles* and created a regulatory mechanism that would grant them an official status if they met some minimal health and safety requirements. Few requests for this status would be turned down, and the *assistantes maternelles* quickly became a government-sanctioned alternative to the highly trained staff of the public *crèches*.[74] This law also established a minimum salary to which these workers were entitled and required that parents pay social security taxes for them.[75] To help parents with this cost, the CNAF created a benefit in 1980 that covered part of these social security taxes.

The Socialist president François Mitterrand continued this approach after a brief flirtation with Swedish-style family policy. In 1981, the first Socialist government of the Fifth Republic came to power with grand ambitions, including promises to create 300,000 new places in public *crèches* and a paid parental leave that would be so generous that men would also take advantage of it. The number of public day care places rapidly grew between 1981 and 1983. However, by 1983, the Socialist government had dramatically reversed course from a program of Keynesian expansion to one of economic austerity. With this U-turn, the commitment to egalitarian family policy faded.[76] A decentralization law of 1983 shifted full responsibility for child care to municipal governments, and the number of new places in *crèches* created each year declined dramatically.[77] The idea of creating a generous parental leave also was dropped.

Instead of more resources being poured into the construction of new day care centers, there were renewed efforts to encourage the use of family day care as both an anti-unemployment measure and a way to relieve the demand for day care. In 1990, the Socialist government replaced the old benefit for family day care with a new one—the *aide à la famille pour l'emploi d'une assistante maternelle agréée* (AFEAMA), which covers the social charges parents pay for a family day care worker.[78] Since 1989, the government has supported *relais assistantes maternelles* (family day care networks), which are places where parents and day care workers can meet and gain information about child care issues and *assistantes maternelles* can sometimes benefit from some training. The emphasis on these more flexible and cheaper forms of care continued under center-right governments, usually under the rubric of promoting parental choice.

Where the parties have differentiated themselves from each other is in the class orientation of these policies. In 1986, a center-right government created the *allocation de garde d'enfant à domicile* (AGED), a payment to cover part of the social security taxes that parents must pay on the nannies they hire. Then, in 1996, another center-right government doubled AGED's reimbursement ceiling and extended its use to cover children aged three to six. The number of families benefiting from the AGED increased by 170 percent in two years.[79] The Socialists have vigorously contested this policy, arguing that it only benefits the upper-income families who are most likely to hire nannies. Seizing the opportunity to differentiate themselves from the center right on this issue, a Socialist government reduced the attractiveness of the AGED in the late 1990s.[80]

Left and Right parties also have created benefits that encourage mothers to retreat from paid employment while their children are young.[81] In 1977, a center-right government created the right for working parents with children under three to suspend work for two years without pay. Then, in 1985, a Socialist government made a renewed effort to draw women out of the labor force by creating the *allocation parentale d'éducation* (APE), a benefit for parents with three or more children who leave the labor market for two years. The leave had a strict work requirement that is revealing of its function as an anti-unemployment policy, but it also had a pronatalist flavor in that it was open only to parents with three or more children. When few parents took advantage of the measure, the center-right government that came to power in 1986 passed a new law that diminished the work requirement and offered the paid leave for three years.[82]

In 1994, another center-right government made the leave open to families with only two children and raised the work requirement—the clear intention being to promote women's exit from the labor market. The value of the benefit also increased substantially, and parents were now able to take it part-time. The measure produced a sharp drop in the employment of mothers with two children. Between 1994 and 1999, the percentage in the labor force of mothers with two children dropped from 74 percent to 56 percent, the first time since the 1970s that there was a downward trend in women's labor force participation.[83] Many on the left, including feminists and the

Communist Party, were sharply critical of this expansion in the APE. However, when a Socialist government returned to power in 1997, it did not repeal the law, trying instead to soften its effects by encouraging the re-entry of women into paid work at the end of this lengthy leave.[84] Despite statements about the importance of public child care, there was virtually no growth in the numbers of public *crèches* during the leftist government's tenure in office.[85] Instead, the use of registered and subsidized family day care increased throughout the 1990s.

In 2003, a center-right government consolidated and extended this approach to work-family policy by expanding the subsidies for family day care, promising greater investments in the public *crèches*, and extending the right to a longer care leave to parents of one child. Labeled a *complément libre choix d'activité* (free-choice benefit), a parent with one child could now cease working for six months following the well-paid maternity leave and receive a flat-rate benefit of about €500 per month. Those with two or more children can still leave work until their children are three, receiving the same flat-rate benefit (which is worth about one-half of the French minimum wage).[86] Alternatively, parents can receive a different free-choice benefit, the purpose of which is to make family day care more affordable for moderate-income families, to subsidize their use of this form of care. At the same time, the government has promised to spend €200 million to create 20,000 more places in the *crèches*.[87]

Although the French approach to work and family has shifted course since the mid-1970s, there never was a very solid vision behind from these policies from the start. The negative economic climate has undermined support among the major political parties for the public *crèches* and other policies that would encourage mothers to work. Nonetheless, even the center-right parties have not fully embraced a conservative familialist vision but have instead sought to meet the preferences of a diverse range of families. In so doing, the language of choice has become a dominant motif in debates over family policy, with parties on both the left and the right competing over how well they meet the needs of French parents. They differ in the class orientation of their policies, but the distinction between the Socialist and center-right family policy is not great. Given the mixed views of French parents about their preferred form of assistance, a proclaimed policy of free choice that provides both benefits for caregivers at home and services and subsidies for those in paid work seems calculated to appeal to French voters.

Social and Political Ramifications of Swedish and French Family Policy

In some areas, Swedish and French work-family policies have produced similar results. Fertility rates in both countries have been high, although Swedish fertility levels dropped in the 1990s during the economic downturn. In general, however, direct financial supports to families and the ability of women with children to work seem conducive to higher birth rates in these countries than in much of continental Europe.[88] Similarly, a number of scholars have noted that single mothers in both countries have lower poverty rates than in the United States owing to the combination of financial subsidies and work supports available to them.[89] Yet another commonality lies in their extensive preschool systems, staffed by highly trained and well-paid workers. By the time Swedish or French children reach the age of two or two and a half, the overwhelming majority of them are in publicly funded services that are heavily subsidized or, in the case of France, free of charge. Observers have lauded the quality of these programs and their affordability for parents.[90] According to Gornick and Meyers, between 80 and 100 percent of the costs of child care are covered by the public sector in both countries, compared to 41 percent of costs in the United States. This substantially lowers the cost of day care to parents, with particular ramifications for low-income families.[91]

Where these countries differ is in the extent of mothers' employment, which is less in France than in Sweden. Swedish family policy clearly has contributed to high employment rates among Swedish mothers because there are few incentives for a parent to leave the labor force entirely.[92] A generous parental leave and options for part-time work allow parents to spend a lot of time with their children while also maintaining their place in paid work. In France, by contrast, the three-year job-guaranteed leave and benefit creates incentives for mothers to leave work for a longer time. As was noted earlier, the extension of the care leave benefit to mothers of two children in the 1990s led to a sharp drop in mothers' employment.[93] Although many of these women return to paid work at the end of the leave period, a study of women six to twelve months after they had received the care allowance showed that only 51 percent were in paid employment, compared to 76 percent who had been employed before they began receiving the benefit.[94] Critics also note that those more likely to take these leaves are women at the lower end of the socioeconomic spectrum, and that they often face difficulties being reintegrated into the workplace after the leave period is over.[95]

This picture of contrasts does need to be modified, however, to take into account the large proportion of Swedish mothers that are absent from paid work during parental leave. French labor force studies do not count women on three-year care leaves as employed, whereas Swedish studies do include mothers on the sixteen-month parental leave as employed. Thus, although 66.2 percent of French mothers with children under three are in paid work, compared to 72 percent of equivalent Swedish mothers, the proportion of Swedish mothers actually *at work*, and not on parental leave, is 45 percent.[96]

Moreover, while Swedish policies have created a child care system in which nearly all children are in either publicly provided or publicly subsidized child care, children enter these services only after they are at least one year old. In 2003, only twenty-five children under the age of one were in center or family day care, and most children do not go to child care before they are one and a half.[97] This means that parents lack much choice about returning to work before one or one and a half years of parental leave. In addition, though most child care centers are open ten to twelve hours per day, the trend is for parents to remove their children from child care by 3:00 or 4:00 P.M. This may reflect the tendency of some municipal governments during the 1990s to introduce time-related fees for child care, so that centers would charge parents less for children who left the centers earlier in the day.[98] It may also be due to norms about the importance of parental caring time.[99] In any case, one parent must have reduced working hours for this to be possible.

In short, rather than create a two-earner world in which both parents are equally engaged in paid work, the Swedish "one-and-three-quarters" model has largely restructured women's work and family time and is slowly changing men's as well. Extensive parental leave and reduced work time are crucial elements of Swedish work-family policy, and women take advantage of both far more than men. As Anita Nyberg has observed, many believe the Swedish welfare state has made it possible for women to be workers, but it also has "enabled women workers to become caregivers" through its generous parental leave system.[100]

Critics also point out that the Swedish labor market is one of the most sex segregated in the world, certainly more so than the French one.[101]

Public-sector jobs are most amenable to reduced and interrupted work schedules and therefore attract a large percentage of women. Additionally, many allege that private firms discriminate against female employees and job applicants. The prevalence of part-time work exacerbates the problem, because certain sectors of the Swedish economy that are organized around the assumption of part-time employment disproportionately draw female workers. In France, by contrast, there is a greater bifurcation of the pool of female workers, with a higher percentage of women at home full-time and high rates of full-time female employment as well. In short, the implications of these two models of public policy for the position of women in paid work are more ambiguous than at first glance. The effect of the models also is a moving target: the proportion of women in part-time work now is declining in Sweden, while it is rising in France.

In thinking about the future of these approaches, there also are important political differences between these two countries that should affect work-family politics in the years ahead. Sweden is better poised to achieve a fundamental transformation of gender roles in the distribution of work and care. The policies of the SAP not only forged a unified constituency of parent-workers, but also brought about larger societal changes that have put gender-egalitarian goals into the heart of Swedish politics. As Helga Hernes describes it, the welfare state has been a source of women's mobilization into the public sphere, bringing about large-scale changes in women's roles in society and politics.[102] One example is the feminization of unions: from 1970 to 1991, women made up 98 percent of new union members, and they now dominate the white-collar unions. Because unions have tremendous influence over the SAP, the feminization of the workforce has helped bring women's concerns into the mainstream of partisan politics.[103] Similarly, there are high proportions of women in parliament, the political parties, and government administration.[104] Although there is no straightforward relationship between the proportion of women in public office and gender-egalitarian policies, the insertion of women into the public sphere contributes, at the very least, to new discourses and understandings of these issues.[105]

The push for gender equality in Sweden increasingly is about not only changing women to make them fit into traditionally male roles, but also changing men and broader societal structures that reproduce traditional gender roles. In addition to the push from feminists on this issue, men's groups have emphasized the importance of paternal care and lobbied for the mandatory father's quota of parental leave.[106] Although critics have noted the shortcomings of the Social Democratic Party in certain areas of gender equality, the party clearly places a high priority on the equal sharing of work and care between men and women.[107] One can expect continued evolution in this regard: more women work full-time and have expectations about their partner's involvement in child care, and men themselves are influenced by new values. Currently, Swedish men take the highest proportion of parental leave of men in any country in Europe.

In France, there is less discussion of the need to change men's behavior or adopt public policies that would encourage men to take up more responsibilities for child care. The extension of paternity leave from a few days to two weeks was one step in this direction, but this limited measure does nothing to change the fact that 98 percent of extended (three-year) leave takers are women.[108] French policies for working mothers remain precisely that— policies to help *mothers* better fit into the world of paid work, without encouraging changes in the behavior of fathers. Such a vision of equal work and care is largely absent from the political scene; the only ones voicing it are a small number of feminists, who lack much influence in mainstream politics. Swedish work-family policies are likely to continue effecting a wide-scale change in gender roles and values, but we should not expect similar changes in the French context. Particularly because of the expanded use of long care leaves by women, current French policies are reinforcing a traditional vision of work and care roles that, for a portion of the public, will likely endure.

CHAPTER FIVE

The Consolidation of the Private Market Model in the United States

Policies for working parents in the United States have hardly changed since the mid-1970s. The American system maximally privileges private decision making, with limited public subsidies to help either parents in paid work or parents at home. In the case of child care, public funds are available only for the very poorest families and have increasingly become a tool of welfare reform. Instead, most parents look for day care services in private markets, receiving at most some tax subsidies to cushion them from the full cost of these programs. One of the few policy changes in recent decades was the creation of a federally mandated family and medical leave of three months and the passing of similar mandates at the state level. These are unpaid leaves, however, so that people depend on the good will or policies of employers for compensation during their absence.[1] This mix of child care and leave arrangements is typical of the American welfare state, with its complex array of privately provided services and benefits, hidden public subsidies through the tax code, and residual public supports for the poor.[2]

The continuity of American work-family policies since the mid-1970s reflects both the ideological changes in American politics and the success of private market solutions in undercutting drives for reform. The mid-1970s marked the beginning of a conservative resurgence in American politics that combines hostility to "big government" and the welfare state with a social traditionalism rooted in a conservative religious revival. Economic and social conservatives have become increasingly prominent in the Republican Party, and they have unified in their opposition to the welfare state—particularly when it comes to federal family policies. Proposals for broad-based child care assistance have ignited opposition in both camps as an expansion of the public sector and federal interference in the family. For social conservatives, the issue is one of both defending stay-at-home mothers and resisting government interference in the family. Thus, direct, public child care subsidies have been acceptable only for very poor parents as part of welfare reform.

In a climate of highly politicized debates about work and family issues, Democrats have largely failed to pass policies and programs that would help working parents. The Democratic Party has become the party of feminism, and Democratic politicians have successfully pushed key elements of the feminist agenda, such as abortion rights. They have had more trouble with issues that require social spending (child care) or labor market regulation (parental leave), because these proposals arouse strong opposition by economic and social conservatives. Democratic difficulties on redistributive questions are reinforced by the way in which private social provision has eroded the constituency for new social spending. With most people reliant on the private sector to meet their human welfare–related needs, support for new welfare state programs often proves soft. The private welfare model is politically self-reinforcing over time, particularly given tax subsidies and regulatory policies that help sustain these private alternatives.

The same has been true for work-family policies. With some government prodding since the 1970s, the child care market has been responsive to growing demand, generating day care programs run by both for-profit and nonprofit organizations. Though often prohibitively expensive for lower-income people, such programs have met the needs of many middle- and upper-income families. The latter also are more likely to be in firms with family leave provisions. This circumstance has undercut the demand by politically important groups—such as middle-class parents—for further government action in this area. The majority of families find some way to put the pieces of the work-family puzzle together, albeit imperfectly.

This is not to say that there is no support for increased federal involvement in helping parents balance work and family. Many parents would undoubtedly welcome paid leave time from work or direct subsidies for child care. What is lacking, however, is sufficiently strong public sentiment to overcome a conservative mobilization against expanded federal family policies. When efforts in the late 1980s to promote child care subsidies for the middle class came to naught, there were no political consequences. By the 1990s, the issue of child care had dropped off the political agenda, and after the Family and Medical Leave Act (FMLA) was signed in 1993, discussion of paid leaves disappeared from the national political scene. Advocacy groups lobby on these issues at the national level, but many of their successes have come in shoring up residual programs for the poor. The political will for a major redistributive effort is lacking, and reform efforts often have foundered in the face of unified conservative opposition.

The Political Context for Work-Family Policies

Despite the lack of federal child care support or paid parental leave, the number of mothers in paid work rose rapidly throughout the 1970s and 1980s. The percentage of mothers in the labor force with children under six went from 32.2 percent in 1970 to 46.8 percent in 1980, and by 1990 it increased another 12 percentage points. There was a parallel trend for mothers with children under three (figure 5.1). Although these figures might seem to indicate a constituency for broad-based programs that help working mothers, these trends were filtered through a new economic and political context. The economic situation in the United States had worsened considerably by the mid-1970s. The oil shocks of the 1970s created the immediate crisis, but the larger malaise affecting the American economy was the slowdown in productivity growth. Throughout the 1980s, the United States experienced slower economic growth and higher unemployment rates. In addition, chronic budget deficits and mounting levels of public debt put pressure on federal spending. The economic and fiscal climate has hardly been conducive to expensive new social programs.[3]

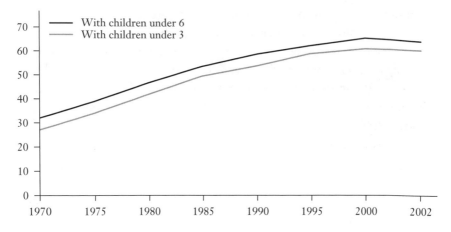

Figure 5.1 Participation in labor force by American women with children, 1970–2002

SOURCE: Committee on Ways and Means, *2004 Green Book.*

At the same time, a political movement was emerging that profoundly shaped American politics by politicizing both economic and social values issues. The mass basis of this movement grew out of the social upheavals of the 1960s, when countercultural movements and Vietnam war protesters sent southern and many blue-collar whites to the Republican Party, while African Americans, feminists, and other social liberals became part of the Democratic coalition.[4] The fight over civil rights lost some intensity by the 1970s, and racial conflicts spread to the sphere of welfare politics, as evidenced by the growing racialization of poverty and social-welfare issues.[5] These conflicts fed negative perceptions among whites about the federal government, the welfare state, and taxation and contributed to some of the tax revolts that took shape at the state level.[6] The apparently antistatist mood among the mass public gave sustenance to conservative elites seeking to rollback the "New Deal order"—the consensus around Keynesian economic policy and a moderately sized welfare state that had characterized American politics for decades. Shedding their previous moderation on social and economic policy, the Republican Party shifted to the right on economic matters and became determined to hold the line on social spending and federal taxes, if not actively dismantle parts of the federal welfare state.[7] This shift dovetailed with and was reinforced by a business mobilization against government regulation and taxation that began in the 1970s and the spread of conservative think tanks in which conservative social and economic policy ideas were nurtured and promoted.[8]

The politicization of social values also began in the 1970s, when a host of gender and family issues erupted onto the scene, including the Equal Rights Amendment (ERA), abortion, homosexuality, and, more broadly, the revolution in sexual mores.[9] These and other issues catalyzed a mobilization in defense of traditional family values in which much conservative animus was directed at feminism and a perceived erosion of parental control over children.[10] The movement emerged in part out of a religious revival, particularly among evangelicals. Although most Western countries have experienced widespread secularization over the past several decades, in the United States rates of religious belief and practice remain high.[11] Of course, American religion is extremely diverse, and people from the various denominations often have quite different political leanings. One of the most important trends in recent decades, however, has been the growing strength of evangelical religions and the decline of liberal Protestant churches. One reason is that evangelicals have built up a network of religiously based institutions, including religious radio stations, television programs, periodicals, colleges, and schools.[12] As James Davison Hunter describes it, in the four decades following the Second World War evangelicalism emerged as a "socio-cultural majority."[13]

The political manifestations of evangelicalism became apparent in the 1970s with the growing political activism of religious conservatives. Initially, some of the most visible activists were fundamentalist Christians such as the Reverend Jerry Falwell, but the excesses and scandals associated with him and other televangelists discredited them in the eyes of the mainstream public. More moderate evangelicals came to the fore by the 1980s, softening the rougher edges of the conservative message while hewing to similarly traditional social values.[14] This new moderation enabled the movement to attract a broader constituency: the pool of evangelical voters who hew to moral traditionalism but reject racism or strident antifeminism. Evangelical leaders also have had some success building a multidenominational coalition by reaching out to Catholics, Mormons, and Orthodox Jews.[15]

Whether or not social conservatives have actually had much influence on American politics has been the source of some debate.[16] Evangelicals make up a significant but not dominant share of the electorate; in the 2004 election, only 23 percent of people surveyed in exit polls identified themselves as evangelicals (with 78 percent of those who identified themselves as evangelicals reporting that they voted for George W. Bush).[17] Although they clearly are not a majority in the Republican Party, the social conservative movement has had a great impact on American politics owing to a number of factors, particularly the coalitional nature of American political parties. Recall from the discussion of Sweden and Norway in chapter 3 how small Christian Democratic parties serving as coalition partners could extract promises on issues of importance to them from the other parties, giving them a weight beyond their actual vote share on certain policies. The same processes are at work *within* American political parties, as horse trading and compromise between groups help shape the overall policy agenda. Even if the social conservatives' views do not represent those of the entire party, they have successfully monopolized certain areas of public policy such that no Republican with national political aspirations can buck their positions on these issues. For example, although the Republican Party was once moderate on most women's equality issues, since the start of the 1980s Republicans have become increasingly pro-life and opposed to the feminist agenda.[18]

Religious conservatives also gained political leverage through their ability to turn out voters at the polls. This has given them a voice during the presidential primaries and can be seen in the steady decrease in the number of moderate Republicans in Congress. Many of these moderates have been replaced by social conservatives elected in districts or states with high proportions of evangelical voters.[19] Moreover, because the antistatism of social conservatives fits well with the free-market, small-government orientation of economic libertarians, the social conservative viewpoint on many issues gained allies in the party. The fusion of social and economic conservatives created a potent electoral coalition for the Republican Party, one unified by opposition to expanded federal power.[20]

How have Democrats treated work-family issues in this new political context? One consequence of the 1970s realignments on social issues was that the Democratic Party became the party of feminism. Democrats may not always listen to the demands of feminist organizations, but they are one interest group within the party coalition and have successfully shifted Democrats toward their views on many issues. Even though Democratic politicians and voters were at least as pro-life as Republicans until the 1970s and the party had long been lukewarm on the ERA, that changed by the 1980s when the Democratic Party began supporting abortion rights and other feminist causes.[21] Democrats also came increasingly to favor supports for working mothers. Throughout the past three decades, Democrats have been at the forefront of all campaigns to increase federal child care subsidies or entitle parents to paid parental leave.

Democrats have gained little traction on the work-family question, however, because of the redistributive aspects of policies such as child care or parental leave. A federal child care program requires some agreement not only on the question of whether or not mothers should work, but also on whether the federal government should expand the scope of federal responsibility to help them do so. On such proposals, Democrats face the unified opposition of social and economic conservatives—as well as fiscal conservatives within their own party—making it that much more difficult to gets these policies enacted. They also run into the limitations imposed by budget deficits and the political obstacles to raising taxes. Thus, although Democrats have had some success promoting abortion rights, affirmative action, and other issues that do not require increased federal spending, the economic-redistributive dimension of the work-family issue generates formidable opposition.

A more fundamental problem for Democrats is the way in which the American system of privately provided welfare undercuts their ability to use the welfare state as a political resource. In much of Western Europe, people live within all-encompassing systems of public social provision that provide income support, cover many of their costs, and protect them from many of the risks they face over the life cycle. The political popularity of the welfare state has made it difficult for neoliberal political movements to take root while giving Left parties a strong position as defenders of beloved social programs.[22] Americans receive substantially less direct support from federal or state government, relying instead on employers for many social benefits and facing costs such as housing, (higher) education, health care, and retirement without direct federal support. This reduces people's dependence on the public sector while also diminishing pressures on government to provide help for social needs.[23] Efforts to promote expensive new social programs run up against the fact that many people are already getting by with various forms of private provision. Democrats therefore have difficulty pushing any expansion of the welfare state beyond such highly popular programs such as Social Security or Medicare.

This dynamic became evident in President Bill Clinton's health reform effort of the early 1990s, which attempted, among other things, to guarantee access to health insurance. Although it initially appeared that there was public support for such a major reform, support vaporized as the legislation became bogged down in controversies over financing and administration. The deeper problem was that although around 15 percent of the public lacked health insurance at any time, the vast majority of people did have health insurance—provided mostly by private employers—and were generally happy with the quality and cost of care they received. Asking them to pay more for an uncertain benefit proved politically unpalatable. In the face of stiff business opposition and lacking a strong grassroots base of support, the Clinton reform effort collapsed.[24]

Leaving it to the private sector to solve parents' work and family needs has proven politically self-reinforcing. It has undermined the advocates for federal family policies, who have also faced an energized movement of economic and social conservatives. As the succeeding section will show, efforts to promote broad-based policies for families were undermined by both strong opposition on the right and the weakness of the advocates on the left.

The Political Debates over Work and Family, 1975–2005

Recurrent debates over work and family issues have not led to many concrete policy changes beyond tax breaks and an unpaid parental leave. Initially, free-market ideas shaped efforts to subsidize private child care markets and thus indirectly support working mothers. With the growing influence of social conservatives in the Republican Party, however, even these policies became controversial. The result has been a policy deadlock, leaving parents to figure out for themselves, with little government assistance, how to fit together their working and family lives.

THE SHIFT TOWARD PRIVATE MARKETS, 1975–1985

As chapter 3 showed, the mobilization of social conservatives helped defeat proposals in the early to mid-1970s to create a broad-based child care system. Toward the end of the decade, Democrats made one more push to expand the federal role in child care. Senator Alan Cranston (D-Calif.) spearheaded the effort, which proposed only modest increases in funding. Even so, the introduction of the bill in 1979 prompted an immediate reaction from conservatives, who sent letters to congressional offices and wrote strongly worded newspaper editorials against the bill.[25] Divisions among advocacy groups further undermined the effort, but what finally doomed the measure was when the Carter administration came out against it.[26] President Jimmy Carter was a born-again Christian whose political appeal in the late 1970s stemmed in part from his image as a social conservative. Although he had temporarily stanched the Democrats' loss of white Protestant votes in the South, he brought a conservative social agenda with him into office.[27] Faced with administration opposition, Cranston abandoned the bill. The only increases in federal spending on child care were minor expansions in day care for poor families or for women receiving public assistance.

Disagreement over the role of the federal government in family policy continued, and Democratic efforts turned to promoting private market alternatives for working parents. The tax break for parents' child care costs was made more attractive in 1976 when the tax deduction was turned into a credit—a boon to upper-income people because, unlike the previous tax deduction, there was no income ceiling on the wages of workers who could receive the credit.[28] Another key development was the 1979 Pregnancy Discrimination Act (PDA), which barred discrimination against women on the basis of pregnancy. Henceforth, when employers provided temporary disability insurance, they had to include pregnant women as a covered category. As Erin Kelly and Frank Dobbin argue, both the PDA and the initial Equal Employment Opportunity Commission (EEOC) ruling on which it was based spurred employers to create maternity leave policies.[29] Figure 5.2 shows this expansion by tracking changes in the leave arrangements taken by women during their first pregnancy. By the 1980s, increasing proportions of women had access to either paid or unpaid leave.

The Reagan administration reinforced the market-based approach to work and family as a way to appeal to both economic and social conservatives. Ronald Reagan, who rode a wave of anti-tax sentiment to office, championed cuts in the welfare state and increased reliance on free markets. His opposition to abortion rights and the ERA also earned him the support of social conservatives, and he was attentive to their concerns.[30] At the same

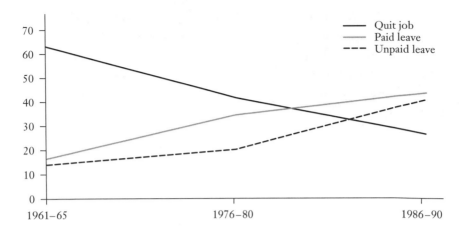

Figure 5.2   Leave arrangements by women working during first pregnancy
  SOURCE: U.S. Census Bureau, "Maternity Leave and Employment Patterns: 1961–1995," *Current Population Reports P70–79*, November 2001, 11.

time, it was clear that employed mothers were a growing proportion of the electorate and could not be ignored. Supply-side economists and other free market advocates were less likely to condemn working mothers; if anything, they believed that having educated mothers at home was a waste of human capital or a source of deadweight loss.[31] The Reagan administration's position on the question of working mothers represented the mix of voices within the party and his administration, oscillating between a market liberal and socially conservative approach.

Initially, Reagan's policies toward working mothers were more in line with the concerns of free market advocates. One of the administration's main priorities was to turn responsibility for human services over to states and private markets. During Reagan's first term, the administration consolidated social services funding in a block grant and cut overall spending. Child care funds now had to compete with other social programs at the state level and received fewer guaranteed federal funds. The result was a sharp drop in spending on public child care as federal spending declined by over 14 percent between 1981 and 1985.[32] The administration also tried to end any direct federal involvement in child care by halting the collection and analysis of child care data.[33]

To shore up the private market, the Reagan administration eliminated the federal regulations attached to public child care funds. There had been disputes over this issue since the late 1960s, when a number of federal government agencies proposed a set of federal standards for child care centers—the Federal Interagency Day Care Requirements (FIDCR). A decade-long battle ensued to pass legislation that would impose the FIDCR on all centers receiving federal funds.[34] But the FIDCR ran into a fundamental obstacle: the unwillingness of policy makers to commit more resources to public day care. Higher standards and requirements for publicly funded day care programs would have run many child care providers out of business in the absence of increased public subsidies. Implementation of these standards was repeatedly delayed through the 1970s. The issue was settled in 1981 when the Reagan administration abolished the FIDCR, assuring that there would be no federal standards on day care centers and leaving the matter entirely up to state governments.

Another way to support the private system was to expand tax breaks for day care costs. The massive tax-cutting bill signed by Reagan in 1981 included a substantial expansion of the Dependent Care Tax Credit (DCTC).[35] The bill also created a new measure that allowed companies to set up tax-favored dependent care assistance programs to help their employees pay for child care. This allowed employees to shelter up to $6,000 a year spent on child care from taxes.[36] Both of these changes to the tax code delivered disproportionate benefits to middle-class parents with child care costs. Working-class families had a lower tax liability and thus benefited less from a nonrefundable tax credit. Throughout the 1980s, the DCTC was the single largest federal expenditure on child care, although the dependent care assistance plans often proved most valuable to better-off families.[37]

Interestingly, the 1981 tax law also created a second-earner tax credit that diminished some of the disincentives against married women's employment. The credit was a response to the "marriage penalty" in the tax code, which affected two-earner couples.[38] With the high inflation of the 1970s, married couples with two incomes faced steep marginal tax rates on the "second income," which is piled on top of the first. This became known as the marriage penalty because an unmarried cohabiting couple could file separately and have a lower tax liability, whereas married couples were essentially forced to file their taxes together.[39] Although the Reagan administration did not ultimately endorse the more radical proposal of mandatory individual taxation—which would have shifted the tax burden from two-earner to one-earner households—it agreed to provide fiscal relief to working wives and mothers through both the second-earner credit and tax breaks for child care costs. Together, these tax provisions signified a degree of acceptance of mothers' employment, at least among some within the Republican camp.

Social conservatives, however, viewed these tax breaks as discrimination against traditional families and encouragement for mothers to work. Their complaints surfaced almost immediately and signaled the growing politicization of the "hidden" side of the American welfare state—the deductions, credits, and other advantages provided through the tax code.[40] Social conservatives favored general tax cuts that would compensate all families for the costs of having children.[41] In a 1985 hearing on tax reform, these conservatives argued that the tax law was antifamily and stacked the deck against stay-at-home mothers. They specifically called for repeal of the DCTC and other changes in the tax code to compensate single-earner married couple families for the lost income of a second earner.[42]

By the mid-1980s, momentum was building for policies more consistent with the social conservative view. Reagan himself gave more attention to family issues in his second term and created a White House Working Group on the Family.[43] The group was headed by Gary Bauer, a key figure in the conservative family movement, and its 1986 report charged that the family had been undermined by "the abrasive experiments of two liberal decades."[44] Echoing the principle of subsidiarity espoused by European Christian Democrats, Bauer argued that only community groups, churches, and local governments should be involved in family affairs. Rather than call for the child-rearing benefits defended by European conservatives, Bauer's group wanted to increase the personal exemption in the tax code from $1,080 to as much as $5,000. The higher exemption would give more money to parents, which they could then spend on day care or use to enable one parent to be home. The working group suggested paying for the increase by repealing the DCTC, which many social conservatives saw as discriminatory because it was available only to working mothers.[45]

The drive for general, family-related tax cuts gained ground in the second Reagan administration. The administration's 1985 tax reform proposal called for eliminating both the two-earner credit and the DCTC, and the two-earner credit was repealed in 1986.[46] Although the DCTC survived, the ceiling on eligible earnings was not increased to keep up with inflation. In addition, eligibility for the DCTC was scaled back in 1988 to help pay for a welfare reform bill. Thus, while the tax code continued to offer some support for child care expenses, its value for parents continually declined. Instead, the 1986 tax law also nearly doubled the personal exemption. The emphasis of the "hidden welfare state" was moving from explicit support for working mothers to general tax cuts to all families, which fit well with the conservative theme of promoting of "parental choice" in matters of child rearing. This theme was to dominate debates in the late 1980s about publicly funded child care.

DEBATES OVER CHILD CARE AND PARENTAL LEAVE, 1986–PRESENT

After lying dormant for several years, the issue of child care came back on the political agenda in the latter half of the 1980s owing to the efforts of children's advocacy groups. Led by Marian Wright Edelman and the Children's Defense Fund, the coalition behind reform included women's organizations, unions, child development advocates, left-leaning churches, antipoverty groups, and other social welfare organizations. Notably, feminist organizations were more engaged and active on the child care issue than they had been in the past.[47] The advocates came together to support the Act for Better Child Care (ABC), a measure that aimed to establish national regulations for day care centers and increase federal spending on child care. In an effort to spread day care funding to a wider swath of families, the legislation would have made all parents earning below 115 percent of the state median income level eligible for child care assistance.[48]

The ABC effort faced stiff opposition from social and economic conservatives alike. In the view of social conservatives, child care assistance took tax dollars from families struggling to get by on one income and gave it to two-earner families who had the "luxury" of a second income. Such a position was espoused not only by conservative think tanks and activists such as Phyllis Schlafly and Gary Bauer, but also by many Republicans in Congress.[49] Economic conservatives opposed the ABC as an expansion of governmental power, arguing that state-level and market solutions could address the needs of most parents.[50] The two groups came together in their opposition to federal regulation of day care centers, arguing that this interfered in markets, state-level affairs, and parental child-rearing practices. Furthermore, the original ABC bill did not allow public funding to be used for any "sectarian purpose." The issue of whether or not church-run day care centers could receive public funding in the form of vouchers led to fierce fights.

Conservatives also argued that most parents preferred care given by relatives, friends, and churches, and that the regulations in the ABC bill threatened this existing fabric of child care services while constraining parental choices. In this, they gained support from the growing sector of private day care companies, which had a strong stake in opposing federal regulations.[51] Conservatives instead advocated child tax credits for all families, which would return income to parents and allow them to choose whatever form of care they preferred, be it from relatives, church-run centers, or parents. As in France or Sweden, the issue of "choice" became an important theme among conservatives, although they emphasized the need for tax breaks rather than direct benefits for families as the way to promote choice. As Elizabeth Dole, the Secretary of Labor, wrote at the time, the Bush administration was a "pro-choice administration" that intended to maximize options for parents in the area of work and family life.[52]

Although opponents maintained a unified front against the legislation, ABC advocates were divided on a number of issues. One of the greatest sources of discord was the issue of whether church-based day care centers should be able to receive public funds and, if so, whether they could have sectarian programs and preferential hiring according to religious membership and belief. The ABC's system of state-funded vouchers for parents also aroused the suspicions of education groups, who saw the measure as a first step toward vouchers in education to the detriment of the public school system.[53] There were other clashes over tactics: Edelman directed a vituperative attack against legislators who favored federal child care assistance but did not adhere to the ABC approach.[54]

The fundamental problem for the ABC advocates was the lack of strong public support for the legislation. On the one hand, higher rates of women's workforce participation since the early 1970s fostered favorable views of mothers' employment, much as had occurred in France or Sweden. In the United States, this came about less because of explicit government policy to promote women's labor force participation, and more because of the necessities of two incomes in a country with a limited safety net, the growing service sector that lured women into paid work, and an antidiscrimination regime that has removed many of the barriers to women's employment.[55] Significant shifts in public opinion followed, as women's labor force partici- pation tends to increase support for feminist ideas, including the notion of mothers remaining in paid employment.[56] Thus, much as in other Western countries, a welfare state regime that promotes women's employment— albeit indirectly in the case of the United States—contributed to changing public perceptions about the acceptability of mothers' employment.

Although there was increasing support for the idea that mothers should work for pay, it did not translate into a groundswell of support for public child care policy because so many parents had found child care in the private mar- ketplace. Government tax subsidies and regulatory measures to support pri- vate options bore fruit in the 1980s. For one thing, the day care market was booming: between 1976 and 1988, jobs in this sector increased by 117 per- cent, exceeding the rate of job growth in the rest of the economy by almost four times.[57] For-profit child care chains did especially well, owing to both the lack of federal regulations that would increase their costs and the child care tax breaks so beneficial for their middle- and upper-income clientele.[58] There also were major expansions in both nonprofit centers and family day care pro- grams.[59] In 1965, only 6 percent of young children with employed mothers were in center care, but by 1993 this figure had risen to 30 percent, while many other children were in family day care and informal arrangements.[60]

Firms increasingly were offering family leave for parents such that, by the end of the 1980s, one-third of medium and large firms had these provisions. Nearly 89 percent of full-time workers in these firms had short-term dis- ability insurance plans, which women could use to take temporary paid leaves from work for pregnancy-related reasons.[61] Of course, not everyone has benefited from private solutions to the same extent. Lower-income people are unable to pay the high fees charged by good-quality day care cen- ters and are less likely to be employed by firms that offer family leave provi- sions. However, the politically important middle class generally has bene- fited from these private alternatives, fragmenting the constituency for universalistic federal family policies.[62]

As a result, intensity over the work-and-family issue has been lacking. On the one hand, people generally agree with the statement that government should spend more on child care programs—a point repeatedly raised by advocates during the debates over the ABC. However, surveys showed an

TABLE 5.1
"Should the government spend more on child care?" American responses

Preschool programs like Head Start for poor children	60%
Child care for poor children	58%
Child care for all children with working parents	35%

SOURCE: General Social Survey, 1988–91.

Percentage answering "spend much more" or "spend more" to the question, "Here are some other areas of government spending. Please indicate whether you would like to see more or less government spending in each area. Remember that if you say 'much more,' it might require a tax increase to pay for it."

equal if not greater proportion agreed with Bush's tax cut proposals for all families, and that most people favored increased spending on child care for the poor, not for the middle class (see table 5.1).[63] In addition, when asked about their child care arrangements, most parents reported that they were satisfied with what they had. A 1988 Louis Harris and Associates poll found that over 83 percent of parents were satisfied with the quality of child care they get, 79 percent were satisfied with the cost, and 78 percent were happy with the availability of these services.[64] Such data should be treated with caution; parents are unlikely to admit to a pollster that they are putting their children in poor-quality day care. Nonetheless, legislators needed political support on such a contentious issue, and a groundswell of opinion in favor of broad-based child care assistance was not apparent.[65]

Without strong enthusiasm for public child care for non-poor families, the Republican proposal to give tax credits to families with children—returning more money to them to make their own decisions about work and family—was a potent alternative. After much legislative haggling, compromise legislation in 1990 combined the Democratic and Republican approaches. A new child care subsidy, the Child Care Development Block Grant (CCDBG), was to be available to those earning up to 75 percent of a state's median income, while more child care dollars were directed at women at risk of going on welfare. Republicans prevailed in removing requirements from the bill that states improve their regulatory standards, but additional funds were earmarked for states to invest in quality improvements. The bill included a major extension of the Earned Income Tax Credit and a supplemental tax credit for families with infants.[66] Both were targeted to low-income families, and they were to prove more valuable than the CCDBG. Appropriations in the first three years for the new child care grant were under $1 billion a year and thus helped a small percentage of children in need.[67] Moreover, the CCDBG is not an entitlement; most of those who meet the income requirements for these services have not actually received them, owing to limited funding.[68]

Advocates had more success with the passage of the Family and Medical Leave Act in 1993, which requires firms with fifty or more employees to provide workers an unpaid leave of three months for family or medical reasons. One reason for the success of this legislation is the broader coalition of support behind the bill. Although feminists and labor unions were some of the most active advocates, the decision to push for a general family-related leave rather than simply a parental or maternity leave created an intergenerational coalition around the bill that included powerful groups such as the AARP.[69] In addition, the FMLA had the support of Catholic pro-life activists. Much like the Pregnancy Discrimination Act of 1978, which they also supported, many Catholic activists viewed the FMLA as a measure that would help prevent women from having abortions. As Anya Bernstein and others have argued, Catholic support was crucial for the bill, and it led high-level pro-life congressmen such as Representative Henry Hyde (R-Ill.) to throw their support behind the bill.[70]

More generally, the legislation successfully united people across the values divide, with feminists and other liberal advocates joining sides with pro-life Catholics. Not all social conservatives were in agreement on the bill—Schlafly labeled it "a windfall for yuppies"[71]—but many were ambivalent about a measure to promote people spending more time with family and did not devote much energy to defeating it, concentrating their efforts instead on the child care legislation being considered at the same time.[72] Without the cross-cutting values issue, conflict over the FMLA centered on economic questions, with business opposing the bill as an unfunded mandate on business while labor unions and women's groups strongly supported it. To appease business groups, the leave remained unpaid, and the FMLA applied only to larger firms. Although this scaling back enabled the FMLA to pass, it also kept the act extremely limited.[73] The United States remains one of the few advanced, industrialized countries in which parents have no entitlement to a paid parental leave.

In short, for non-poor families, the debates over child care and parental leave in the 1980s and 1990s brought limited policy changes. During the

Clinton years, the issue of providing broad-based support to working parents was low on the political agenda once Clinton had signed the FMLA. In 1998, his administration proposed expansions in the CCDBG and the Dependent Care Tax Credit, worth $21.7 billion over five years. The plan was immediately attacked by Republicans in the House and Senate as discrimination against stay-at-home mothers—an argument that also attracted centrist Democratic support.[74] A House resolution that any child care plan must also give support to parents at home passed 409 to 0—a sign that no one wanted to be on the record as being less than supportive of full-time motherhood.[75] Republicans also voiced concern about a measure that would encourage parents to put their children in child care. As the co-chairperson of the Republican National Committee said, "A lot of experts are saying this is a very scary experiment. . . . Uncle Sam was never meant to be a parent."[76] At the same time, however, Republicans were careful not to assail working parents, and their counterproposal of expanded tax breaks for all families appealed to mothers at home without alienating working mothers.[77] Although Democrats asserted that failure to act on this issue would have electoral consequences, Republicans argued that the issue was off voters' radar screen.[78] The latter proved true, in part because the initiative was eclipsed by the Monica Lewinsky scandal. Even before that, however, the proposal was going nowhere in Congress.

Instead, residual child care supports for the poor were shored up as part of welfare reform efforts in the 1990s. As early as 1988, the Family Support Act intensified efforts to get poor welfare mothers into paid work and provided increased funding for welfare-related child care. The act also created an entitlement for single mothers to receive child care assistance when participating in a job training program or in the first twelve months after starting work.[79] In 1996, the Clinton administration and the Republican Congress agreed to eliminate the federal entitlement to welfare (Aid to Families with Dependent Children) but included increased resources for child care and other supports that aimed to help poor mothers remain in paid work. The Personal Responsibility and Work Opportunity Reconciliation Act of 1996 rolled together a number of different child care programs into one block grant, the CCDBG, and substantially increased its funding. Since then, debate has continued about whether the government is spending enough on child care and other work supports for women on public assistance. Even with recent funding increases, the proportion of parents benefiting from direct public subsidies appears to be extremely low. One recent survey found that only 12 percent of parents with children under thirteen who are using child care programs get help from the government or other organizations, such as charities.[80]

Consequences of the Private Model of Work and Family Policy

The American model of work and family policy has had numerous social and economic consequences. One result has been fairly high rates of female employment, including that of mothers with children. American mothers' participation in the workforce is comparable to that of women in continental European countries, and the United States even stacks up well against the Nordic countries if the long leaves in many of these countries are taken into account. As chapter 4 showed, 45 percent of Swedish mothers with a child under three are actually at work (compared to 72 percent counted as employed), while the proportion of equivalent American mothers in the labor force is just over 60 percent.[81] In fact, some have argued that the absence of a lengthy and well-paid parental leave in the United States works to the advantage of American women by reducing the incentives for private employers to discriminate against women. In general, higher percentages of American women are in managerial positions than women in other Western countries. As Margarita Estevez-Abe has argued, this is due, in part, to the lack of extended parental leaves.[82]

Although a high percentage of mothers are working in the United States, there are some necessary caveats to the figures. The first is that half of employed mothers with children under six work part-time.[83] Thus, although at first glance it seems that most women are maintaining their place in paid labor when they have children, the reality is that one-third are out of the labor force, one-third work full-time, and one-third work at reduced hours. This reliance on part-time work among mothers is similar to the behavior of mothers in Sweden or the Netherlands, but part-time workers in the United States are more vulnerable than equivalent workers in many Western European countries. As chapter 6 will show, the Netherlands passed laws in the 1990s requiring part-time workers to have the same wages and social protections as those enjoyed by full-time employees; in the United States, these

workers typically lack health insurance and private pensions, and they receive lower hourly wages than their full-time equivalents.

The lack of public supports for mothers helps explain why American
women experience a high "baby penalty" on their wages relative to women
in other countries. Much of the wage gap between men and women is experienced by women with children. One estimate holds that women without
children earn 91 percent of what men do, but women with children earn
only about 73 percent, and that American women face a higher penalty for
having children than women in many European countries.[84] When these
lower earnings are accumulated over fifteen years, a recent study shows,
American women earn 38 percent of what men do owing to reduced working time and concomitant disinvestment in work-related skills.[85]

The American system not only fails to redress the gendered economic
consequences of having children, but also reinforces class and racial strati-
fication. Recall that the ability of many American women to combine work
and family life is due in large part to the availability of a private child care
market. Although federal tax credits provided some impetus for the development of this market, the key to these programs is the availability of a low-
wage labor force. The economics of child care are such that there are no
gains to be had by technology or productivity increases; personnel costs
make up nearly the entire budget of most centers. Because most centers are
dependent on the fees parents pay for care, a direct relationship is set up between the price parents pay and the wages received by child care workers.[86]
To maintain profitability, centers must find ways to keep these costs down,
or they will quickly find parents shopping around for cheaper forms of care
(baby-sitters, relatives, family day care, etc.).[87]

The United States' private day care system has been made possible by
a low-wage, flexible workforce that can shift in and out of child care employment as needed. Of particular importance is the lack of a vocational education system or other training requirements that would create barriers to entry into the child care profession.[88] Almost anyone can get a job in a child
care center, and many do so for short-term employment before moving into
another field. One study in the 1990s found that annual turnover of staff in
all day care centers is around 30 percent, with as many as 45 percent of
staff leaving for-profit chains each year and 35 percent leaving independent
for-profits.[89] Thus, not only do many child care workers lack skills upon

entering into the profession, they do not acquire on-the-job knowledge either, nor do they have time to take advantage of programs to upgrade skills.[90]

With this lack of barriers to entry into the child care profession, day care is one of the lowest paying jobs in the United States. In the 1990s, studies show, only one-third of child care workers earned the minimum wage, and many have earnings that would put them below the poverty line.[91] As Gornick and Meyers have calculated, the wages of child care workers and preschool teachers are worth between 53 and 66 percent of the wages of all employed women, considerably lower than the comparable figures for European countries.[92] In addition, fewer than a third of child care centers offer fully paid health insurance, and even fewer provide pension benefits,[93] which has particular ramifications for the welfare of low-income minority women. Studies show that minorities make up a disproportionate percentage of child care workers, with particularly high representation in the "informal" and lowest-paid sector of home-based care and work as nannies.[94]

When services are distributed by private markets, income determines both access to services and the quality of services received. One study shows that non-poor parents pay, on average, 6.6 percent of household income on child care; that figure is more than 28 percent of household income for those below the poverty line.[95] Yet, while paying nearly five times as much of their income on care, poor families spend less in dollar amounts, often on lower-quality services. Middle- and upper-class children tend to be in better-quality services, while lower-income children are found predominantly in the least-regulated programs—usually family day care.[96] Studies find that most of the family day care experienced by poor children is of poor quality, and because minority children are overrepresented among the poor they are more likely than white children to experience inadequate care.[97] The current move to shift more low-income women into paid work requires them to put very young children into often inferior forms of child care so that these mothers can work in low-paying jobs.

In short, the private model in the United States holds advantages for some women, particularly those higher up on the educational and income ladder. They are more likely to work in firms that provide maternity leaves, can pay for high-quality child care (albeit often at a steep price), and can therefore continue the investment in their working lives that will pay off for them down the road. Low-income women have a harder time finding and paying for quality care, and they tend to work in the low-wage sector of the economy, which provides few fringe benefits for workers. Job interruptions hit these women particularly hard, but sustaining the work-family balance is particularly difficult for them. The American system may promote women's equality and advancement in the world of paid work in many ways, yet it comes at the price of intensifying inequality.

CHAPTER SIX

Openings for Change? The Politics of Mothers' Employment in the Netherlands

Since the 1990s, the Netherlands has experienced significant changes in the area of work and family, with a rapid rise in women's employment—including that of mothers—and new policies to encourage this trend. Day care provision has increased from previously low levels, and parents have gained expanded rights to parental leave and to part-time work. Overall rates of women's employment now exceed those of many Western European countries—a dramatic turnaround from the situation in the 1970s and 1980s. These changes contradict what we might expect of a conservative welfare regime dedicated to "passive" income assistance and the support of the male-breadwinner family. The Dutch case shows that change is possible in the social policy arrangements of advanced industrialized states.

A closer look at Dutch work-family policies, however, reveals considerable continuities with the past. Women's employment has increased dramatically, but this is overwhelmingly in part-time work. More than 70 percent of women work part-time, including nearly all mothers with young children.

Rather than abolish the male-breadwinner model, Dutch public policies have modernized it, encouraging a one-and-a-half-earner model that largely restructures women's time without changing that of men. Although access to child care clearly has expanded, most places are part-time, and almost no children attend child care four or five days a week. Dutch child care policy avoids entangling the central state in the direct subsidy or provision of these programs. In a renewed subsidiarity model, non-state actors in society—in this case, private firms and nonprofit organizations—are encouraged to organize the provision, and much of the funding, of these services.

In short, Dutch work-family policies since the 1990s have exemplified the "bounded change" typical of many policy reforms. This leaves us asking not only why there has been change, but also why so much has stayed the same. To answer the first question, this chapter traces shifts in the social and political mechanisms that had long reproduced the Dutch model of work and family policy. For decades, the male-breadwinner model of both social relations and public policy was reinforced by high rates of societal religiosity, the power of the Christian Democratic Party, and economic structures that enabled families to live on one income. All of this began changing by the 1980s as rapid secularization and the rise of women's employment undermined the foundations of the male-breadwinner model. These changes also eroded the traditional constituencies for the major political parties, leading to shifts in party orientation on the question of working mothers. Together, such changes opened up new spaces for political competition around the needs of working parents, disrupting the apparent path dependency of the Dutch welfare state.

Despite significant social change, however, Dutch society has not experienced an overnight revolution in values. Preferences for the maternal care of young children remain strong, as do beliefs about the importance of allowing families to determine their own care arrangements. Rather than sharply contravene these preferences, Dutch policy modernizes the male-breadwinner model by reorganizing women's caring time around a modified work schedule. In addition, the principle of subsidiarity has been reworked through a policy that encourages private-sector provision of child care services, rather than directly state-funded or state-provided services. Although current Dutch policies are a clear departure from the past, they bear the clear imprint of past family and social service policies.

Changing Welfare States

As the previous two chapters showed, France, Sweden, and the United States have shown considerable continuities in their policies for wage-earning mothers over the past three decades. Although there have been some shifts in specific policies, the overall paradigm has remained the same, whether it be the promotion of the universal-parent-worker model in Sweden, the mixed model in France, or reliance on private markets to solve these problems in the United States. In the Netherlands, there have been significant policy changes since the 1990s. This fact contravenes assumptions that welfare states are "frozen" in their current shape, fated to reproduce themselves through mechanisms of path dependency, and it raises questions about how we should understand and explain these changes.

A growing literature on contemporary welfare states has been grappling with the degree to which social policy regimes are changing. Globalization, the deteriorating economic climate in Western Europe since the 1970s, and the rise of neoliberal political movements had led some to predict the imminent demise of the welfare state. Paul Pierson's essential insight about the difficulties of slashing the welfare state has, however, proven true thus far. In almost no Western country has there been a dramatic rolling back of the welfare state or significant privatization of public functions.[1] At the same time, the policies and programs of the welfare state are not cast in stone. As Karl Hinrichs has put it, the "elephants are on the move" as policy makers attempt to reform huge public pension and health insurance systems, redirect public resources from passive to active employment policy, and shore up minimum income provisions so as to combat poverty and social exclusion.[2] In so doing, policy makers in most Western European countries have not sought to tear down the edifice of social policy, but rather to "recalibrate" or "recast" the welfare state so that it is better able to cope with contemporary and future challenges.[3]

Gender arrangements have been at the heart of these reform debates, particularly in the continental European countries but also in the United Kingdom.[4] With the aging of the population and declining fertility rates, many analysts have looked toward their northern neighbors and decided that helping women combine work and family is the key to higher fertility rates.[5] Economic arguments against maintaining a large "inactive" population also have propelled moves to augment the female labor supply; women at home increasingly are viewed as wasted labor that should instead be contributing to the economy and tax system through paid work. These concerns have dovetailed with debates about the need to help single mothers attain self-sufficiency. Governments now increasingly privilege labor market *activation*—increasing the proportion of the population in paid work—with a particular emphasis on women's employment.[6] This entails not only helping mothers to work who might like to, but also requiring work from low-income single parents who had previously relied on state support to be at home.[7]

To some extent, the drive to recast the welfare state has been influenced by ideas about the causes of the economic and demographic malaise in Western Europe and new beliefs about the best remedies for it.[8] It also reflects deeper social and political changes that are generating new social needs and shifting the constituencies of the political parties. In all Western countries, women's participation in the labor force has continued to rise, regardless of whether state policy has encouraged it or not. This has created a growing constituency of wage-earning women and two-earner couples who are more favorable to the idea of mothers' employment and would appreciate more state-supported child care or a generous parental leave. For Social Democratic parties, who face continual erosion of their blue-collar base, these white-collar workers are a key constituency to be courted.[9] At the same time, secularization continues to gnaw away at the religious foundations of Western societies, spurring crises in Christian Democratic parties and churches. As figure 6.1 shows, support for the traditional organization of the family has been in continual decline over the past decade. This poses challenges to conservative and Christian Democratic parties, which can no longer assert the immorality of mothers' employment but must find ways to address the real needs of today's parents.

This changing social and political context may help us understand why governments have devoted attention, at least rhetorically, to questions of work and family. It has been particularly true of leftist governments as Social Democratic parties have shed their prior indifference to the question of how to help parents balance their work and family lives. Conservative governments also have moderated their tone; they no longer openly condemn working mothers, but instead espouse policies that enable maximum parental

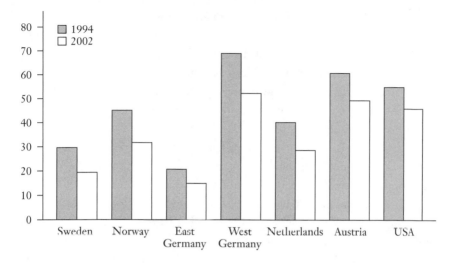

Figure 6.1   Percent of respondents who believe a mother with preschool-aged children should be at home, 1994 and 2002
  SOURCE: ISSP, Family and Changing Gender Roles II and III.

"choice."[10] The result has been that governments in many formerly male-breadwinner welfare regimes are taking an increasingly active role in helping working parents. In Germany, for example, the Social Democratic–Green coalition government increased spending on child care and kindergartens. In the United Kingdom, the Labour government has significantly expanded paid parental leave and increased investments in child care and early education programs.

What remains to be seen is how much change is actually occurring. In Germany's western *Länder*, for example, recent data show that there has been virtually no increase in the proportion of young children in child care, despite promised investments.[11] In the United Kingdom, most expansions of the child care system have come through part-day preschools that are of little help to many working parents, and government investment in full-time child care remains limited.[12] The small-scale changes we see today may ultimately add up to a more significant reform down the road, but it is hard to argue that a fundamental paradigm shift has occurred in the policies of these countries. Many analysts argue that public policy in a number of continental European countries is effectively modernizing the male-breadwinner model rather than challenging it in a more fundamental way.[13] Recent developments in child care and parental leave policies are examples of what Kathleen Thelen has called bounded change.[14] Clearly, policy shifts are occurring in many countries, but they have not produced radical disjunctures with the past.

Why has the degree of change proven limited? One reason is that although governments have adopted an interest in promoting mothers' employment, they are less willing to spend the necessary resources to ensure that parents have all the resources and services they need to effectively balance work and family. As Jane Lewis has put it, many policy makers have accepted the idea that mothers should work—and should even be forced to work—but the policy instruments that would enable this have been slow to develop.[15] To some degree, this can be explained by fiscal constraints and a cautious approach to social spending. In most countries, social spending has not declined in recent decades, but the welfare state is no longer expanding the way it did during its golden era, which means that new spending must come through cuts in other programs. Although some policy makers have sought to turn "vice into virtue" by redirecting existing programs toward new goals, such efforts may also face entrenched interests that will defend their piece of the budgetary pie.[16]

Another source of constraint is that although social values about gender roles clearly are changing, they do not radically transform overnight. In many Western countries, people have not fully embraced the idea that mothers of young children should work full-time; rather, the shift is toward first supporting part-time work for mothers, and perhaps eventually there will be growing acceptance of the idea that mothers should work longer hours.[17] These views may simply represent the realities on the ground: it is difficult for parents to both work full-time and raise children. For women, the fact that the gender division of labor in the home has only minimally changed is another source of constraint. The time women spend doing housework has declined over the past three decades, while the involvement of men in both housework and child care has increased. Still, even in households where both parents are employed full-time, women do substantially more of the household labor than men in all Western countries.[18] Men in Sweden do the same proportion of home labor as men in the United States.[19] This may be the result of parental choices about the division of labor in the workplace and home, but it also reveals the slow pace of change in deeply rooted societal patterns and behavior. Public policy has a limited capacity to alter these patterns and beliefs.

The Dutch case offers an example of these political and social dynamics. The rise of women's workforce participation and of secularization opened up a widow of opportunity for policies that support wage-earning mothers, yet the pace of change has been constrained.

Bounded Policy Change in the Netherlands

Dutch policy makers were slow to respond to the growth of mothers' employment. By the late 1980s, however, continuing social changes and new ideas about economic policy created an opening for new child care and working time policies. Rather than fully overhaul the old male-breadwinner model of social relations, however, the new policy orientation would modernize this model through high rates of part-time work for mothers and continued reliance on much maternal care of children.

THE DECLINE OF THE MALE-BREADWINNER MODEL

Throughout the 1980s, policies for working mothers in the Netherlands hardly changed, and the question of mothers' employment was only minimally on the political agenda. In part, this was due to continuing low rates of mothers' employment. By 1980, only 32 percent of married women were in the labor force, compared to 50 percent in France and 76 percent in Sweden.[20] Even lower proportions of mothers were in paid work.[21] Because few people believed that mothers should work while their children were young, there was little political demand for child care or parental leave. Although it is hardly surprising that the Christian Democrats continued to oppose mothers' employment, the very low percentages of women in paid work help explain Social Democratic indifference to this issue. According to Jet Bussemaker, feminist lobbying in trade unions and leftist political parties for expanded public child care in the late 1970s and early 1980s came to naught. Faced with such strong resistance, even the women's movement gave up on the issue.[22]

In addition, the deteriorating economic situation proved particularly damaging to any claims that the government should spend money on new programs to promote women's employment. Although the economic shocks of the 1970s hit all Western countries, the Netherlands was afflicted with the famous "Dutch disease"—a situation in which the exploitation of a natural resource generates not growth but economic stagnation. Natural gas revenues in the 1970s initially cushioned the Netherlands from the effects of the oil shocks but put upward pressure on the currency, making Dutch manufacturing exports more expensive. The availability of these revenues also encouraged greater social spending and higher wages to meet union demands, which further hurt the manufacturing sector.[23] By the early 1980s, the Dutch economy was in shambles, with high unemployment, stagnant growth, and large budget deficits.

In response, the Christian Democratic–Liberal coalitions that governed through most of 1980s broke with the Keynesian consensus of years past.[24] These governments adopted wage austerity measures while leveling a more general critique against the welfare state. The situation had implications for family policies: some Christian Democrats called for the renewal of a "caring society," in which families would take care of themselves rather than look to the state for assistance. The Christian Democratic minister of health and welfare asserted that use of day care was a sign that parents were giving up responsibility for their children.[25] Some child psychiatrists claimed that day care was bad for children and that mothers who worked were egotistical.[26] High unemployment also gave rise to complaints about couples with two incomes.[27]

At the same time, however, social changes were eroding the foundations of the Dutch male-breadwinner model. One major trend was the ongoing secularization of Dutch society. Church membership and regular church attendance had plunged dramatically since the 1970s, matched by changing values on a host of moral questions, including divorce, abortion, and homosexuality. Secularization also produced de-pillarization as people's identities became detached from the subcultural pillars that had dominated Dutch life for decades.[28] Many point to the mid-1960s as the period when de-pillarization began, but the full effects of the trend were felt in the 1980s and 1990s. For the main political parties, this meant the loss of their original class- or religiously based constituencies. In 1970, 65 percent of Catholics identified with one of the confessional parties, while 67 percent of the non-church-attending working class supported the PvdA. By the mid-1990s, these proportions had

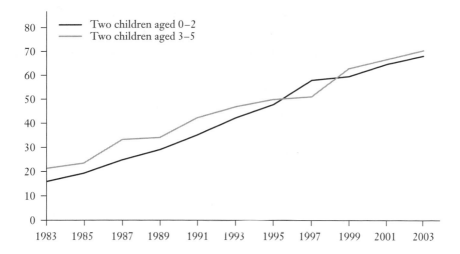

Figure 6.2   Proportion of Dutch mothers with two children in paid work
 SOURCE: Eurostat, EU Labour Force Survey.

dropped to 35 and 39 percent.[29] De-pillarization also was reflected in the rise of new social parties outside the dominant pillars, such as D66 and the Green Left Party (discussed below). More generally, de-pillarization signified that people would no longer live within their particular subcommunity, absorbing its values through community-run media and voluntary associations.

Another major change in Dutch society was the steady rise in women's employment, including that of married women. As figure 6.2 shows, even without supportive services or other policies, the percentage of married women in paid work climbed steadily throughout the 1970s and 1980s. Broadly speaking, the rise in married women's employment was due to rising education levels, declining fertility rates, and increasing wages.[30] Economic recession in the 1980s also led more mothers to try to stay in paid work because their husbands had lost their jobs and/or the women feared leaving their jobs because of the risk of never being able to return.[31] In addition, the growth of part-time work opportunities was critical to drawing in married women with children, and much of the increase in women's employment was through part-time work. The social reality was one of growing rates of women's participation in the labor force and changing expectations on the part of many women about their place in paid employment.

Some of these demands were channeled through markets, as occurred in the American context. Employers began offering paid and unpaid leaves, part-time work, and subsidies for child care, reflecting the pressures of union demands in collective bargaining. The development of private child care markets was slow, however; by 1990, only around 1 or 2 percent of children under the age of four were in commercially run, unsubsidized day care, and another 1 percent were in employer-provided services.[32] Private, for-profit child care has not developed much in European countries owing to their more tightly regulated labor markets. The highly regulated labor market keeps wages higher than in the United States, which makes private child care more difficult to sustain.[33] The gap between incomes also is narrower than in the United States, so many parents do not have the incomes to pay for unsubsidized services.[34] In the 1980s, the child care available in private markets was too expensive for most people. Tax breaks for these costs, granted in 1984, did little to further stimulate this market, and most working mothers continued to cobble together child care from family, friends, or unregulated family day care. The lack of private options thus reinforced the mismatch between social realities and government policy.

These social changes and tensions created openings for new issues to become the source of political competition. Starting in the late 1980s, the political spectrum shifted on the issue of mothers' employment, with first the Social Democratic (PvdA) and Liberal (VVD) parties embracing the goal of increasing women's employment, and then the Christian Democrats (CDA) moderating their opposition to these aims. The ideological change in the PvdA is notable given its previous indifference or opposition to mothers' employment, a position that made sense given that, as in other European countries, many in the party's working-class constituency were not particularly interested in promoting mothers' employment. As figure 6.3 shows, education correlates with views on mothers' employment, and less-educated people make up a substantial share of the PvdA's voting base.

Several different forces led the party to change its views. One was electoral competition for the growing share of white-collar voters. As in Sweden, the Netherlands experienced a massive decline in both secular working-class and religious voters and a dramatic increase in the secular middle class (table 6.1). Not only did the pool of working-class voters shrink, but also the proportion of them voting for the PvdA has continually declined, pushing

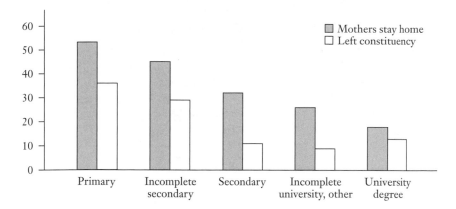

Figure 6.3   Opinions of left voters on mothers' employment

SOURCE: ISSP, Family and Changing Gender Roles II, 1994.

Percentage of respondents who believe mothers with preschool-aged children should be home full-time, by level of education.

the PvdA to reach out to better-educated middle-class voters by embracing a host of "new politics" issues such as the environment and women's rights.[35] This reaching out was particularly essential given the development of two new competitors—the Green Left Party and Democrats '66 (D66). The Green Party is a conglomeration of Left parties that first came together in the 1989 election and gained votes throughout the 1990s. D66 is largely a party of white-collar public-sector voters, but its electoral fortunes have varied widely depending on the level of discontent toward the established parties. The party experienced an electoral spurt in the late 1980s and the first half of the 1990s, stealing voters away from the "mainstream" parties. Both the Green Left and the D66 parties have competed with the PvdA for educated middle-class voters.[36]

Stable party attachments have been declining and electoral competition has been growing since the late 1960s. However, the very low percentage of women who were in the workforce during that period meant that there was little interest in the issue of mothers' employment. Electoral competition in the 1970s centered on other new issues—the environment, nuclear energy, and other gender-equality issues, such as abortion.[37] As women's employment grew in the 1980s, however, attention turned to the situation of working parents, and the PvdA's efforts to attract younger and better-educated voters led the party to alter its stance on mothers' employment policies. As was noted

TABLE 6.1
The changing identities of Dutch voters

	1956	1968	1972	1977	1982	1989	1994	1998
Catholic	30	30	25	24	16	14	13	11
Dutch Reformed	12	16	7	9	7	8	6	6
Reformed	10	12	7	9	7	7	5	7
Secular working class	33	25	28	28	27	24	23	21
Secular middle class	15	18	32	30	42	48	54	55

SOURCE: Thomas R. Rochon, *The Netherlands: Negotiating Sovereignty in an Interdependent World* (Boulder, CO: Westview Press, 1999), 80.

earlier, higher levels of education are an important predictor of views on the suitability of working mothers. In addition, as figure 6.4 shows, voters for the PvdA's competitors—the Greens and D66—are generally more favorable toward mothers' employment. Not surprisingly, both parties have been strong advocates for child care, parental leave, and flexible work-time.

While these changes were taking place at the base of society, political party elites were debating the future of the welfare state. Budget deficits and concern about high tax rates in the 1980s fueled concern with the size of the public sector. Much of the focus was on the burgeoning disability insurance system, which underwent major reforms in the early 1990s.[38] Although many Christian Democrats and Liberals advocated fiscal austerity measures, Social Democrats began developing an alternative vision of active state intervention to reduce dependency on the welfare state.[39] Child care and other supportive policies were presented as a way to cut welfare costs for the state while increasing tax revenues through the mobilization of new workers— married women. These arguments of economic efficiency gained strength in the late 1980s and were espoused by a series of government reports.[40] One highly influential report from the government's policy research unit argued that the aging of the population posed a threat to the labor supply and that measures to stimulate women's employment were needed.[41] With this new focus on economic productivity and reducing welfare costs, all the major political parties agreed on the need to promote mothers' employment. For the PvdA, such an approach had the added political payoff of addressing feminist demands within the party and unions while appealing to the burgeoning middle class.[42]

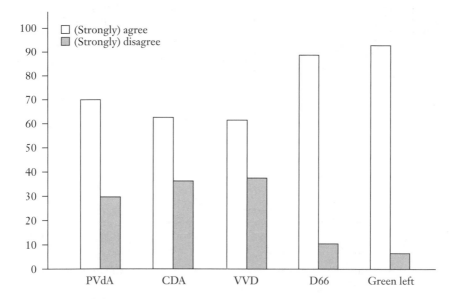

Figure 6.4 Views on whether working mothers can have a good relationship with their children, 1990

SOURCE: World Values Survey 1990.

Question asks if working mothers can establish just as warm a relationship with their children as mothers who don't work.

The dilemma facing these parties was that despite the support for mothers' employment policies among at least part of the population, much of Dutch society remained skeptical, if not opposed, to mothers' working while their children were young. Figure 6.5 shows the evolution of views on the question of whether mothers should work if they have to put their children in day care. Although the degree of opposition was lower than in the past, by the 1990s, nearly 40 percent of the population found the idea unacceptable, while more than 40 percent thought that it was, at best, not unacceptable. About 20 percent of those sampled thought it was a good idea for mothers to work while their children are in day care. In short, the change in views has not led to widespread acceptance of mothers' employment. Other studies find that some parents regard child care with considerable skepticism.[43]

What enabled the dominant parties to negotiate these complex and potentially controversial questions was the growth of women's part-time work. Throughout the 1980s, the growth of married women's participation in

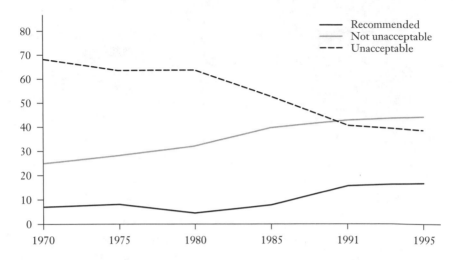

Figure 6.5   Dutch views on married women working while their children are in day care, 1970–95
  SOURCE: Carlo van Praag and Wilfried Uitterhoeve, *Een kwart eeuw sociale verandering in Nederland: De kerngegevens uit het "Sociaal en Cultureel Rapport 1998"* (Nijmegen: Uitgeverij SUN 1999), 114.

the labor force was due largely to expanded part-time work opportunities. Although unions initially opposed this development, Jelle Visser argues that employers outmaneuvered them in offering women the reduced hours of employment they sought. Otherwise, they would be unlikely to work outside the home, particularly when they had young children. Thus, long before government policy began to encourage part-time work in the 1990s, it was a growing reality on the ground, embraced by employers as a way to get a more flexible workforce and by women as a way to balance work and home life.[44]

The expansion of women's part-time work had a number of political consequences. One was to change the composition of unions and their views on the issue. Initially, the unions opposed part-time employment, lobbying instead for a reduction in work time for all. Once union women decided to support part-time work, though, their growing significance in the union movement helped bring the unions around, and unions affected the views of the PvdA on part-time work and women's employment more generally.[45] Part-time work then became part of the bargain between employers, unions, and the state over how to jump-start the Dutch economic and fight unemployment. These negotiations would produce the so-called Poldermodel—a set of economic and social policies whose foremost aims were to promote economic growth and fight unemployment. Wage restraint was central to the model, but part-time work also was seen as a way to combat chronically high unemployment by introducing more flexibility into labor markets and ensuring that most people had at least a part-time job.[46]

Part-time work also offered a way to stimulate women's employment without running contrary to the norms and values of Dutch society.[47] All could agree on the importance of child care and other measures to promote mothers' employment, because some of the perceived negative effects of mothers' employment on young children would be mitigated as long as mothers could be home for a substantial part of the week. Thus, rather than developing a Scandinavian-style system of public care services, Dutch parents would still provide much care for their children, facilitated by restructured working time.[48] Such an arrangement would also save the Dutch state considerable resources because it would not need to develop an extensive system of public child care. With most children attending programs only part of the week, day care centers could provide services to twice as many children.

The first changes came under a CDA-PvdA coalition government in 1989, largely on the initiative of the PvdA. In 1989, parents got the right to a six-month, unpaid, and part-time leave, while paid maternity leave was extended from 12 to 16 weeks. The coalition government also increased child care funding through a temporary child care stimulation scheme; the measure sought to more than double the number of child care places within four years.[49] More fundamental changes came when the CDA lost power in the 1994 elections and the Liberals and Social Democrats formed the first "purple coalition" government in Dutch history.[50] This brought together two parties increasingly committed to women's equality and employment, albeit with different emphases—the VVD preferring free market solutions and lower taxes and the PvdA advocating active labor market measures. The new government created a Committee for the Redivision of Unpaid Work, which in 1995 called for a new *combinatie scenario* (combination scenario) for working parents. In this new vision, both parents would work 32 hours a week while sharing child care duties at home. To the extent that parents could not be at home, there should be day care options available for them, although they would make up only a small amount of the care provided to children.[51]

The purple coalition endorsed this view and took steps to put it in practice. As early as 1993, the government eliminated working-hours thresholds for a worker's entitlement to social benefits and the minimum wage. A 1996 law further banned any discrimination against workers based on the number of hours they worked. The crowning measure came in the Working Hours Adjustment Act of 2000, which gave all employees the right to ask for reduced or increased work time, a request employers could refuse only if they had strong economic reasons to do so.[52] Now everyone, men and women alike, had the right to work part-time. Notably, the act also allowed workers to request full-time hours, a measure fought for by feminist politicians to ensure that involuntary part-time work would not become a trap for women.

There were additional government measures to encourage the development of child care services. The general orientation of child care policy has been to prod unions and employers to include child care measures in collective agreements. Although the government initially increased funds to municipalities to provide child care services, direct public subsidies were reduced in the mid-1990s, and employers were granted a tax deduction for a portion of their costs.[53] Typically, employers pay some percentage of their payroll into a child care foundation, which then purchases child care for employees of the firm.[54] Since the mid-1990s, the share of collective agreements containing child care provisions continually increased, reaching 76 percent in 2003.[55] The availability of child care also expanded: although fewer than 6 percent of children under the age of three were in child care in 1991, nearly 22 percent were in these services just ten years later.[56]

Other changes in tax and social spending policies revealed a widespread assumption among policy makers that women are in paid work and that they should be. One social policy trend has been toward individualizing the entitlement to social benefits. Although not a coherent or consistent trend, one's right to receive benefits is less linked to familial relations and more based on one's own work history than in the past.[57] In addition, joint taxation of married couples' income was replaced in January 2001 with a more individualized tax system, removing one of the significant financial disincentives to married women's employment.[58] Further evidence of the shift in policy makers' assumptions about wage-earning mothers is the push to get single mothers on public assistance into the labor market. For decades, single mothers received state support to compensate for the absence of a male breadwinner. The situation changed in 1996, when a new government law required mothers of children above the age of five to be in, or actively seeking, paid work. In return, these mothers receive a tax break, while city governments get funds to provide child care for their children.[59]

These policy changes have contributed to a dramatic rise in women's employment. The Netherlands long had some of the lowest rates in Europe of women's participation in the workforce, yet, by the end of the 1990s, the Dutch had equaled or surpassed many countries on this measure. Although work requirements for single mothers receiving public assistance have not been vigorously enforced, their employment rates also have increased. In 1990, only 18 percent of single mothers with at least one child under five were in paid work. By 2003, that figure had risen to 39 percent—well below the figure of 60 percent for mothers with partners, but a marked change nonetheless.[60]

Although these figures signify an important shift in policies for working mothers, a closer look at the nature these changes reveals considerable continuities with the past, making the Dutch reforms an example of "bounded change."

THE BOUNDED NATURE OF DUTCH POLICY CHANGE

In a situation of bounded change, a seeming departure from the past is in fact constrained by the weight of past arrangements, perhaps because policy makers view new issues from the standpoint of previous approaches. Rather than effect a radical departure from the status quo, policy makers may be more likely to redeploy an existing repertoire of policy instruments toward new aims. These continuities also may reflect the strength of particular constituencies or social values, which limit the likelihood of a sharp change from the past. In the case of Dutch family policy, the rise in women's employment challenged two long-standing values: the importance of maternal care of young children and the idea of subsidiarity in the provision of services for children and families. Rather than sharply contravene these two values, policy makers have crafted a response that alters the Dutch model of work and care while maintaining significant continuities with the past.

The linchpin of policy makers' response has been to encourage women's part-time work, which has led to far higher rates of women's employment than in the past, though they often work limited hours. In 2003, nearly 60 percent of employed Dutch women worked part-time compared to

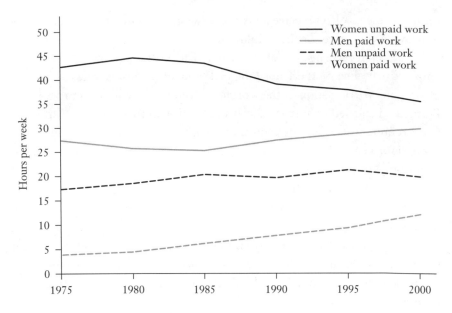

Figure 6.6   Gendered division of labor in the Netherlands, 1975–2000
SOURCE: Sociaal en Cultureel Planbureau, *Emancipatiemonitor*, 93.
The data are for all people above the age of 25.

21 percent in Sweden, 23 percent in France, and 19 percent in the United States.[61] When women's employment is measured in terms of full-time equivalents, Dutch women's full-time employment rate is 41.6 percent compared to 50.8 percent in France, and 63 percent in Sweden.[62] In addition, although both men and women have the right to ask for reduced working time, the most common practice is for women to either cease working or reduce their work time upon the birth of a child. In 85 percent of Dutch couples with children, the woman works part-time or not at all.[63] The *combinatie scenario* was envisioned as a way to restructure the work and caring time of both men and women, but only a very small proportion of couples actually live this scenario. As of 2003, in only 6 percent of couples with young children do both parents work part-time, compared to 45 percent doing the one-and-a-half-earner model (usually with the man in full-time work), 6 percent the two-full-time-earner model, and 34 percent the one-earner model.[64] In fact, as figure 6.6 shows, men's hours of paid work have increased in the past decades. Their contribution to unpaid work in the

home has increased some, but it remains much lower than women's hours of unpaid work.

In short, the one-and-a-half-earner model is the predominant approach to combining work and care, with women making up the half. Although this was long true in Sweden, women in part-time work usually have worked a six-hour day. In the Netherlands, 35 percent of employed women work fewer than 20 hours per week, compared to only 6 percent working similarly few hours in Sweden.[65] In addition, Swedish women are increasingly working full-time, while the generalization of part-time work in the Netherlands is such that very few women work full-time, particularly when they have children.

Although Swedish Social Democrats are increasingly critical of part-time work, there is still a broad political consensus around women's part-time work in the Netherlands, despite the fact that the *combinatie scenario* has not materialized. As was noted earlier, part-time work made mothers' employment acceptable both to Dutch society and to the political parties. The proportion of people who are involuntarily working part-time is extremely low in the Netherlands; only 1 percent of employed women currently work part-time and prefer full-time work, compared to 13 percent in Sweden and 11 percent in France.[66] Given Dutch society's increased secularization, satisfaction with the current arrangements can no longer be said to reflect the strength of religiosity; rather, we can see here the enduring power of traditional gender ideologies that were institutionalized through the policies of the welfare state. Although the idea of mothers' employment has gained theoretical acceptance, it has not fully entered into practice.[67]

Given the unpopularity of the idea of mothers working full-time, it is hardly surprising that the dominant political forces do not challenge the spread of the one-and-a-half-earner model. The current coalition government has raised concern about the low average number of hours worked in the Netherlands, but it has focused on extending the workweek or raising the retirement age. There is little discussion of the low number of hours worked by women. The PvdA and VVD remain the parties that are most supportive of wage-earning mothers, but they do not challenge the one-and-a-half earner model either. Certainly, Social Democrats are stronger champions of a more gender-egalitarian vision, which is constantly pushed by feminist advocates within the party.[68] However, the party's lack of concern over the unequal position of women in paid work reveals the limits of its commitment and its acceptance of different roles in society for men and women. The CDA remains less favorable to mothers working while their children are young, although the party encompasses multiple views on the matter.[69] However, many in the CDA see part-time work as a way to mitigate the negative effects of non-maternal care.[70] The larger political consequence is that the possibility of part-time work has sapped the strength of other initiatives—such as a well-paid, Scandinavian-style parental leave or greater child care subsidies. Having most mothers in part-time employment and still performing most of the care work reduces the pressure for the development of public services or other policies.[71]

Another source of institutional continuity is the enduring commitment of the main political forces to the decentralized provision of social and education services. As chapter 3 described, the principle of subsidiarity was a founding principle of the Dutch welfare state. Moreover, as chapter 2 showed, publicly funded but privately provided services—particularly in the area of education—were essential to maintaining political peace in this religiously divided country. Despite secularization and de-pillarization, the practice of local and non-governmental solutions to social problems has been maintained in the area of child care. Rather than construct a set of universal, publicly run programs, Dutch governments of all ideological colors have instead used public subsidies to encourage private market solutions. This has entailed prodding employers to subsidize a portion of the costs of child care for their workers. Parents then pay a certain amount for these services, with public subsidies covering the rest. Through this system, the Dutch government avoids responsibility for direct provision of public care services.

Reliance on non-governmental actors to provide social services reflects in part the growing fiscal conservatism of the main political parties. Since the 1990s, governments have prioritized fiscal restraint, with tax cuts favored as a way to stimulate economic growth. This leaves little room for new public spending and has influenced the strategies of all the political parties on social policy. Even the PvdA has accepted that markets are essential for the development of Dutch child care, rather than publicly funded and provided programs.[72] In addition, the party of neoliberalism, the VVD, has been in all coalition governments since 1994, and it has opposed the growth of the public sector.

The decentralized child care system also reflects the deeply rooted antipathy of many Dutch parents to excessive state intervention in children's education.[73] For nearly 100 years, the solution has been to decentralize responsibility for educational and welfare services and to delegate it instead to the subcultural pillars that made up Dutch society. Voluntary organizations within these pillars received public funds to provide these programs, ensuring that they would be in tune with the preferences and beliefs of parents. Now, with the collapse of these pillars, a modernized version of this model has emerged in which markets are charged with the task of providing services for working parents, assuring maximum parental choice and autonomy.[74]

The modern market-based approach transcends partisan divisions, for both center-left and center-right coalition governments embrace this model. Recently, a center-right (CDA-VVD) government has transformed the child care subsidy system into a set of demand subsidies that will maximize parental autonomy in selecting services. Since January 2005, parents have been reimbursed for part of the costs of child care through the tax system, and the centers are no longer directly subsidized. The Left has opposed elements of the new policy, such as a measure that removed all national regulations on the new services. It also has opposed allowing employers to decide whether they will offer subsidies to their employees, rather than compelling them to do so. However, the demand-subsidy system was hatched first under a center-left government, with a Social Democratic minister of social affairs in charge of the policy.[75] The shared orientation of these governments has been to stimulate market provision of child care through demand subsidies instead of through public supply-side measures that would assure a certain level of provision.

Although this approach has stimulated an expansion in the supply of services, the Dutch state spends less on these services than France or Sweden; only the United States spends less per child on child care.[76] As a result, the cost of care to parents in the Netherlands is high, contributing to the tendency for one parent to work part-time.[77] However, as many analysts have emphasized, the high prevalence of part-time work is not simply a consequence of the price of care. Many parents continue to regard child care with suspicion and prefer to maximize parental caring time while minimizing that of outside caregivers. Statements by child psychologists in recent years about the nefarious effects of day care on young children only reinforce this tendency.[78] In short, despite social changes in the past few decades, the model of maternal care and subsidiarity in the provision of social services is alive and well in the Netherlands.

Conclusion

The Dutch case is revealing of the complex mix of stability and change that characterizes many policy reforms. On the one hand, Dutch policy clearly has moved away from the male-breadwinner assumptions that shaped the structures of the welfare state for decades. Changes in the Netherlands show that despite the extremely low rates of women's participation in the work-force only two or three decades ago and the lack of day care or other mea-sures for working mothers, welfare regimes are not forever locked in place. At the same time, this chapter has shown that Dutch policies demonstrate considerable continuities with the past, evidenced by the continuing weak role of the state in service provision and the nearly universal practice of part-time work among mothers. These continuities illustrate the importance of a historical perspective on the Dutch welfare state, one sensitive to both contemporary dynamics and the institutional legacies of the past.

Conclusion: The Future of Policies for Working Parents

Why are policies for working mothers so different, in different countries? This book has sought to answer the question by probing the politics of an issue that often has been highly controversial. Public child care and other measures that encourage mothers' employment tap politically sensitive questions about gender roles and the boundaries between the state and the family. Should states attempt to change the gendered division of labor in the workplace and home or be involved in the education and care of young children? Swedish policy answers both questions in the affirmative, as evidenced by its extensive public child care system, generous parental leave, and other policies that have eliminated the male-breadwinner model and now push men to do a greater share of the caring work. France also has a long tradition of active state involvement in family policy and the early education of children, although policy makers have not tried to remake French society along gender-egalitarian lines. The United States lies on the opposite end of the spectrum: aversion to government policy on families has repeatedly blocked efforts to expand public child care or otherwise involve the federal govern-ment in the work-family issue. In the Netherlands, there has been a similar reticence toward central state involvement in children's education, yet for years the welfare state actively sustained the male-breadwinner model. More recently, policy makers have encouraged changes in traditional gender roles without involving the state too directly in the provision of social and educa-tional services for families.

To explain these differences, this book has adopted a historical approach to locate the origins of ideologies about gender roles and the relationship be-tween the state and the family that would shape the politics of this issue. Most scholars view 1945 to 1975 as a critical period of welfare state expan-sion, but the dominant political forces and ideologies of that period grew out of political cleavages that arose during the late nineteenth and early twenti-eth centuries. That was a period of intense conflict over religion as states were expanding their role in children's and family affairs—areas over which churches had traditionally had responsibility. Chapter 1 identified four pat-terns of religious conflict and church-state relations that shaped the inten-sity and nature of these disputes and that had a lasting impact on the role of religion in these four polities. The subordination of religious to secular au-thorities in both France and Sweden facilitated active state involvement in family affairs while contributing to the secularization of politics and society, although the latter went further in Sweden than in France. In the Nether-lands and the United States, religious pluralism resulted in the decentraliza-tion of family issues to lower levels of society, such as local governments and the voluntary sector. Socially conservative forces also continued to play a greater role in politics, particularly in the Netherlands.

The consequences could be seen in the expansion of the welfare state during the three decades after the Second World War. Initially, the male-breadwinner model was hegemonic in both society and public policy, but by the late 1960s, welfare states began diverging in their treatment of working mothers. In both France and Sweden, an activist family policy tradition and political secularization facilitated the expansion of child care and other poli-cies in support of mothers' employment. This expansion went furthest in Sweden, where the state effectively dismantled the male-breadwinner model and sought to upend the gender division of labor in work and care. In France, policy makers adopted more limited yet supportive policies for working mothers without attempting a broader transformation of gender roles. The opposite occurred in the Netherlands, as politically dominant Christian Democratic parties opposed both mothers' employment and direct state provision of social care services. In the United States, efforts to increase the federal role in child care in the 1970s also met with fierce opposition to what was perceived as undue state intervention in the family. This opposition was the first strike of a growing mobilization of social conservatives around gender and family issues that has continued to the present day.

These policy decisions were consequential because they put countries on different paths of public policy—paths they largely followed in the ensuing decades. Such stability reflects in part the change in the political and economic climate since the mid-1970s, a change marked by high unemployment, fiscal constraints on the public sector, and the ascendance of neoliberal ideas. Chapters 4 and 5 traced the institutionalization of policies for working parents in this context, identifying the mechanisms that solidified different policy approaches. Path dependence is shaped by the way the programs of the welfare state intersect with social forces, creating constituencies in support of particular programs or in opposition to others. In Sweden, the rapid elimination of the male-breadwinner model created a unified constituency for child care, parental leave, and other policies that support mothers' employment, enabling the Swedish approach to endure in an often adverse economic and political environment. Such a constituency became fragmented in France because of the state's more tentative policies in this area. French society, rather than favoring a system of universal breadwinners, evinced continued support for full-time homemaking, leaving programs such as public child care vulnerable to the deteriorating economic climate. The United States took yet a different turn as the expansion of private market solutions undercut the constituency for a greater federal role. Coming at a time of mobilization by social conservatives against mothers' employment, policy makers have tried to place responsibility for this area on the marketplace, shifting the issue of child care from the public sphere back to the private one.

Although the embeddedness of welfare state programs in supportive social constituencies helps explain their continuity, autonomous social change can be a source of dynamism in public policy. Such was the case in the Netherlands during the 1990s, when governments abandoned the male-breadwinner model that had informed earlier policies and adopted other measures to encourage women's, and especially mothers', employment. As chapter 5 showed, rapid secularization and the growth of women's employment in the Netherlands undermined support for the previous model of public policy, creating openings for political competition around new issues. Even so, Dutch policy since the 1990s has been an example of bounded change, in which institutional legacies have conditioned policy reform. Rather than overturn the male-breadwinner model, Dutch policy has modernized it through the expansion of women's part-time work. Similarly, rather than engage direct state resources in the provision of social care services, policy makers reworked the principle of subsidiarity to justify market-provided services.

Thus, despite persistent secularization across much of the Western world, the religious roots of the welfare state have endured and continue to shape both public policy and societal organization.

Contributions to Intellectual Inquiry

One contribution of this book has been to investigate the forces shaping gendered dimensions of the welfare state. There is now a rich and varied literature about the ways welfare regimes affect gender relations and the place of women in the public and private spheres. But there are fewer cross-national comparative studies that seek to explain differences between countries in these policies. At the same time, mainstream research into the origins of social policy has largely neglected policies for women and children. This study has filled the gap between these two bodies of work by investigating the origins of public policies that influence the gendered effects of the welfare state.

In so doing, this project drew attention to a variable that has received insufficient attention in comparative research: religion. Neglect of this factor reflects in part the preeminent attention paid to the Left in political research. Library shelves overflow with books on Social Democratic and other Left parties, and there is a growing body of work on the extreme right, but there have been few volumes on the politics of the moderate center right.[1] Similarly, in research on the welfare state, much research focuses on the role of Left parties and labor unions in the creation of social programs, with only a few noting the impact of religious forces on social policy.[2] Recent work has focused exclusively on Christian Democratic parties rather than on considering how religious cleavages shaped European and American political development in a broader sense. As this study has shown, religious divisions affected political outcomes as much by their absence in countries such as Sweden as by their presence in the Netherlands. Viewing the actions of Left parties in isolation leaves us with an incomplete picture, particularly of the nature of political competition over gender and family issues. The ways in which these questions are treated in party politics reflect the spectrum of views represented in politics. A focus on religion not only helps us understand patterns of gendered public policy, but also enhances our understanding of politics in advanced industrialized states and the origins of the welfare state.

Although this book focused specifically on four countries, its arguments could apply to a wider range of cases and contribute to a larger account of how religion has shaped the foundations of the gendered welfare state. The Nordic countries generally share a similar history of early church-state fusion, religious homogeneity, and early secularization, although Norway experienced more religiously based conflict.[3] Religious homogeneity inhibited the growth of religious cleavages in society and thus limited the development of a religiously based voluntary sector or Christian political parties.[4] One consequence was that the central state in most of these countries gained responsibility for educational and family policy, rather than leaving it in the ambit of the voluntary sector, and did so in a relatively peaceful way. These countries also were pioneers in the extension of individual rights to women and children early in the twentieth century, including suffrage rights for women, which some argue reflects the already waning influence of the church.[5]

Later in the twentieth century, all of these countries would develop programs and policies to support mothers' employment, although there are some important variations among them. Norway and Finland have been less enthusiastic champions than Sweden of mothers' employment, and were slower to develop public child care. Instead, governments in both countries have created two- or three-year paid care leaves for parents.[6] As chapter 2 argued, the Norwegian case can be explained by its more fractious history of religious conflict, which produced a stronger Christian Democratic party. Despite the political strength of the Norwegian Social Democrats, they faced greater societal and political divisions over the question of mothers' employment as well as a more entrenched sector of voluntary organizations with responsibility for child care. In Finland, the strength of agrarian parties posed a similar challenge to a considerably weaker Social Democratic party, although their orientation was rooted less in religion than in the preferences of their rural constituency.[7] The result was that although all these countries have large welfare state and active labor market policies that reflect the strength of Social Democratic power, they differ in their approach to mothers' employment.

Some of the continental European countries—such as Austria, Germany, and Italy—resemble the Netherlands in their histories of religious conflict. Generally, religious forces prevailed in these political struggles, and the conflicts themselves generated a rich sector of voluntary organizations that asserted responsibility for the provision of educational and social services.[8] The Catholic principle of subsidiarity (and related Protestant notions in Germany) shaped the organization of the welfare state, and Christian Democratic parties played a preeminent role in the politics of these countries.[9] Later in the twentieth century, Social Democratic parties were considerably more reticent toward mothers' employment than their Nordic equivalents. The male-breadwinner model was more entrenched in both public policy and societal practice, and although currently some reform efforts are underway in these countries, the pace of change is slow. Public child care remains limited, lengthy care leaves encourage mothers to temporarily exit the workforce when they have children, and other policies such as the joint taxation of income discourage married women's employment.[10]

One exception is Belgium, whose family and educational policies resemble those of France. Public child care is extensive in Belgium, particularly in the preschool sector. There also has been some development of public child care for children below the age of entry into preschool (two and a half). As in France, Belgian politics was wracked by sharp clerical-anticlerical conflicts in the late nineteenth century, centered largely on the question of education, that endured well into the 1950s. One consequence of this competition over children's education was the early development of preschool programs that became part of the national education system in the late nineteenth century.[11]

These preschools make a major contribution to the child care system, although they follow school hours and are thus not perfectly suited to working parents' schedules. Belgium also developed a tradition of active family policies that were a compromise between clerical and anticlerical forces.[12] Where Belgium differs from France is in the greater influence of religious parties and civil society throughout the twentieth century. Christian Democratic parties have been politically powerful, and religious organizations maintained a greater role in the provision of educational and social services than in France. Belgium differs from its continental neighbors, however, in that its Social Democratic Party has long posed sharp challenges to conservatives on the issue of mothers' employment, perhaps reflecting the continuing strength of anticlericalism through much of the twentieth century.[13]

Finally, the liberal countries resemble each other in their religious pluralism, the importance of Protestant sects, their lack of established churches (or a weak established church, in the case of England), and their often higher rates of religious practice and belief (again, with the exception of the United Kingdom).[14] These countries also share a leeriness toward national or federal family policies—with a tendency to employ the individual as the category of social policy, rather than the family—and a rich sector of voluntary organizations that provide many social services.[15] The relationship between their religious heritage and their approach to child and family policy remains a largely unexplored area of research. The implication of the argument developed for the United States would be that in all these countries, religious pluralism and the early separation of church and state (or weakening of the established church in the case of England) created a desire to leave matters of familial morality at lower levels of society. At the same time, the continuing vitality of religion in many of these countries injects a more conservative and interventionist strand of thought about family affairs, shaping campaigns to restrict abortion access, fight changing mores about sexuality and familial morality, and preserve the traditional family.[16] Such forces appear to be considerably stronger in the United States than in other English-speaking countries, however, and a number of them have moved toward greater public involvement in promoting mothers' employment, albeit through public-private partnerships that assign a strong role to the voluntary sector.[17]

Although this project focused specifically on the programs of the welfare state, its findings could inform future research on other gendered policy areas. One implication of this study is the need to be attentive to the structural dimensions of politics. In recent years, scholars have focused increasingly on the role of women's agency in the policy-making process—an antidote to the heavily structural feminist analyses of earlier times.[18] This project serves as a reminder that feminists and other women's groups operate within political structures that often are historically rooted and that shape prospects for political influence. Thus, although American feminists often failed to make headway on the issue of work and care, focusing their energies on liberal "body rights" provided them with greater successes. Swedish women were better able to make claims about the importance of female employment and the need for public child care—perhaps to the detriment of the liberal rights that became well established in the United States.[19] Future research could profitably probe the ways in which different kinds of gender issues make their way into mainstream politics. In particular, we should learn more about the relationship of feminists and other women's groups to political parties, as well as the incentives for those parties to incorporate feminist concerns into their party platforms.[20]

This project also contributes to a growing body of research on historical institutionalism. There is now a large literature in political science and sociology about path dependence—the notion that public policies are "sticky" and difficult to change. The theory of path dependence has led to a view of welfare states as locked into place, following pathways determined in the distant past. The empirical reality, however, is one of both continuity and change: countries experience long periods of stable policy arrangements, but also moments of dynamism and reform. The central task for researchers is to identify the mechanisms that produce the institutionalization of public policy but that can also be a source of change.[21] This project focused on the role of social constituencies that form around existing policy arrangements. Given the size and reach of the welfare state, it is hardly surprising that its programs often shape politics themselves, becoming part of the fabric of social divisions that give rise to political identities and activism. Even so, societies are neither static nor shaped solely by the institutional structures of the welfare state. Autonomous social change can create new tensions and needs, generating political competition around previously ignored social questions.

The stability of social arrangements and identities can make them political forces in their own right. The gender division of paid work and care is one area of striking social stability that has evolved very slowly in most countries. Even in Sweden, where supportive public policies and active state campaigns have sought to alter the division of labor between men and women, the pace of change has been sluggish. This reality poses a challenge for those who aim to restructure work and caring arrangements, not only as a way to further women's integration into the public sphere of work, but also as a way to transform society around a vision of shared work and care.[22] Many policy makers seeking to augment women's employment have turned to mandating part-time work and lengthy parental leaves as a way to attract female workers. Often these provisions are officially gender neutral, with men and women both eligible for parental leave or reduced working hours, yet women are far more likely to take advantage of these opportunities than men. Such policies may help increase women's participation in the labor force as a whole but do not guarantee much change in the gendered distribution of work and care.

What policies for working parents can we expect in the future in advanced industrialized states?

The Future of Work-Family Policies

One notable trend is the growing assumption that women are, or should be, in paid work. In fact, as chapter 5 noted, one goal of policy makers in many of these countries has been "activation"—getting women, and especially mothers, into the labor market. One example of activation is welfare reform in the United States, which eliminated poor single mothers' entitlement to public assistance. The emphasis on activation in Western Europe informs a wider set of policies aiming not only to end welfare "dependency," but also to encourage all mothers to work for pay. Demographics form the crucial backdrop to these debates: policy makers worry about declining fertility rates and their consequences for both the fiscal sustainability of the welfare state and shortages of skilled workers. Because nations that do the least to support mothers' employment often have the lowest fertility rates, this has sparked interest in the French and Nordic models of work-family policies.

The European Union is an additional source of pressure on these states because official EU policy now advocates increased rates of female employment. This marks a departure from how the European Union's past treatment of women's employment issues, which was limited to antidiscrimination measures and workplace regulations that eliminate barriers to women's employment. Lacking both independent fiscal capacity and the support of the member states, the European Union generally has stayed out of redistributive politics. Since the 1997 Amsterdam Treaty, however, the member states have sought to augment the social dimension of European integration without violating the primary role of domestic governments in this area. The result has been the open method of coordination (OMC)—a system in which the member states voluntarily seek to meet agreed-upon targets without facing sanctions for their failure to do so.[23] This approach has been applied to a number of areas, including that of women's employment and child care. By 2010, the EU's goal is to have 60 percent of women in the EU area in paid employment, with access to child care for one-third of children below the age of three and for 90 percent of children between the age of three and the mandatory school age.

The impact of the OMC on domestic policy-making remains to be seen. One the one hand, the OMC's benchmarking and peer review processes may become a source of policy learning on the part of elites, especially if pressures from the supranational level are matched by the lobbying of activists within these countries.[24] However, without the kinds of sanctions that apply to EU directives, this "soft law" approach to women's equality may produce few changes outside of what otherwise would have happened in these countries. In addition, critics have noted that the European Union's drive to increase women's employment is part of a larger agenda of fighting unemployment through increasing flexibility in labor markets. These authors argue that the mobilization of women's employment will come through part-time and other flexible jobs, rather than through a commitment to a fundamental rethinking of the gender division of labor.[25]

Although European countries are under increasing pressure to promote mothers' employment, they also are under economic pressure to contain the growth of the welfare state and even to cut taxes and public spending. Many of these countries have made generous pension and health care commitments that will explode with the aging of the population. Real or perceived international competitive pressures also fuel a sense that these economies need to follow the American model of more labor market deregulation, tax cuts, and private market stimulation. The European Union contributes to this sentiment, requiring states within the common currency to keep budget deficits down and thus further reducing the margin of maneuver for these governments. Another influential actor at the international level, the OECD, also pressures its member states to restrain spending and promote private market solutions. Recently, an OECD study scolded Sweden for its generous spending on public child care.[26]

How will these various pressures shape the politics of work and family in advanced industrialized countries? In the Scandinavian countries, where mothers' employment rates are high and provisions for parents are well developed, there are few reasons to expect much retrenchment. Strong public expectations about state responsibilities in this area should preserve existing policies, and we can imagine expansions in these provisions. In Sweden, the supply of publicly funded child care is close to meeting the demand. In Norway, where child care provision long lagged behind that of Sweden and Denmark, these services have continually expanded since the 1990s.[27] One development in these countries could be increased requirements for men to take a larger share of parental leave time. This would be a further extension of the principles of existing policy, however, rather than a challenge to them.

More change could be forthcoming in continental Europe, given pressures on systems of social provision and concerns about low fertility rates. We probably should not expect Scandinavian-style family policies in these countries, however, but rather an attempt to follow the Dutch model of policy change. There is still a good deal of popular skepticism in many of these countries about the idea that mothers should work full-time while their children are young.[28] Many people favor the idea that mothers should work part-time, and some continue to endorse the model of the full-time caregiver. The Dutch model of widespread part-time work may satisfy a number of political and economic imperatives in these countries because it offers the possibility of higher rates of mothers' participation in the workforce without extensive state spending on child care. Part-time care can be made available to more children, and the state also gains revenues from the taxes paid by working mothers. Similarly, policy makers may seek to create their own "Dutch miracle" of high economic growth and low unemployment by using part-time work to introduce greater labor market flexibility. Although we can expect continued policy change in continental Europe, these countries are likely to try modernizing the male-breadwinner model rather than fully overthrowing it. Part-time work, extended care leaves, and part-time child care arrangements provide one way for these states to address social change without taking on huge financial burdens or wholly contravening traditional social values.

There are few reasons to expect the United States to swerve from its current trajectory of work-family policy. The current political climate is one in which free market advocates and social conservatives dominate both the Republican Party and the current government. These conservatives have long opposed federal child care funds for any but very poor children and just as vigorously object to the idea of a paid parental leave or other direct supports for working parents. However, even before conservative Republicans came to power, the work-family issue was moribund in national politics.[29] Private child care and employer-provided parental leaves have met at least some of the needs of working parents. These arrangements are a patchwork, not a guaranteed system, and access to this patchwork varies by socioeconomic class. Still, the availability of private options has stifled campaigns for greater federal involvement in child and family policy. The near absence of these questions from the political agenda at either the federal or the state level speaks to the difficulties of rousing public concern about this issue.

Political Lessons for the United States

Does the United States need to learn anything from other countries? Some might say no, given that market-based approaches in the United States have produced fairly high employment rates of women and a varied array of child care services. Currently, about one-third of women with young children are at home full-time, while another two-thirds are at work either part- or full-time—a diverse set of approaches to balancing work and family needs that perhaps mirrors the diversity of American society and its values. Moreover, it is difficult to use policy lessons from other countries to encourage their adoption in the United States: it appears that one of the quickest ways to doom a policy idea in the United States is to note that other countries actually do things this way. Many analysts of American family policy have pointed to the menu of child care and parental leave options available elsewhere in the world, to little avail.[30]

What the United States might learn from other countries is less about specific policy options and more about the way different societies have dealt with the contentious politics of this issue. In the United States, it often seems there is a zero-sum division between advocates of full-time motherhood and full-time female employment, such that resources delivered to one group are viewed as an insult to the life choices of the other. Yet, nearly all European countries have experienced similar debates and divisions at some point in their history, with advocates for full-time motherhood arrayed against those favoring public child care and other supports to working mothers. Polities have treated these divisions in different ways. In Sweden, calls for extended care leaves were rejected, but parents have the possibility of spending extensive time at home through part-time work and a long and generous parental leave. In France, current policy offers subsidies both for public child care and for parents who care for their children at home. Rather than ignore the difficulties facing French parents, public policy attempts to satisfy a diverse range of needs.

In the United States, difficulties reaching agreement on the question of mothers' employment have paralyzed policy such that there are few public supports for any parents, regardless of the choice they make in matters of work and family. Elements of the tax code subsidize one-earner families and offer limited child care subsidies for those who need them. These subsidies pale, however, in comparison to the degree of public support for families in other nations, with predictable consequences for poverty and inequality in the United States. In addition, as chapter 5 showed, some of the greatest costs of the American private model of child care are borne by child care workers themselves, who earn far less than their equivalents in other countries and tend to lack training or develop a lasting place in the profession. As a result, the quality of care suffers, particularly in the cheaper services that are available to lower-income families.

Efforts to redress this situation need not result in a one-size-fits-all approach that endorses one form of family or another or that directly involves the federal government in the provision of child care. Combining tax credits for one-earner families with greater subsidies for child care could bridge the divide between social conservatives and feminists on child care policy. Paid parental leave should be viewed not only as helping working mothers, but as enabling greater time for everyone to spend with family. In addition, government support for child care does not necessarily entail government provision.

In many European countries, publicly funded voluntary organizations are a critical layer between the state and the family and make possible publicly funded programs that offer a pluralistic range of services. In short, federal family policy need not represent the governmental Leviathan reaching into the family and its child-rearing practices but can instead help parents make their own decisions about work and family. Such policies, aimed at the broad middle class, could be politically popular, too, especially if they reflect the diversity of preferences parents have in matters of work and care.[31]

A final political lesson for the United States is the political potential of a campaign around early childhood education.[32] The United States was the original innovator in the development of public mass education. In the nineteenth century it surpassed most European countries in the proportion of children in public schools. When it comes to early education programs, though, the United States is a laggard. Access to early education programs has stagnated, and given the fiscal difficulties facing state governments in recent years, any change in this situation is unlikely. In other countries, educational programs have the ability to unify groups that are divided on the contentious question of mothers' employment. In Germany, belief in the importance of full-time maternal care of young children remains strong in the western *Länder*, yet there is also strong support for educational programs for preschool-aged children. This has enabled greater government investments in this area, to the benefit of all families who seek these services. In France, universal preschool has long been a popular part of the French education system, and all children attend these programs whether their mothers are in paid work or not. Educational programs can be designed to meet the needs of all families and can thereby serve as a way to unify people rather than divide them.

In short, the historical legacies of a reticent state in the United States need not preclude action to improve the well-being of families. Other elements of American political culture—such as the high value placed on education or the oft-stated concern with family values—can be mobilized around campaigns to expand subsidies and services for children and families. Examples from other nations show that public policy can be mindful of pluralism and diversity by finding ways to address the concerns and needs of all families.

Notes

1. Janet C. Gornick, Marcia K. Meyers, and Katherin E. Ross, "Public Policies and the Employment of Mothers: A Cross-National Study," *Social Science Quarterly* 79, no. 1 (March 1998): 35–54; Florence Jaumotte, "Female Labor Force Participation: Empirical Evidence on the Role of Policy and Other Determinants in OECD Countries," *OECD Economic Studies* 37 (February 2003): 51–107.

2. Jane Waldfogel, "Understanding the 'Family Gap' in Pay for Women with Children," *Journal of Economic Perspectives* 12, no. 1 (Winter 1998): 137–56.

3. Arlie Hochschild, *The Second Shift: Working Parents and the Revolution at Home*, with Anne Machung (New York: Viking, 1989); Janeen Baxter, "Gender Equality and Participation in Housework: A Cross-National Perspective," *Journal of Comparative Family Studies* 28, no. 3 (Autumn 1997): 220–48; Nancy Burns, Kay Lehman Schlozman, and Sidney Verba, "The Public Consequences of Private Inequality: Family Life and Citizen Participation," *American Political Science Review* 91, no. 2 (June 1997): 373–89.

4. Jane Waldfogel, "The Effect of Children on Women's Wages," *American Sociological Review* 62, no. 2 (April 1997): 209–17. The smallest gap is in Sweden. See Waldfogel, "Understanding the 'Family Gap,'" 140.

5. Barbara Hobson, "No Exit, No Voice: Women's Economic Dependency and the Welfare State," *Acta Sociologica* 33, no. 3 (1990): 235–50.

6. Jane Lewis with Barbara Hobson, introduction to *Lone Mothers in European Welfare Regimes: Shifting Policy Logics*, ed. Jane Lewis (London: Jessica Kingsley Publishers, 1997), 4–6; Gøsta Esping-Andersen, "A Child-Centered Investment Strategy," in *Why We Need a New Welfare State*, ed. Gøsta Esping-Andersen, Duncan Gallie, Anton Hemerijck, and John Myers (Oxford: Oxford University Press, 2002), 26–67.

7. Gøsta Esping-Andersen, *The Social Foundations of Postindustrial Economies* (Oxford: Oxford University Press, 1999).

8. Some argue that women delay childbirth in countries with high job insecurity, because they fear they will not be able to reenter the labor market after a period of

child rearing. High unemployment in Continental Europe leads couples to delay having children, whereas job-protected parental leaves in Scandinavia and the relatively flexible employment market in the United States allow women greater confidence in their ability to return to paid work. Alícia Adserà, "Changing Fertility Rates in Developed Countries: The Impact of Labor Market Institutions," *Journal of Population Economics* 17, no. 1 (2004): 17–43.

9. Rianne Mahon, "The OECD and the Reconciliation Agenda: Competing Blueprints," in *Children in Context: Changing Families and Welfare States*, ed. Jane Lewis (London: Edward Elgar, forthcoming).

10. Jane Jenson and Denis Saint-Martin, "New Routes to Social Cohesion? Citizenship and the Social Investment State," *Canadian Journal of Sociology* 28, no. 1 (Winter 2003): 77–99.

11. Given the now vast size of this literature, one way to approach it is through review essays. See Lynne Haney, "Engendering the Welfare State," *Comparative Studies in Society and History* 40, no. 4 (1998): 748–68; Felicia A. Kornbluh, "The New Literature on Gender and the Welfare State: The U.S. Case," *Feminist Studies* 22, no. 1 (Spring 1996): 171–97; Kimberly Morgan, "Gender and the Welfare State: New Research on the Origins and Consequences of Social Policy Regimes," *Comparative Politics* 34, no. 1 (October 2001): 105–24.

12. For criticism of the excessive focus of feminist welfare state research on motherhood, see Lisa Brush, "Changing the Subject: Gender and Welfare Regime Studies," *Social Politics* 9 (2002): 161–86. Some alternative approaches focus more on rights involving sexuality or one's body. For example, see Kathrin Zippel, *The Politics of Sexual Harassment: A Comparative Study of the United States, the European Union, and Germany* (Cambridge: Cambridge University Press, 2006).

13. Ann Shola Orloff, "Gender and the Social Rights of Citizenship: The Comparative Analysis of Gender Relations and Welfare State," *American Sociological Review* 58 (June 1993): 303–28.

14. Other measures of women friendliness have often come up with a different ordering. See, for example, R. Amy Elman, "Debunking the Social Democrats and the Myth of Equality," *Women's Studies International Forum* 16, no. 5 (September–October 1993); Zippel, *Politics of Sexual Harassment.*

15. For some of the debates about care, see Jane Jenson, "Who Cares? Gender and Welfare Regimes," *Social Politics* 4 (Summer 1997): 182–87; Trude Knijn and Monique Kremer, "Gender and the Caring Dimension of Welfare States: Toward Inclusive Citizenship," *Social Politics* 4 (Fall 1997): 328–61; Joya Misra, "Caring about Care," *Feminist Studies* 29, no. 2 (Summer 2003): 387–401.

16. Ingela K. Naumann, "Child Care and Feminism in West Germany and Sweden in the 1960s and 1970s," *Journal of European Social Policy* 15, no. 1 (2005): 47–63. The literature on maternalism offers a historical perspective on these differences. See Theda Skocpol, *Protecting Soldiers and Mothers: The Political Origins of Social Policy in the United States* (Cambridge: Belknap Press of Harvard University Press, 1992);

Seth Koven and Sonya Michel, *Mothers of a New World: Maternalist Politics and the Origins of Welfare States* (New York: Routledge, 1993).

17. Other authors have examined in detail the range of tax and benefit policies that also affect women's social citizenship. See Julia O'Connor, Ann Shola Orloff, and Sheila Shaver, *States, Markets, Families. Gender, Liberalism and Social Policy in Australia, Canada, Great Britain, and the United States* (Cambridge: Cambridge University Press, 1999); Diane Sainsbury, *Gender, Equality and Welfare States* (Cambridge: Cambridge University Press, 1996).

18. Yet another form of care is more informal—parents hiring babysitters or nannies who come to a parent's home to look after their child or children. Some countries subsidize this, either through direct payments or tax breaks on the cost of hiring these workers. Usually it is not counted as part of a country's official child care system, although the availability of subsidies for these forms of care can be an important aid to working parents.

19. Not all countries have done this. Sweden, for example, had only a parental leave and offered women no specific entitlement to a maternity leave. This was changed in 1995 to comply with the European Union's pregnancy directive, which mandated that member states provide women the right to fourteen continuous weeks of maternity leave.

20. For the distinction between conventional parental leave and care leave, see Kimberly J. Morgan and Kathrin Zippel, "Paid to Care: The Origins and Effect of Care Leave Policies in Western Europe," *Social Politics* 10, no. 1 (Spring 2003): 49–85.

21. For discussion of the effects of parental leave on women's employment, see "Perspectives: Parental Leave," *International Labour Review* 136, no. 2 (Spring 1997): 109–28; "Long-Term Leave for Parents in OECD Countries," *OECD Employment Outlook* (July 1995): 171–202.

22. Harald Bielenski, Gerhard Bosch, and Alexandra Wagner, *Working Time Preferences in Sixteen European Countries* (Dublin: European Foundation for the Improvement of Living and Working Conditions, 2002), 53.

23. A recent study showed that although 71.9 percent of Austrian mothers with a youngest child under the age of three were counted as "employed," 40 percent were on parental leave, 17.2 percent worked part-time, and 14.7 percent worked full time. *Babies and Bosses: Reconciling Work and Family Life*, vol. 2, *Austria, Ireland, Japan* (Paris: OECD, 2003), 48.

24. Gøsta Esping-Andersen, *Three Worlds of Welfare Capitalism* (Princeton, NJ: Princeton University Press, 1990).

25. Ibid., 82–88.

26. This typology has been much contested since it first appeared, but in many ways it captures important elements of these systems. Support for the typology can be found in Kees van Kersbergen, *Social Capitalism: A Study of Christian Democracy and the Welfare State* (London: Routledge, 1995); Evelyn Huber, Charles Ragin,

and John Stephens, "Social Democracy, Christian Democracy, Constitutional Structure, and the Welfare State," *American Journal of Sociology* 99, no. 3 (November 1993): 711–49. Critics include Jane Lewis, "Gender and the Development of Welfare Regimes," *Journal of European Social Policy* 2, no. 3 (1992): 159–73; Julia O'Connor, "Gender, Class and Citizenship in the Comparative Analysis of Welfare State Regimes: Theoretical and Methodological Issues," *British Journal of Sociology* 44 (September 1993): 501–18; Orloff, "Gender and the Social Rights of Citizenship."

27. Sainsbury, *Gender, Equality, and Welfare States.*

28. Juhani Lehto, Nina Moss, and Tine Rostgaard, "Universal Public Social Care and Health Services," in *Nordic Social Policy: Changing Welfare States*, ed. Mikko Kautto, Matti Heikkilä, Bjørn Hvinden, Staffan Marklund, and Niels Ploug (London: Routledge, 1999): 104–32.

29. Arnlaug Leira, *Welfare States and Working Mothers: The Scandinavian Experience* (Cambridge: Cambridge University Press, 1992).

30. Leira, "Caring as Social Right: Cash for Child Care and Daddy Leave," *Social Politics* 5, no. 3 (1998): 367–78; Jacqueline Heinen and Heini Martiskainen de Koenigswarter, "Framing Citizenship in France and Finland in the 1990s: Restructuring Motherhood, Work, and Care," *Social Politics* 8, no. 2 (Summer 2001): 170–81.

31. Kersbergen, *Social Capitalism.*

32. Bérengère Marques-Pereira and Olivier Paye, "Belgium: The Vices and Virtues of Pragmatism," in *Who Cares? Women's Work, Childcare, and Welfare State Redesign*, ed. Jane Jenson and Mariette Sineau (Toronto: University of Toronto Press, 2001), 56–87.

33. Jane Lewis, "Developing Early Years Childcare in England, 1997–2002: The Choices for (Working) Mothers," *Social Policy and Administration* 37, no. 3 (June 2003): 219–38.

34. *Babies and Bosses: Reconciling Work and Family Life*, vol. 1, *Australia, Denmark and the Netherlands* (Paris: OECD, 2002), 86–87.

35. Jane Jenson, "Against the Current: Child Care and Family Policy in Quebec," in *Child Care Policy at the Crossroads: Gender and Welfare State Restructuring*, ed. Rianne Mahon and Sonya Michel (New York: Routledge, 2002), 309–31; Daniel Wincott, "Reshaping the Public Space? Devolution and Policy Change in British Early Childhood Education and Care," *Regional and Federal Studies* 15, no. 4 (December 2005): 453–70.

36. William Goodman, "Boom in Day Care Industry the Result of Many Social Changes," *Monthly Labor Review* 118, no. 8 (August 1995): 7–8.

37. Deborah Brennan, *The Politics of Australian Child Care*, 2d ed. (Cambridge: Cambridge University Press, 1998), chap. 10; Lewis, "Developing Early Years Childcare."

38. Wolfgang Tietze and Debby Cryer, "Current Trends in European Early Child Care and Education," *Annals of the American Academy of Political and Social Sciences* 563 (May 1999): 180.

NOTES TO PAGES 16-20

39. Gøsta Esping-Andersen and Kees van Kersbergen, "Contemporary Research on Social Democracy," *Annual Review of Sociology* 18 (1986): 187–208; Walter Korpi, "Power, Politics, and State Autonomy in the Development of Social Citizenship," *American Sociological Review* 54, no. 3 (1989): 309–28; John D. Stephens, *The Transition from Capitalism to Socialism* (Atlantic Highlands, NJ: Humanities Press, 1980).

40. Kimberly J. Morgan, "The Production of Child Care: How Labor Markets Shape Social Policy and Vice Versa," *Social Politics* 12, no. 2 (Summer 2005): 243–63.

41. Jean Quataert, "Socialisms, Feminisms, and Agency: A Long View," *Journal of Modern History* 73, no. 3 (Sept 2001): 603–17.

42. This discussion of ideology was informed by John Gerring, "Ideology: A Definitional Analysis," *Political Research Quarterly* 50, no. 4 (Dec 1997): 957–99.

43. Ann Shola Orloff, *The Politics of Pensions: A Comparative Analysis of Britain, Canada, and the United States, 1880–1940* (Madison: University of Wisconsin Press, 1993), 58.

44. Gerring, "Ideology," 980.

45. More generally, there appears to be no linear relationship between women's movement organizing and policy outcomes: differences in the nature of these movements, their alliances with other organizations, and state structures play a critical mediating role. See Mary Fainsod Katzenstein, "Comparing the Feminist Movements of the United States and Western Europe: An Overview," in *The Women's Movements of the United States and Western Europe: Consciousness, Political Opportunity, and Public Policy*, ed. Mary Fainsod Katzenstein and Carol McClurg Mueller (Philadelphia: Temple University Press, 1987), 3–20.

46. Amy Mazur and Dorothy McBride Stetson, *Comparative State Feminism* (Thousand Oaks, CA: Sage, 1995); Amy Mazur, ed., *State Feminism, Women's Movements, and Job Training: Making Democracies Work in the Global Economy* (New York: Routledge, 2001); Dorothy McBride Stetson, ed., *Abortion Politics, Women's Movements, and the Democratic State: A Comparative Study of State Feminism* (Oxford: Oxford University Press, 2001).

47. Kristi Andersen and Elizabeth A. Cook, "Women, Work, and Political Attitudes," *American Journal of Political Science* 29, no. 3 (August 1985): 606–25; David De Vaus and Ian McAllister, "The Changing Politics of Women: Gender and Political Alignment in 11 Nations," *European Journal of Political Research* 17, no. 3 (May 1989): 241–62; Max Haller and Franz Hoellinger, "Female Employment and the Change of Gender Roles: The Conflictual Relationship between Participation and Attitudes in International Comparison," *International Sociology* 9, no. 1 (March 1994): 87–112; Mahshid Jalilvand, "Married Women, Work, and Values," *Monthly Labor Review* 123, no. 8 (August 2000): 26–31.

48. The few exceptions include van Kersbergen, *Social Capitalism*; Birgit Fix, "The Institutionalization of Family Welfare: Division of Labour in the Field of Child Care in Austria and Germany," Working paper 1, no. 24 (Mannheim Center for European Social Research, 1998); Philip Manow, "The Good, the Bad, and the

Ugly: Esping-Andersen's Regime Typology and the Religious Roots of the Western Welfare State," unpublished manuscript (Max Planck Institute for the Study of Societies, 2004).

49. Arland Thornton, William G. Axinn, and Daniel H. Hill, "Reciprocal Effects of Religiosity, Cohabitation, and Marriage," *American Journal of Sociology* 3 (November 1992): 628–51; Merlin B. Brinkerhoff and Marlene MacKie, "Religion and Gender: A Comparison of Canadian and American Student Attitudes," *Journal of Marriage and the Family* 47, no. 2 (May 1985): 415–30.

50. Paul Butts, "The Social Origins of Feminism and Political Activism: Findings from Fourteen Countries," in *Citizen Politics in Post-Industrial Societies*, ed. Terry Nichols Clark and Michael Rempel (Boulder, CO: Westview Press, 1997), 209–44; Haller and Hoellinger, "Female Employment and the Change of Gender Roles"; Ronald Inglehart and Pippa Norris, *Rising Tide: Gender Equality and Cultural Change around the World* (Cambridge: Cambridge University Press, 2003), chap. 3; Clyde Wilcox, "Support for Gender Equality in West Europe: A Longitudinal Analysis," *European Journal of Social Research* 20 (1991): 127–47; Loek Halman and Thorleif Pettersson, "Differential Patterns of Secularization in Europe: Exploring the Impact of Religion on Social Values," in *Religion in a Secularizing Society: The European's Religion at the End of the 20th Century*, ed. Loek Halman and Thorleif Pettersson (Tilburg: Tilburg University Press, 1999), 41–65.

51. Thornton, Axinn, and Hill, "Reciprocal Effects."

52. Arland Thornton, "Reciprocal Influences of Family and Religion in a Changing World," *Journal of Marriage and the Family* 47, no. 2 (May 1985): 381–94.

53. Michael Minkenberg, "The Policy Impact of Church-State Relations: Family Policy and Abortion in Britain, France, and Germany," *West European Politics* 26, no. 1 (January 2003): 195–217; Irene Wennemo, *Sharing the Costs of Children* (Stockholm: Swedish Institute for Social Research, 1994); Francis G. Castles and Michael Flood, "Why Divorce Rates Differ: Law, Religious Belief and Modernity," in *Families of Nations: Patterns of Public Policy in Western Democracies*, ed. Francis G. Castles (Aldershot: Dartmouth, 1993), 293–326.

54. Mattei Dogan, "The Decline of Traditional Values in Western Europe," *International Journal of Comparative Sociology* 39, no. 1 (February 1998): 77–91; Ronald Inglehart, *Culture Shift in Advanced Industrialized Societies* (Princeton, NJ: Princeton University Press 1990), chap. 6.

55. Paul Pierson, "The New Politics of the Welfare State," *World Politics* 48 (January 1996): 595–628; Andrea Louise Campbell, *How Policies Make Citizens: Senior Political Activism and the American Welfare State* (Princeton, NJ: Princeton University Press, 2003); Skocpol, *Protecting Soldiers and Mothers.*

56. Suzanne Mettler, *Dividing Citizens: Gender and Federalism in New Deal Public Policy* (Ithaca, NY: Cornell University Press, 1998); Mettler and Joe Soss, "The Consequences of Public Policy for Democratic Citizenship: Bridging Policy Studies and Mass Politics," *Perspectives on Politics* 2, no. 1 (March 2004): 55–73.

57. Seymour M. Lipset and Stein Rokkan, *Party Systems and Voter Alignments: Cross-National Perspectives*, ed. Seymour M. Rokkan Lipset and Stein Rokkan (New York: Free Press, 1967).

58. Kathleen Thelen, "How Institutions Evolve: Insights from Comparative-Historical Analysis," in *Comparative Historical Analysis in the Social Sciences*, ed. James Mahoney and Dietrich Rueschemeyer (New York: Cambridge University Press, 2002): 208–40. See also Wolfgang Streeck and Kathleen Thelen, "Introduction: Institutional Change in Advanced Political Economies," in *Beyond Continuity: Institutional Change in Advanced Political Economies*, ed. Wolfgang Streeck and Kathleen Thelen (Oxford: Oxford University Press, 2005), 1–39.

59. Esping-Andersen, *Three Worlds*, 141.

60. Gøsta Esping-Andersen, *Politics against Markets* (Princeton, NJ: Princeton University Press, 1985); Paul Pierson, "When Effect Becomes Cause: Policy Feedback and Political Change," *World Politics* 45, no. 4 (July 1993): 595–628.

61. Heidi Gottfried and Jacqueline O'Reilly, "Reregulating Breadwinner Models in Socially Conservative Welfare Systems: Comparing Germany and Japan," *Social Politics* 9, no. 1 (Spring 2002): 29–59.

62. Wincott, "Reshaping the Public Space?"

63. Lipset and Rokkan, *Party Systems and Voter Alignments*.

CHAPTER TWO

1. Seymour M. Lipset and Stein Rokkan, "Cleavage Structure, Party Systems, and Voter Alignments: An Introduction," in *Party Systems and Voter Alignments: Cross-National Perspectives*, ed. Seymour M. Lipset and Stein Rokkan (New York: Free Press, 1967), 15, 19.

2. See, for example, James L. Sundquist, *Dynamics of the Party System: Alignment and Realignment of Political Parties in the United States*, rev. ed. (Washington, DC: Brookings, 1983).

3. Chris Pierson, "On the Origins of the Welfare State, 1880–1975," in Pierson, *Beyond the Welfare State? The New Political Economy of Welfare* (University Park, PA: Pennsylvania State University Press, 1998).

4. Seth Koven and Sonya Michel, eds., *Mothers of a New World: Maternalist Politics and the Origins of the Welfare State* (New York: Routledge, 1993).

5. Theda Skocpol, *Protecting Soldiers and Mothers: The Political Origins of Social Policy in the United States* (Cambridge, MA: Belknap Press, 1992); Sonya Michel, *Children's Interests/Mothers' Rights: The Shaping of America's Child Care Policy* (New Haven, CT: Yale University Press, 1999), chap. 2; Ann-Sofie Ohlander, "The Invisible Child? The Struggle for a Social Democratic Family Policy in Sweden, 1900–1960s," in *Maternity and Gender Policies: Women and the Rise of the European Welfare States, 1880s–1950s*, ed. Gisela Bock and Pat Thane (London: Routledge, 1991), 65–68.

6. Seymour M. Lipset and Stein Rokkan, "Cleavage Structure, Party Systems, and Voter Alignments: An Introduction," in Lipset and Rokkan, *Party Systems and Voter Alignments*, 15.

7. On the impact of these cleavages on the growth of the voluntary sector and its relationship with the welfare state, see Josef Schmid, "Verbändewohlfahrt im modernen Wohlfahrtsstaat: Strukturbildende Effekte des Staat-Kirche-Konflicts," *Historical Social Research* 20, no. 2 (1995): 88–118; Schmid, "Two Steps Forward—One Step Back?" *European Journal of Political Research* 30, no. 1 (July 1996): 103–9.

8. Theodore Zeldin, introduction to *Conflicts in French Society: Anticlericalism, Education and Morals in the Nineteenth Century*, ed. Theodore Zeldin (London: George Allen & Unwin, 1970), 9–11, 36–37; René Rémond, *L'anticlércalisme en France, de 1815 à nos jours* (Paris: Editions Complexe, 1985). Zeldin also emphasizes the ways in which boundaries blurred between these two worlds.

9. One of the classic works on republicanism and education is that of Mona Ozouf, *L'école, l'eglise et la république, 1871–1914* (Paris: Éditions Cana/Jean Offredo, 1982).

10. Zeldin, introduction, 13–14; Robert Andersen, "The Conflict in Education," in Zeldin, *Conflicts in French Society*, 89.

11. Antoine Prost, *Histoire de l'enseignement en France, 1800–1967* (Paris: Librairie Armand Colin, 1968), 192–93; Ozouf, *L'École, l'église*, 55–92.

12. This was in large measure because of the Dreyfus affair—the false accusation and conviction for treason of an Alsatian Jew that divided the nation. Monarchists, the Catholic clergy, and the army resolutely stood by the conviction of Dreyfus against the fervent defense of Dreyfus by many intellectuals, republicans, and leftists.

13. There were limits to how well these measures actually eliminated religious teachers from schools. Sarah A. Curtis, "Lay Habits: Religious Teachers and the Secularization Crisis of 1901–1904," *French History* 9, no. 4 (December 1995): 478–98.

14. Subsidies would be restored to Catholic schools under the Vichy government and maintained by a series of laws in the 1950s that, though at times hotly contested, paved the way for some degree of reconciliation between Catholics and defenders of secular public education. See Antoine Prost, *Éducation, société et politiques: Une histoire de l'enseignement de 1945 à nos jours* (Paris: Editions du Seuil, 1997), 64. Even with public subsidies, only about 15 percent of primary school pupils have been in privately run schools. *Repères et références statistiques* (Paris: Ministère de l'Education Nationale, 1997).

15. Sudhir Hazareesingh, *Political Traditions in Modern France* (Oxford: Oxford University Press, 1994), 83–84.

16. Edith Archambault, *Le secteur sans but lucratif: Associations et fondations en France* (Paris: Economica, 1996), 25, 32–33. Despite some rapprochement between anticlerical and Catholic forces after 1914, restrictions on the religious congregations remained.

17. Suzanne Berger, "Religious Transformation and the Future of Politics," in *Changing Boundaries of the Political: Essays on the Evolving Balance between the State and Society, Public and Private, in Europe*, ed. Charles Maier (Cambridge: Cambridge Univ. Press, 1987), 107–49.

18. Jean-Noël Luc, *L'invention du jeune enfant au XIXe siècle: De la salle d'asile à l'école maternelle* (Paris: Belin, 1997), 42. Prost, *Histoire de l'enseignement*, 284.

19. Raymond Grew and Patrick J. Harrigan, "The Catholic Contribution to Universal Schooling in France, 1850–1906," *Journal of Modern History* 57, no. 2 (June 1985): 219–24.

20. Frédéric Dajez, *Les origines de l'école maternelle* (Paris: Presses Universitaires de France, 1994), 142–45.

21. Ibid., 161–65. Technically, all communes with at least 2,000 inhabitants were supposed to create an *école maternelle*, although this did not always occur.

22. Hazareesingh, *Political Traditions*, 85, 88.

23. Bonnie G. Smith, *Ladies of the Leisure Class: The Bourgeoises of Northern France in the Nineteenth Century* (Princeton, NJ: Princeton University Press, 1981), 149–51; 153–56; John H. Weiss, "Origins of the French Welfare State: Poor Relief in the Third Republic, 1871–1914," *French Historical Studies* 13, no. 1 (Spring 1983): 47–78; Timothy B. Smith, "Republicans, Catholics, and Social Reform: Lyon, 1870–1920," *French History* 12, no. 3 (September 1998): 247–48.

24. Rachel G. Fuchs, *Poor and Pregnant in Paris: Strategies for Survival in the Nineteenth Century* (New Brunswick, NJ: Rutgers University Press, 1992), 142.

25. Smith, *Ladies of the Leisure Class*, 149; Fuchs, *Poor and Pregnant*, 142.

26. Siân Reynolds, "Who Wanted the Crèches? Working Mothers and the Birth-Rate in France, 1900–1950," *Continuity and Change* 5, no. 2 (1990): 178–86.

27. Mary Daly, "The Functioning Family: Catholicism and Social Policy in Germany and Ireland," *Comparative Social Research* 18 (1999): 108–9.

28. Robert Talmy, *Histoire du mouvement familial en France, 1896–1939* (Paris: Union Nationale des Caisses d'Allocations Familiales, 1962), 1:60–61.

29. Richard Tomlinson, "The 'Disappearance' of France, 1896–1940: French Politics and the Birth Rate," *Historical Journal* 28, no. 2 (1985): 405–15; Karen Offen, "Depopulation, Nationalism, and Feminism in Fin-de-siècle France," *American Historical Review* 89, no. 3 (June 1984): 648–76.

30. Véronique Antomarchi, "La famille et le Parlement de 1870 à 1914," *Recherches et prévisions* 44 (June 1996): 41; Rémi Lenoir, "La question familiale: Familialisme d'Église, familialisme d'état," *French Politics, Culture, and Society* 17, nos. 3–4 (Summer–Fall 1999): 79.

31. Lenoir, "La question familiale," 78–79; Catherine Rollet-Echalier, *La politique à l'égard de la petite enfance sous la Troisième République* (Paris: PUF-INED, 1990).

32. Lenoir, "La question familiale," 90.

33. Mary Lynn McDougall, "Protecting Infants: The French Campaign for Maternity Leaves, 1890s–1913," *French Historical Studies* 13, no. 1 (Spring 1983): 79–105.

34. Susan Pedersen shows that employers created these benefits as a means of labor control. State policies to extend the system in the 1930s reflected the strength of pro-natalist anxieties within the governing class. *Family, Dependence, and the Origins of the Welfare State* (Cambridge: Cambridge University Press, 1993), chaps. 5, 7.

35. Pedersen, *Origins of the Welfare State*, 414–15.

36. Louise A. Tilly and Joan W. Scott, *Women, Work, and Family* (New York: Holt, Rinehart & Winston, 1978).

37. Ibid., 70–72.

38. Ibid., *Origins of the Welfare State*, 16.

39. Jane Jenson, "Gender and Reproduction: Or, Babies and the State," *Studies in Political Economy* 20 (Summer 1986): 9–46.

40. James F. McMillan, *Housewife or Harlot: The Place of Women in French Society, 1870–1940* (New York: St. Martin's Press, 1981), 26–27, 129.

41. James F. McMillan, "Religion and Gender in Modern France: Some Reflections," in *Religion, Society, and Politics in France since 1789*, ed. Frank Tallett and Nicholas Atkin (London: Hambledon Press, 1991), 55–66.

42. Steven C. Hause with Anne R. Kenney, *Women's Suffrage and Social Politics in the French Third Republic* (Princeton: Princeton University Press, 1984), 98–99. Hause and Kenney do not argue that anticlericalism was the sole barrier to female suffrage; they offer a nuanced account of how Catholicism, the legacy of Roman law, and political geography stymied the movement for women's right to vote.

43. John T. S. Madeley, "Scandinavian Christian Democracy: Throwback or Portent?" *European Journal of Political Research* 5, no. 3 (1977): 273–74; Susan Sundbeck, "Tradition and Change in the Nordic Countries," in *The Post-War Generation and Establishment Religion: Cross-Cultural Perspectives*, ed. Wade Clark Roof, Jackson W. Carroll, and David A. Roozen (Boulder, CO: Westview Press, 1995), 87.

44. Madeley, "Scandinavian Christian Democracy," 273.

45. Ibid., 274.

46. John T. S. Madeley, "A Framework for the Comparative Analysis of Church-State Relations in Europe," *West European Politics* 26, no. 1 (January 2003): 23–50.

47. Loek Halman and Ole Riis, "Contemporary European Discourses on Religion and Morality," in *Religion in a Secularizing Society: The Europeans' Religion at the End of the 20th Century*, ed. Loek Halman and Ole Riis (Tilburg: Tilburg University Press, 1999), 6–7.

48. David Martin, "Notes for a General Theory of Secularisation," *Archives Européennes de Sociologie* 10 (1969): 192–201; Sundbeck, "Tradition and Change," 87–91.

49. Leon Boucher, *Tradition and Change in Swedish Education* (Oxford: Pergamon, 1982), 5; John D. Stephens, "Religion and Politics in Three Northwest European Democracies," *Comparative Social Research* 2 (1979): 129–57.

50. Göran Gustafsson, "Church-State Separation Swedish-Style," *West European Politics* 26, no. 1 (January 2003).

51. Madeley, "Scandinavian Christian Democracy," 279–80.

52. John Boli, *New Citizens for a New Society: The Institutional Origins of Mass Schooling in Sweden* (Oxford: Pergamon, 1989), 227, 241–42; Göran Gustafsson, "Religious Change in the Five Scandinavian Countries, 1930–1980," *Comparative Social Research* 10 (1987): 145.

53. Gustav Sundbärg, ed., *Education in Sweden* (Stockholm: Kungl Boktryckeriet, 1904), 3–7.

54. Boli, *New Citizens*, 68, 84, 139–40; Gustafsson, "Religious Change," 166.

55. Filip Wijkstrom, "Changing Focus or Changing Role? The Swedish Nonprofit Sector in the 1990s," *German Policy Studies* 1, no. 2 (May 2000).

56. Estelle James, "The Private Provision of Public Services: A Comparison of Sweden and Holland," in *The Nonprofit Sector in International Perspective: Studies in Comparative Culture and Policy*, ed. Estelle James (New York: Oxford University Press, 1989), 37.

57. Wijkstrom, "Changing Focus."

58. Anita Nyberg, "From Foster Mothers to Child Care Centers: A History of Working Mothers and Child Care in Sweden," *Feminist Economics* 6, no. 1 (2000): 11–12.

59. Lars Gunnarsson, "Sweden," in *International Handbook of Child Care Policies and Programs*, ed. Moncrieff Cochran (Westport, CT: Greenwood Press, 1993), 501.

60. Tessa Blackstone, "Some Aspects of the Structure and Extent of Nursery Education in Five European Countries," *Comparative Education* 7, no. 3 (December 1971): 91–105; OECD, *Reviews of National Politics for Education: Sweden* (Paris: OECD, 1969), 31; Boucher, *Tradition and Change*, 63.

61. Kimberly J. Morgan, "Forging the Frontiers between State, Church, and Family: Religious Cleavages and the Origins of Early Childhood Care and Education Policies in France, Sweden, and Germany," *Politics and Society* 30, no. 1 (March 2002): 113–48.

62. Nyberg, "From Foster Mothers to Child Care Centers," 12.

63. Göran Therborn, "The Politics of Childhood: The Rights of Children in Modern Times," in *Families of Nations: Patterns of Public Policy in Western Democracies*, ed. Frances Castles (Aldershot: Dartmouth, 1993), 258; Kari Melby, Anu Pylkkänen, Bente Rosenbeck, and Christina Carlsson Wetterberg, eds., *The Nordic Model of Marriage and the Welfare State* (Copenhagen: Nordic Council of Ministers, 2000).

64. Christina Carlsson Wetterberg, Kari Melby, and Bente Rosenbeck, "The Nordic Model of Marriage and the Welfare State," paper presented at "Alva Myrdal's Questions to Our Time," conference at Uppsala University, Sweden, March 6–8, 2002.

65. Melby et al., introduction to *Nordic Model of Marriage*, 20 21.

66. Helena Bergman and Barbara Hobson, "Compulsory Fatherhood: The Coding of Fatherhood in the Swedish Welfare State," in *Making Men into Fathers: Men,*

Masculinities, and the Social Politics of Fatherhood, ed. Barbara Hobson (Cambridge: Cambridge University Press, 2002), 93–94.

67. David Bradley, "Family Laws and Welfare States," in *Nordic Model of Marriage*, 37–66.

68. Melby et al., introduction to *Nordic Model of Marriage*, 15.

69. Wetterberg, Melby, and Rosenbeck, "Nordic Model of Marriage," 10. See also Therborn, "Politics of Childhood," 258.

70. Diane Sainsbury, *Gender, Equality, and Welfare States* (Cambridge: Cambridge University Press, 1996), 63–64.

71. Urban Lundberg and Klas Åmark, "Social Rights and Social Security: The Swedish Welfare State, 1900–2000," *Scandinavian Journal of History* 26, no. 3 (September 2001): 160.

72. Ohlander, "The Invisible Child?" 68–69; Rita Liljeström, "Sweden," in *Family Policy: Government and Families in Fourteen Countries*, Sheila B. Kamerman and Alfred J. Kahn (New York: Columbia University Press, 1978), 25–26.

73. Herman Bakvis, *Catholic Power in the Netherlands* (Kingston, ON: McGill-Queen's University Press, 1981), 13.

74. E. H. Kossmann, *The Low Countries, 1780–1940* (Oxford: Clarendon Press, 1978), 208–10.

75. Joos van Vugt, "For Charity and Church: The Brother Teachers of Maastricht, 1840–1900," *History of Education* 20, no. 3 (1991): 226–27.

76. Kossman, *Low Countries*, 301–2; Abram de Swaan, *In Care of the State: Health Care, Education, and Welfare in Europe and the USA in the Modern Era* (New York: Oxford University Press, 1988), 101–2. De Swaan's study emphasizes how conflicts between the central state and local elites underpinned religiously based divisions over education.

77. John Valk, "Religion and the Schools: The Case of Utrecht," *History of Education Quarterly* 35, no. 2 (Summer 1995): 159–77.

78. De Swaan, *In Care of the State*, 211.

79. Kossman, *Low Countries*, 355.

80. Arend Lijphart, "Consociational Democracy," *World Politics* 21, no. 2 (January 1969): 207–25.

81. In return for Social Democratic support for this agreement, universal suffrage was granted.

82. Estelle James, "Benefits and Costs of Privatized Public Services: Lessons from the Dutch Educational System," *Comparative Education Review* 28, no. 4 (1984): 609.

83. Vincent, 223–24; Lily E. Clerkx and Marinus H. van Ijzendoorn, "Child Care in a Dutch Context: On the History, Current Status, and Evaluation of Non-maternal Child Care in the Netherlands," in *Child Care in Context: Cross-Cultural Perspectives*, ed. Michael E. Lamb, Kathleen J. Sternberg, Carl-Philip Hwang, and Anders G. Broberg (Hillsdale, NJ: Lawrence Erlbaum Associates, 1992), 58–59.

84. *Statistical Yearbook of the Netherlands;* Jean-Pierre Briand, Jean-Michel Chapoulie, Françoise Huguet, Jean-Noël Luc, and Antoine Prost, *L'enseignement primaire et ses extensions, 19e–20e siècles: Annuaire statistique* (Paris: Economica, 1987).

85. Blackstone, "Structure and Extent of Nursery Education."

86. Maria Brenton, "Changing Relationships in Dutch Social Services," *Journal of Social Policy* 11, no. 1 (1982): 60–61.

87. Kees van Kersbergen, "The Causes and Consequences of Prolonged yet Interrupted Christian Democratic Rule in the Netherlands," presented at The Western Welfare State and Its Religious Roots, Max Planck Institute for the Study of Societies, Cologne, Germany, April 30–May 1, 2004.

88. Thomas R. Rochon, *The Netherlands: Negotiating Sovereignty in an Interdependent World* (Boulder, CO: Westview Press, 1999), 33.

89. The Catholic and Protestant pillars were the strongest, while the liberal pillar was somewhat incomplete, making the Netherlands a society of three and a half pillars. See Rochon, *The Netherlands*, 33.

90. James, "Private Provision of Public Services," 31–60.

91. Hettie A. Pott-Buter, *Facts and Fairy Tales about Female Labor, Family and Fertility* (Amsterdam: Amsterdam University Press, 1993), 201.

92. Jet Bussemaker, "Gender and the Separation of Spheres in Twentieth-Century Dutch Society: Pillarisation, Welfare State Formation and Individualisation," in *Gender, Participation, and Citizenship in the Netherlands*, ed. Jet Bussemaker and Rian Voet (Hants., England: Ashgate, 1998), 28–29, 31.

93. Quoted in Janneke Plantenga, "Double Lives: Labor Market Participation, Citizenship and Gender," in Bussemaker and Voet, *Gender, Participation, and Citizenship*, 51.

94. A. James Reichley, *Faith in Politics* (Washington, D.C.: Brookings Institution, 2002), 103–5; James W. Fraser, *Between Church and State: Religion and Public Education in a Multicultural America* (New York: St. Martin's Press, 1999), 12, 17.

95. Stanley Rothman, "The Politics of Catholic Parochial Schools: An Historical and Comparative Analysis," *Journal of Politics* 25, no. 1 (February 1963): 55.

96. Max Weber, "The Protestant Sects and the Spirit of Capitalism," in *From Max Weber: Essays in Sociology*, ed. H. H. Gerth and C. Wright Mills (New York: Oxford University Press, 1958), 302–3; Edward A. Tiryakian, "American Religious Exceptionalism: A Reconsideration," *Annals of the American Academy of Political and Social Science* 527 (May 1993): 41–43.

97. Tiryakian, "American Religious Exceptionalism," 47.

98. Virginia A. Hodgkinson and Kathleen D. McCarthy, "The Voluntary Sector in International Perspective: An Overview," in *The Nonprofit Sector in the Global Community: Voices from Many Nations*, ed. Kathleen D. McCarthy, Virginia A. Hodgkinson, Russy D. Sumariwalla (San Francisco: Jossey-Bass, 1992), 8–9; Michael O'Neill, *The Third America: The Emergence of the Nonprofit Sector in the United States* (San Francisco: Jossey-Bass, 1989).

99. This is not to neglect the large membership organizations that extended over a wide range of territory. The point is a comparative one—that civil society did not become pillarized in the way it was in Netherlands, Germany, or Belgium. On the growth of American voluntary associations in the nineteenth century, see Theda Skocpol, Marshall Ganz, and Ziad Munson, "A Nation of Organizers: The Institutional Origins of Civic Voluntarism in the United States," *American Political Science Review* 94, no. 3 (September 2000): 527–46.

100. On the origins of the American education system, see Carl F. Kaestle, *Pillars of the Republic: Common Schools and American Society, 1780–1860* (New York: Hill and Wang, 1983).

101. John W. Meyer, David Tyack, Joane Nagel, and Audri Gordon, "Public Education as Nation-Building in America: Enrollments and Bureaucratization in the American States," *American Journal of Sociology* 85, no. 3 (1979): 591–613.

102. Paul Kleppner, "Partisanship and Ethnoreligious Conflict: The Third Electoral System, 1853–1892," in *Evolution of American Electoral Systems*, ed. Paul Kleppner (Westport, CT: Greenwood Press, 1981), 133–35.

103. Tiryakian, "American Religious Exceptionalism," 47.

104. Carl F. Kaestle, *Pillars of the Republic: Common Schools and American Society, 1780–1860* (New York: Hill and Wang, 1983); Meyer et al., "Public Education as Nation-Building."

105. Rogers Smith, *Civic Ideals: Conflicting Visions of Citizenship in U.S. History* (New Haven, CT: Yale University Press, 1997), 216–20; Marvin Lazerson, "Understanding American Catholic Educational History," *History of Education Quarterly* 17, no. 3 (Fall 1977): 297–317; Stanley Rothman, "The Politics of Catholic Parochial Schools: An Historical and Comparative Analysis," *Journal of Politics* 25, no. 1 (Feb. 1963): 56.

106. Smith, *Civic Ideals*, 218.

107. Fraser, *Between Church and State*, 25–26.

108. Ibid., chap. 3.

109. Kleppner, "Partisanship and Ethnoreligious Conflict," 137–38.

110. David Tyack and Thomas James, "State Government and American Public Education: Exploring the 'Primeval Forest,'" *History of Education Quarterly* 26, no. 1 (Spring 1986): 39–69.

111. Fraser, *Between Church and State*, 13; Charles L. Glenn, "Public Education Changes Partners," *Journal of Policy History* 13, no. 1 (2001): 136.

112. Linda Gordon, *The Great Arizona Orphan Abduction* (Cambridge, MA: Harvard University Press, 1999).

113. Fraser, *Between Church and State*, 58.

114. Maris A. Vinovskis, "Early Childhood Education: Then and Now," *Daedalus* 122, no. 1 (Winter 1993): 152, 154–56; Barbara Beatty, *Preschool Education in America: The Culture of Young Children from the Colonial Era to the Present* (New Haven: Yale University Press, 1995), 23.

115. Kaestle, *Pillars of the Republic*, 112.

116. See Beatty, *Preschool Education*, chaps. 4–5.

117. Marvin Lazerson, "Urban Reform and the Schools: Kindergartens in Massachusetts, 1870–1915," *History of Education Quarterly* 11, no. 2 (Summer 1971): 121.

118. Beatty, *Preschool Education*, 111.

119. Morton Keller, *Regulating a New Society: Public Policy and Social Change in America, 1900–1933* (Cambridge, MA: Harvard University Press, 1994), 4–6.

120. Lynn Dumenil, "'The Insatiable Maw of Bureaucracy': Antistatism and Education Reform in the 1920s," *Journal of American History* 77, no. 2 (September 1990): 499–524; David J. O'Brien, *American Catholics and Social Reform: The New Deal Years* (New York: Oxford University Press, 1968), 43–45.

121. Dumenil, "'Insatiable Maw,'" 516. While most Catholics were uniformly opposed to a federal education department, there was greater diversity of opinion on the Sheppard-Towner Act and the child labor amendment.

122. Stanley Coben, "A Study in Nativism: The American Red Scare of 1919–20," *Political Science Quarterly* 79, no. 1 (March 1964): 52–75.

123. Clyde Wilcox, *God's Warriors: The Christian Right in Twentieth-Century America* (Baltimore: Johns Hopkins University Press, 1992), 4–5.

124. Paul H. Douglas, *Wages and the Family* (Chicago: University of Chicago Press, 1923); Abraham Epstein, *Insecurity: A Challenge to America; A Study of Social Insurance in the United States and Abroad* (New York: Harrison Smith and Robert Haas, 1933).

125. *Low-Income Families*, hearings before the Subcommittee on Low-Income Families of the Joint Committee on the Economic Report (U.S. GPO, 1959); *Low-Income Families*, hearings before the Subcommittee on Low-Income Families of the Joint Committee on the Economic Report (U.S. GPO, 1955); Richard L. Neuberger, "Family Allowances," *America* 97, no. 6 (May 11, 1957): 189–91; "Family Allowances Stalled," *America* 95, no. 1 (April 7, 1956): 8.

126. "Who Wants Subsidies for Children?" *Christian Century* 74, no. 22 (May 29, 1957): 676.

127. Winifred Bell, *Aid to Dependent Children* (New York: Columbia University Press, 1965), 3–9. Linda Gordon, *Pitied but not Entitled: Single Mothers and the History of Welfare, 1890–1935* (New York: Free Press, 1994).

128. Randall Hansen and Desmond King, "Eugenic Ideas, Political Interests, and Policy Variance: Immigration and Sterilization Policy in Britain and the U.S.," *World Politics* 53, no. 2 (January 2001): 237–63. Sweden also maintained a program of eugenic sterilization for decades.

129. Sainsbury, *Gender Equality, Welfare States*; Michel, *Children's Interests/ Mothers' Rights*, chap. 4.

130. The mandatory school age was seven, but in many areas preschools were available for children between the ages of three and six.

131. Pedersen, *Origins of the Welfare State*, 368–71.

132. Anna-Lisa Kalvesten, "Family Policy in Sweden," *Marriage and Family Living* 17, no. 3 (August 1955): 250–54.

133. The assistance single mothers received depended on whether they were widows, divorced or never married, or lacked an acknowledged father for their child(ren). Widows received a children's pension, divorced or never-married mothers could get an advance on child support, while all others had to rely on poor relief. See Celia Winkler, *Single Mothers and the State: The Politics of Care in Sweden and the United States* (Lanham: Rowman & Littlefield, 2002), 46–47.

134. J. M. L. Jonker, "The Netherlands," in *Family Policy in the EEC Countries* (Brussels: Commission of the European Community, 1990), 278–79.

135. Vernon Mallinson, *The Western European Idea in Education* (Oxford: Pergamon Press, 1980), 106.

136. Gordon, *Pitied but Not Entitled*, 281.

137. Ibid., 95, 207.

138. Gilbert Steiner, *The Children's Cause* (Washington, D.C.: Brookings, 1976), 8–10.

139. *Children's Interests/Mothers' Rights*, chap. 4.

140. Emilie Stoltzfus, *Citizen, Mother, Worker: Debating Public Responsibility for Child Care after the Second World War* (Chapel Hill: University of North Carolina Press, 2003).

141. Bernard Greenblatt, *Responsibility for Child Care* (San Francisco: Jossey-Bass, 1977), 66–69.

142. Véronique Aubert, "Système professionnel et esprit de corps: le rôle du syndicat national des instituteurs," *Pouvoirs* 30 (1984) : 79–89.

143. Michel, *Children's Interests/Mothers' Rights*, chap. 2.

144. Kerstin Holmlund, "Don't Ask for Too Much! Swedish Pre-School Teachers, the State, and the Union, 1906–1965," *History of Education Review* 29, no. 1 (2000): 54–64.

145. Jean-Claude Chamboredon and Jean Prévot, "Le 'métier d'enfant': Définition sociale de la prime enfance et fonctions différentielles de l'école maternelle," *Revue française de sociologie* 14 (1973): 295–335. There often are no classes one day or afternoon a week so that parents can arrange for religious education if they choose. Although few do so today, the schedule remains.

146. Blackstone, "Structure and Extent of Nursery Education," 95–96.

147. Clerkx and Van Ijzendoorn, "Child Care," 64.

148. Kerstin Holmlund, "Swedish Pre-School Teachers."

149. Gilbert R. Austin, *Early Childhood Education: An International Perspective* (New York: Academic Press, 1976), 163.

150. De Swaan, *In Care of the State*, 210–11.

151. Kees van Kersbergen, *Social Capitalism: A Study of Christian Democracy and the Welfare State* (London: Routledge, 1995).

152. John D. Stephens, "Religion and Politics in Three Northwest European Democracies," *Comparative Social Research* 2 (1979): 129–57.

153. R. E. M. Irving, *Christian Democracy in France* (London: George Allen & Unwin, 1973), 36–45.

CHAPTER THREE

1. Diane Sainsbury, *Gender, Equality and Welfare States* (Cambridge: Cambridge University Press, 1996), chap. 3; Julia O'Connor, Ann Shola Orloff, and Sheila Shaver, *States, Markets, Families. Gender, Liberalism and Social Policy in Australia, Canada, Great Britain and the United States* (Cambridge: Cambridge University Press, 1999), 110–11.

2. John Bowlby, *Maternal Care and Mental Health* (Geneva: World Health Organization, 1952).

3. Siv Gustafsson, "Childcare and Types of Welfare States," in *Gendering Welfare States*, ed. Diane Sainsbury (London: Sage, 1994): 51.

4. Barbara Hobson, "Feminist Strategies and Gendered Discourses in Welfare States: Married Women's Right to Work in the United States and Sweden," in *Mothers of a New World: Maternalist Politics and the Origins of Welfare States*, ed. Seth Koven and Sonya Michel (New York: Routledge, 1993), 396–429.

5. Marolein Morée, "A Quiet Revolution: Working Mothers in the Netherlands 1950–1990," *Netherlands Journal of Social Sciences* 30, no. 1 (August 1994): 27.

6. Sainsbury, *Gender, Equality, and Welfare States*, 51–54, 59–63.

7. Antoine Prost, "L'évolution de la politique familiale en France de 1938 à 1981," *Le mouvement social* 129 (October–December 1984): 13–15. Child allowances were available only starting with the second child.

8. Christina Bergqvist and Anita Nyberg, "Childcare and Welfare State Restructuring in Sweden: From Universalism, Generosity and Egalitarianism to a Mean, Lean and Stratifying Welfare State?" unpublished paper, 2000; Mary Ruggie, *The State and Working Women: A Comparative Study of Britain and Sweden* (Princeton: Princeton University Press, 1984), 254–55.

9. Jet Bussemaker, "Rationales of Care in Contemporary Welfare States: The Case of Childcare in the Netherlands," *Social Politics* 5, no. 1 (Spring 1998): 71, 76–77.

10. Normal school hours were from 8:30 or 9:00 A.M. until 4:30 or 5:00 P.M., with a one-and-a-half-hour lunch break. Some students could stay at school for lunch. Certain programs were also open as early as 7:00 A.M. and stayed open until 7 P.M. Services outside normal school hours would be staffed by assistants, not regular preschool teachers. Gilbert R. Austin, *Early Childhood Education: An International Perspective* (New York: Academic Press, 1976), 188.

11. Jean-Claude Chamboredon and Jean Prévot, "Le 'métier d'enfant': Définition sociale de la prime enfance et fonctions différentielles de l'école maternelle,"

Revue française de sociologie 14 (1973): 299–303; Eric Plaisance, *L'enfant, la maternelle, et la société* (Paris: PUF 1986).

12. Livia Oláh, "Gender Neutral and Gender Specific Categories in Swedish and Hungarian Law: The Case of Parental Leave," Stockholm University Demographic Department Internal Memorandum, November 4, 1994.

13. Elisabetta Vezzosi, "Why Is There No Maternity Leave in the United States? European Models for a Law That Was Never Passed," paper presented at the annual meeting of the International Sociological Association's Research Committee on Poverty, Social Welfare, and Social Policy, Chicago, Illinois, September 8–10, 2005.

14. Evelyne Huber and John D. Stephens, "Partisan Governance, Women's Employment, and the Social Democratic Service State," *American Sociological Review* 65, no. 3 (2000): 323–42.

15. Jonas Hinnfors, "Stability through Change: The Pervasiveness of Political Ideas," *Journal of Public Policy* 19, no. 3 (1999): 293–312.

16. Christina Florin and Bengt Nilsson, "'Something in the Nature of a Bloodless Revolution . . .': How New Gender Relations Became Gender Equality Policy in Sweden in the Nineteen-Sixties and Seventies," in *State Policy and Gender System in the Two German States and Sweden, 1945–1989*, ed. Rolf Torstendahl (Uppsala, Sweden: University of Uppsala Department of History, 1999) 57.

17. Florin and Nilsson, "Bloodless Revolution," 71; Hinnfors, "Stability through Change," 294.

18. Annika Baude and Per Holmberg, "The Positions of Men and Women in the Labour Market," in *The Changing Roles of Men and Women*, Edmund Dahlström (Boston: Beacon Press, 1971), 116, 130.

19. Dahlström, *Changing Roles of Men and Women*; Helena Bergman and Barbara Hobson, "Compulsory Fatherhood: The Coding of Fatherhood in the Swedish Welfare State," in *Making Men into Fathers: Men, Masculinities and the Social Politics of Fatherhood*, ed. Barbara Hobson (Cambridge: Cambridge University Press, 2002), 104–5.

20. Rianne Mahon, "Child Care in Canada and Sweden: Policy and Politics," *Social Politics* 4, no. 3 (Fall 1997); Florin and Nilsson, "Bloodless Revolution."

21. The report stirred some controversy, however, even among social democrats. See Sissela Bok, *Alva Myrdal: A Daughter's Memoir* (Cambridge, MA: Perseus, 1991), 298–99.

22. Given that one earner, usually the woman, earns less, the woman's income is often viewed as the secondary one. Adding this income to that of the primary earner pushes couples into higher tax rates, thereby imposing steep marginal rates on the second earner. As a result, in evaluations of whether or not to remain in paid employment, couples often face the prospect of almost all of the second salary going to taxes, child care, and other work-related expenses. In such a situation, many opt for one earner to stay home.

23. Sara Brachet, "Politiques familiales et assurance parentale en Suède," *CAF Dossier d'Etudes* no. 21 (June 2001); Florin and Nilsson, "Bloodless Revolution," 75.

24. Siv Gustafsson and Roger Jacobsson, "Trends in Female Labor Force Participation in Sweden," *Journal of Labor Economics* 3, no. 1, part 2 (January 1985): S256–S274.

25. Victor Pestoff and Peter Strandbrink, "The Politics of Swedish Child Care," report prepared for the EMES Research Network, 2002, p. 7.

26. Hillevi Lenz Taguchi and Ingmarie Munkammar, "Consolidating Governmental Early Childhood Education and Care Services under the Ministry of Education and Science: A Swedish Case Study," *UNESCO Early Childhood and Family Policy Series* no. 6 (Paris: April 2003), 8.

27. Loek Halman and Thorleif Pettersson, "Differential Patterns of Secularization in Europe: Exploring the Impact of Religion on Social Values," in *Religion in a Secularizing Society: The European's Religion at the End of the 20ᵗʰ Century*, ed. Loek Halman and Ole Riis (Tilburg: Tilburg University Press, 1999), 41–65.

28. Esping-Andersen, *Politics against Markets* (Princeton, NJ: Princeton University Press, 1985), 89–90.

29. Lauri Karvonen, "Trade Unions and the Feminization of the Labour Market in Scandinavia," in *Women in Nordic Politics: Closing the Gap*, ed. Lauri Karvonen and Per Selle (Aldershot, England: Dartmouth, 1995), 137.

30. Hinnfors, "Stability through Change," 301.

31. Christina Bergqvist, Jaana Kuusipalo, and Auður Styrkarsdóttir, "The Debate on Childcare Policies," in *Nordic Democracies: Gender and Politics in the Nordic Countries*, ed. Christina Bergqvist Jaana Kuusipalo, and Auður Styrkarsdóttir (Oslo: Scandinavian University Press, 1999), 138–39.

32. Kerstin Sörensen and Christina Bergqvist, *Gender and the Social Democratic Welfare Regime: A Comparison of Gender-Equality Friendly Policies in Sweden and Norway* (Stockholm: National Institute for Working Life, 2002), 11.

33. A conversation with Irene Wennemo of the central labor confederation (LO) was invaluable in clarifying my thoughts on this point.

34. Baude and Holmberg, "Positions of Men and Women," 112.

35. Anne-Marie Daune-Richard and Rianne Mahon, "Sweden: Models in Crisis," in *Who Cares? Women's Work, Childcare, and Welfare State Redesign*, ed. Jane Jenson and Mariette Sineau (Toronto: University of Toronto Press, 2001), 152–53; Yvonne Hirdman, *Women: From Possibility to Problem? Gender Conflict in the Welfare State* (Stockholm: Swedish Center for Working Life, 1994), 26–27.

36. Hinnfors, "Stability through Change," 304.

37. One of the pivotal moments was a speech by Olof Palme embracing this new agenda. According to Hinnfors, however, gender equality goals continued to be controversial in the party until 1980.

38. Sörensen and Bergqvist, *Gender and the Social Democratic Welfare Regime*, 10–11. There also was no recourse to immigrant employment to cope with labor

212 NOTES TO PAGES 80–82

shortages. See Arnlaug Leira, *Models of Motherhood* (Oslo: Institute for Social Research, 1989), 131, 136–40.

39. Stein Rokkan, "Norway: Numerical Democracy and Corporate Pluralism," in *Political Oppositions in Western Democracies*, ed. Robert G. Dahl (New Haven, CT: Yale University Press, 1966), 74–78; John D. Stephens, "Religion and Politics in Three Northwest European Democracies," *Comparative Social Research* 2 (1979): 136–37. Kerstin Sörensen develops a more elaborate account of the way in which center-periphery and religious cleavages shaped economic policy, with consequences for the participation of women in paid work and policies on mothers' employment. See "Gender Ideology and Economic Policy in the Making of the Welfare State: Multiple Social Democratic Paths to Policy Development," paper presented at the annual meeting of the International Sociology Association's Research Committee 19, Chicago, Illinois, September 8–10, 2005.

40. Susan Sundback, "Nation and Gender Reflected in Scandinavian Religiousness," in *Scandinavian Values: Religion and Morality in the Nordic Countries*, ed. Thorleif Pettersson and Ole Riis (Uppsala, Sweden: S. Academiae Ubsaliensis, 1994): 129–50.

41. Lars Svåsand, "The Center-Right Parties in Norwegian Politics: Between Reformist Labor and Radical Progress," in *The European Center-Right at the End of the 20th Century*, ed. Frank L. Wilson (New York: St. Martin's Press, 1998), 188; Kaare Strøm and Jørn Y. Leipart, "Ideology, Strategy and Party Competition in Postwar Norway," *European Journal of Political Research* 17, no. 3 (May 1989): 278.

42. Bente Blanche Nicolaysen, "Voluntary Service Provision a Strong Welfare State," Working Paper no. 35 (Mannheim Center for European Social Research, 2001).

43. Lauri Karvonen, "Christian Parties in Scandinavia: Victory over the Windmills?" in *Christian Democracy in Europe: A Comparative Perspective*, ed. David Hanley (London: Pinter, 1994), 126.

44. Sörensen and Bergqvist, *Gender and the Social Democratic Welfare Regime*, 12–13.

45. Anne Lise Ellingsæter, "Dual Breadwinner Societies: Provider Models in the Scandinavian Welfare States," *Acta Sociologica* 41, no. 1 (1998): 62–63.

46. Nicolaysen, "Voluntary Service Provision," 12.

47. Jens Alber, "A Framework for the Comparative Study of Social Services," *Journal of European Social Policy* 5 (1995): 131–49.

48. Kerstin Holmlund, "Don't Ask for Too Much! Swedish Pre-School Teachers, the State, and the Union, 1906–1965," *History of Education Review* 29, no. 1 (2000): 52–54.

49. Anita Nyberg, "From Foster Mothers to Child Care Centers: A History of Working Mothers and Child Care in Sweden," *Feminist Economics* 6, no. 1 (2000): 13–14; Holmlund, "Swedish Pre-School Teachers," 59.

50. Janneke Plantenga, "Double Lives: Labour Market Participation, Citizenship, and Gender," in *Gender, Participation, and Citizenship in the Netherlands*, ed. Jet Bussemaker and Rian Voet (Hants., England: Ashgate, 1998), 56–57.

51. Bussemaker, "Rationales of Care," 78–80.

52. Lily E. Clerkx and Marinus H. Van Ijzendoorn, "Child Care in a Dutch Context: On the History, Current Status, and Evaluation of Nonmaternal Child Care in the Netherlands," in *Child Care in Context: Cross-Cultural Perspectives*, ed. Michael E. Lamb, Kathleen J. Sternberg, Carl-Philip Hwang, and Anders G. Broberg (Hillsdale, NJ: Lawrence Erlbaum Associates, 1992), 66–67; Bussemaker, "Rationales of Care," 79.

53. There was one brief government in 1939 in which Catholics did not participate. See Hans-Martien ten Napel, "The Netherlands: Resilience against Change," in *Changing Party Systems in Western Europe*, ed. David Broughton and Mark Donovan (London: Pinter, 1999), 170.

54. Ten Napel, "Resilience against Change," 176.

55. Kees van Kersbergen, *Social Capitalism: A Study of Christian Democracy and the Welfare State* (London: Routledge, 1995), 90–93.

56. Clerkx and Ijzendoorn, "Child Care in a Dutch Context," 63.

57. Van Kersbergen and Uwe Becker, "The Netherlands: A Passive Social Democratic Welfare State in a Christian Democratic Ruled Society," *Journal of Social Policy* 17, no. 4 (1988): 478.

58. The most comprehensive account of the Dutch model is in Sainsbury, *Gender, Equality, and Welfare States*, 50–55.

59. Bussemaker, "Gender and the Separation of Spheres in Twentieth Century Dutch Society: Pillarisation, Welfare State Formation and Individualisation," in Bussemaker and Voet, *Gender, Participation, and Citizenship*, 27–28.

60. Maria Brenton, "Changing Relationships in Dutch Social Services," *Journal of Social Policy* 11, no. 1 (1982): 59–80.

61. Austin, *Early Childhood Education*, 301.

62. Van Kersbergen, "The Causes and Consequences of Prolonged yet Interrupted Christian Democratic Rule in the Netherlands," presented at the conference "The Western Welfare State and its Religious Roots," Max Planck Institute for the Study of Societies, Cologne, Germany, April 30–May 1, 2004.

63. Bussemaker, "Rationales of Care," 74–75.

64. Austin, *Early Childhood Education*, 302; Tessa Blackstone, "Some Aspects of the Structure and Extent of Nursery Education in Five European Countries," *Comparative Education* 7, no. 3 (December 1971): 95.

65. Clerkx and Ijzendoorn, "Child Care in a Dutch Context," 64. By the 1970s, these programs usually were open from 9:00 to 12:00 A.M., and again from 2:00 to 4:00 P.M., with no lunch available at school. Austin, *Early Childhood Education*, 311.

66. Bussemaker, "Rationales of Care," 77.

67. Bussemaker, "Rationales of Care," 80–82; Clerkx and Van Ijzendoorn, "Child Care in a Dutch Context," 66.

68. Van Kersbergen, "Causes and Consequences."

69. Arend Lijphart, *The Politics of Accommodation: Pluralism and Democracy in the Netherlands*, 2d ed. (Berkeley: University of California Press, 1975).

70. Van Kersbergen and Becker, "A Passive Social Democratic Welfare State," 483–85.

71. Bussemaker, "Rationales of Care," 71.

72. Plantenga, "Double Lives," 61–63.

73. Morée, "Quiet Revolution," 28.

74. Sainsbury, *Gender Equality*, 184.

75. Ibid., 98.

76. Pierre Strobel, "Les mésaventures de Monsieur Gagnepain," in *Démographie et politique*, ed. Francis Ronsin, Hervé Le Bras, and Elisabeth Zucker-Rouvillois (Dijon: Editions Universitaires de Dijon 1997), 177–78.

77. Edith Archambault, *Le Secteur sans but lucratif: Associations et Fondations en France* (Paris: Economica, 1996), 15–17.

78. Olivier Büttner, Marie-Thérèse Letablier, and Sophie Pennec, "L'action publique face aux transformations de la famille en France," Research paper no. 2 (Paris: Centre d'Etudes de l'Emploi, 2003), 32.

79. Jacqueline Ancelin, *L'action sociale familiale et les caisses d'allocations familiales* (Paris: Documentation Française, 1997). Initially, this institution was called the Union nationale des Caisses d'allocations familiales.

80. Liliane Périer, Technical Advisor in the CNAF, interview by the author, Paris, April 19, 1998.

81. Austin, *Early Childhood Education*, 186.

82. R. E. M. Irving, *Christian Democracy in France* (London: George Allen & Unwin, 1973), 36–45.

83. Ibid., 21.

84. Ibid., 14, 65; Suzanne Berger, "Religious Transformation and the Future of Politics," in *Changing Boundaries of the Political: Essays on the Evolving Balance Between the State and Society, Public and Private, in Europe*, ed. Charles Maier (Cambridge: Cambridge University Press, 1987), 120–21.

85. Carolyn M. Warner, *Confessions of an Interest Group: The Catholic Church and Political Parties in Europe* (Princeton: Princeton University Press, 2000), 87–92, 114.

86. The Fifth Republic's electoral system also helped assure the demise of the centrist MRP as the *scrutin d'arrondissement à deux tours* (1958), and direct election of the president (starting in 1962) encouraged a bipolarization of the electorate. Nonetheless, the question remains as to why the dominant party on the right in this new bipolar system was not a Christian Democratic one, as in virtually every other continental European country.

87. Berger, "Religious Transformation and the Future of Politics."

88. Amy Mazur's study of gender equality policies shows how the Left at times embraced feminist causes but abandoned them once the electoral payoffs declined. See Mazur, *Gender Bias and the State: Symbolic Reform at Work in Fifth Republic France* (Pittsburgh: University of Pittsburgh Press, 1995).

89. Michalina Vaughan, "Gaullism," in *Social and Political Movements in Western Europe*, ed. Martin Kolinsky and William E. Paterson (London: Croom Held, 1976), 113; Peter Alexis Gourevitch, "Gaullism Abandoned, or the Costs of Success," in *The Fifth Republic at Twenty*, ed. William G. Andrews and Stanley Hoffmann (Albany: SUNY Press, 1981), 113; Philip Cerny, "Modernization and the Fifth Republic," in *France and Modernization*, ed. John Gaffney (Aldershot: Avebury, 1988): 21.

90. Pierre Birnbaum, *Les sommets de l'Etat: Essai sur l'eilite du pouvoir en France* (Paris: Seuil, 1977), 204.

91. Sudhir Hazareesingh, *Political Traditions in Modern France* (Oxford: Oxford University Press, 1994), 274. De Gaulle, however, was certainly no feminist, and he personally believed mothers should be at home with their children. See Mazur, *Gender Bias*, 29.

92. Rémi Lenoir, "Family Policy in France since 1938," in *The French Welfare State: Surviving Social and Ideological Change*, ed. John S. Ambler (New York: New York University Press, 1991), 146; Strobel, "Les mésaventures de Monsieur Gagne-pain," 177.

93. Virginie Bussat and Michel Chauvière, *Les intérêts familiaux à l'épreuve d'une comparaison France-Angleterre* [Family Interests as Seen through a French-British Comparison] (Report for the CNAF, January 1997).

94. Lenoir, "Family Policy in France," 153, 161.

95. Antoine Prost, "L'évolution de la politique familiale en France de 1938 à 1981," *Le mouvement social* 129 (October–December 1984): 8–15.

96. One of the more conservative associations, Familles de France, does sometimes separate itself from UNAF when strongly opposed to a particular government policy, so as to speak with its own voice. Claude Martin and Patrick Hassenteufel, *La représentation des intérêts familiaux en Europe: Allemagne, Belgique, Grande-Bretagne, France, Portugal* (Report for the European Commission, General Division 5, September 1997), 84, 113.

97. Claire Duchen, *Women's Rights and Women's Lives in France, 1944–1968* (New York: Routledge, 1994), 105; Lenoir, "Family Policy in France," 160–62.

98. Jacqueline Martin, "Politique familiale et travail des femmes mariées en France: Perspective historique, 1942–1982," *Population* 53 (November–December 1998): 1137–38.

99. *Journal officiel* (1970): 3581; Centre des Archives Contemporaines, no. 870176, art. 15, "Documents de synthèse Education Nationale sur le Cinquième Plan: Note pour M. Delors de M. Lasry," December 14, 1964; Jean-Marie Poirier, Report for the Commission of Cultural, Family and Social Affairs, Ministry of National Education, *Journal officiel* (1965): 3794.

100. Ralf Dahrendorf, *Society and Democracy in Germany* (New York: Doubleday, 1967), 314.

101. The education sector is highly unionized compared to the rest of the French workforce: Nearly 80 percent of elementary and preschool school teachers belong to the main teachers' union, which is highly influential on the committees that determine local educational needs. Véronique Aubert, "Système professionel et esprit de corps: Le rôle du syndicat national des instituteurs," *Pouvoirs* 30 (1984); Antoine Prost, *Histoire du l'enseignement en France, 1800–1967* (Paris: Librairie Armand Colin, 1968), 392–93.

102. Commissariat Général du Plan, *Quatrième plan de développement économique et social (1962–1965): Rapport général de la Commission de la main d'oeuvre* (Paris: Imprimerie Nationale, 1961), 13–14, 19, 28, 66–67.

103. Commissariat général du plan, *Sixième plan de développement économique et social* (Paris: Documentation Française, 1971), 44.

104. Jacqueline Ancelin, former CNAF administrator, interview by the author, Paris, March 9, 1998; Evelyne Sullerot, sociologist, interview by the author, Paris, April 22, 1998; Jacqueline Farrache, *Confédération générale du travail*, interview by the author, Paris, April 22, 1998.

105. Sidney Tarrow, "Social Protest and Policy Reform: May 1968 and the *Loi d'Orientation* in France," *Comparative Political Studies* 25, no. 4 (January 1993): 579–607.

106. Duchen, *Women's Rights*, 194.

107. See, for example, Jacqueline de Linares, "Le droit d'avoir des enfants," *L'Express*, November 6, 1972, 102; "Enfance telle que je la rêve," *Reforme*, February 24, 1973; Christine Sacase, "Des crèches sauvages pour les enfants de Mai," *L'Express*, December 8, 1969, 99.

108. Liane Mozère, *Le printemps des crèches: Histoire et analyse d'un mouvement* (Paris: Editions L'Harmattan, 1992).

109. Evidence for growing use of public day care by the middle class in the 1970s is also in Evelyne Sullerot and Michèle Saltiel, *Les crèches et les équipement d'accueil pour la petite enfance* (Paris: Hachette, 1974).

110. Mazur, *Gender Bias*, 77–78; *Le Monde*, April 2, 1974; *L'Humanité*, October 13, 1972; *L'Humanité*, December 11, 1970; *Rouge*, June 9, 1977.

111. *Le Monde*, February 1, 1974; *Le nouvel observateur*, May 13, 1974.

112. Jill Lovecy, "'*Citoyennes à part entière?*' The Constitutionalization of Gendered Citizenship in France and the Parity Reforms of 1999–2000," *Government and Opposition* 35, no. 4 (2000): 439–62.

113. Xavier Gardette, "The Social Policies of Giscard d'Estaing," in *Continuity and Change in France*, ed. Vincent Wright (London: George Allen & Unwin, 1984), 129, 132–33.

114. *Le Monde*, April 26, 1975.

115. Jane Jenson and Mariette Sineau, "France: Reconciling Republican Equality with 'Freedom of Choice,'" in Jenson and Sineau, *Who Cares*, 90.

116. Ancelin, *L'action sociale familiale*, 274–77, 294.

117. Ancelin, interview by the author.

118. Ancelin, *L'action sociale familiale*, 294.

119. Julian E. Zelizer, *Taxing America: Wilbur D. Mills, Congress, and the State, 1945–1975* (Cambridge: Cambridge University Press 1998).

120. Graham Wilson, "Why Is There No Corporatism in the United States?," in *Patterns of Corporatist Policy-Making*, ed. Gerhard Lehmbruch and Philippe C. Schmitter (London: Sage, 1982), 219–35.

121. Jacob S. Hacker, *The Divided Welfare State: The Battle over Public and Private Social Benefits in the United States* (Cambridge: Cambridge University Press, 2002).

122. Christopher Leman, "Patterns of Policy Development: Social Security in the United States and Canada," *Public Policy* 25 (Spring 1977): 261–91.

123. Joan Hoff, *Nixon Reconsidered* (New York: Basic Books, 1994), chap. 4.

124. Gilbert V. Steiner, *The Children's Cause* (Washington, DC: Brookings, 1976), 11.

125. "Poverty Message," *Congressional Quarterly Almanac 1969*, 34-A.

126. Christina Wolbrecht, *Politics of Women's Rights: Parties, Positions, and Change* (Princeton, NJ: Princeton University Press, 2000), 23–44.

127. Sainsbury, *Gender Equality*, 59–63.

128. Susan M. Hartmann, *From Margin to Mainstream: American Women and Politics since 1960* (New York: McGraw-Hill, 1996), 99–129; Joyce Gelb and Marian Lief Palley, *Women and Public Policies: Reassessing Gender Politics*, new ed. (Charlottesville: University of Virginia Press, 1996).

129. Morgan, "A Child of the Sixties: The Great Society, the New Right, and the Politics of Child Care," *Journal of Policy History* 13, no. 2 (March 2001): 225; Carol Joffe, "Why the United States Has No Child-Care Policy," in *Families, Politics, and Public Policy*, ed. Irene Diamond (New York: Longman, 1983), 177–78.

130. *Congressional Record*, 84th Cong., 1st sess., June 14, 1955, vol. 101, part 6: 8139–43; "Family Allowances Stalled," *America* 95, no. 1 (April 7, 1956): 8; *Conference Proceedings of the White House Conference on Children and Youth* (March 27–April 2, 1960), 138.

131. Martin Gilens, *Why Americans Hate Welfare: Race, Media, and the Politics of Antipoverty Policy* (Chicago: University of Chicago Press, 2000).

132. Jill Quadagno, *The Color of Welfare: How Racism Undermined the War on Poverty* (New York: Oxford University Press, 1994); Thomas Byrne Edsall with Mary D. Edsall, *Chain Reaction: The Impact of Race, Rights, and Taxes on American Politics* (New York: W. W. Norton, 1991).

133. For descriptions of this legislation, see Quadagno, *Color of Welfare*, 149–53; Michel, *Children's Interests*, 247–51; and Morgan, "Child of the Sixties."

134. Morgan, "Child of the Sixties," 225–28.

135. Quadagno, *Color of Welfare*, 152–53.

136. As in other policy areas, however, the Nixon White House was quite divided, with different factions pushing for different aims. There were both advocates

of the Child Development Act and strong opponents, which created a power struggle within the White House.

137. Dave Keene, interview by the author, Washington, DC, September 24, 1997. Keene was an aide to Nixon's vice president, Spiro Agnew.

138. *Congressional Record*, 92nd Cong., 1st sess., 1971, vol. 117, part 34: 38170.

139. Steiner, *Children's Cause*, 114–15.

140. "Veto of the Economic Opportunity Amendments of 1971," in *Public Papers of the Presidents: Richard Nixon, 1971* (Washington, DC: U.S. GPO, 1972), 1176–78.

141. Steiner, *Children's Cause*, 116.

142. John K. Iglehart, "Expensive Senate Child-Care Package Faces Dim Prospects in House," *National Journal* (July 22, 1972): 1202–5.

143. Rosalind Pollack Petchesky, "Antiabortion, Antifeminism, and the Rise of the New Right," *Feminist Studies* 7, no. 2 (Summer 1981): 207.

144. Kenneth D. Wald, *Religion and Politics in the United States* second edition (Washington DC: CQ Press, 1992), chap. 7.

145. Paul Weyrich, "Family Issues," in *The New Right at Harvard*, ed. Howard Phillips (Vienna, VA: Conservative Caucus, 1983), 21.

146. *Human Events*, 35, no. 2 (October 18, 1975): 22.

147. U.S. Senate Committee on Labor and Public Welfare, *Background Materials Concerning the Child and Family Services Act, 1975*, 94th Cong., 2d session (Washington, DC: U.S. GPO, 1976), 17, 68–69; Steiner, *The Futility of Family Policy* (Washington, DC: Brookings, 1981), 92.

148. Kristin Luker, *Abortion and the Politics of Motherhood* (Berkeley, CA: University of California Press, 1984), chap. 6; Jane J. Mansbridge, *Why We Lost the ERA* (Chicago: University of Chicago Press, 1986).

149. Edwin J. Feulner, Jr., *Conservatives Stalk the House: The Republican Study Committee, 1970–1982* (Ottawa, IL: Green Hill, 1983), 50–54; Bruce Biggs, "'Child Care': The Fiscal Time Bomb," *Public Interest* 49 (Fall 1977): 90–93.

150. See Michel, *Children's Interests*, 205–9.

151. Michel, *Children's Interests*, 274–78.

152. James J. Kilpatrick, "Nixon was Right to Reject Child Care Bill," *Human Events*, January 1 1972, 6.

153. Keene, interview by author.

CHAPTER FOUR

1. Gøsta Esping-Andersen, *The Social Foundations of Postindustrial Economies* (Oxford: Oxford University Press, 1999).

2. Paul Pierson, *Dismantling the Welfare State? Reagan, Thatcher and the Politics of Retrenchment* (Cambridge: Cambridge University Press, 1994).

3. Wolfgang Streeck and Kathleen Thelen, "Introduction: Institutional Change in Advanced Political Economies," in Streeck and Thelen, eds., *Beyond Continuity:*

Institutional Change in Advanced Political Economies (Oxford: Oxford University Press, 2005), 1–39.

4. Kathleen Thelen, "How Institutions Evolve: Insights from Comparative Historical Analysis," in James Mahoney and Dietrich Rueschemeyer, eds., *Comparative Historical Analysis in the Social Sciences* (Cambridge: Cambridge University Press, 2003), 208–40.

5. Andrea Louise Campbell, *How Policies Make Citizens: Senior Political Activism and the American Welfare State* (Princeton, NJ: Princeton University Press, 2003).

6. Gøsta Esping-Andersen, *Politics against Markets* (Princeton, NJ: Princeton University Press, 1985); Marie Gottschalk, *The Shadow Welfare State: Labor, Business, and the Politics of Health-Care in the United States* (Ithaca, NY: ILR Press, 2000).

7. Pierson, *Dismantling the Welfare State.*

8. Knud Knudsen and Kari Wærness, "National Context, Individual Characteristics, and Attitudes on Mothers' Employment: A Comparative Analysis of Great Britain, Sweden, and Norway," *Acta Sociologica* 44 (2001): 67–79; Brian Powell and Lala Carr Steelman, "Testing an Undertested Comparison: Maternal Effects on Sons' and Daughters' Attitudes toward Women in the Labor Force," *Journal of Marriage and the Family* 44, no. 2 (1982): 349–55.

9. Stephanie Coontz, *The Way We Never Were: American Families and the Nostalgia Trap* (New York: Basic Books, 2000); Birgit Pfau-Effinger, "The Modernization of Family and Motherhood in Western Europe," in *Restructuring Gender Relations and Employment: The Decline of the Male Breadwinner*, ed. Rosemary Crompton (Oxford: Oxford University Press, 1999), 61–62.

10. Crompton, *Restructuring Gender Relations.*

11. Mattei Dogan, "The Decline of Traditional Values in Western Europe," *International Journal of Comparative Sociology* 39, no. 1 (February 1998): 77–91; Ronald Inglehart, *Culture Shift in Advanced Industrialized Societies* (Princeton, NJ: Princeton University Press 1990), chap. 6.

12. Peter Hall, "Policy Paradigms, Social Learning, and the State: The Case of Economic Policymaking in Britain," *Comparative Politics* 25, no. 3 (April 1993): 278–80.

13. Streeck and Thelen, "Introduction: Institutional Change," 6–9.

14. Evelyne Huber and John D. Stephens, *Development and Crisis of the Welfare State: Parties and Policies in Global Markets* (Chicago: University of Chicago Press, 2001), chap. 6.

15. Huber and Stephens, *Development and Crisis*, 241–42.

16. Huber and Stephens, "Welfare State and Production Regimes in the Era of Retrenchment," in Pierson, *New Politics of the Welfare State*, 107–45.

17. Anita Nyberg, "Parental Leave, Public Childcare, and the Dual-Earner/Dual-Carer Model in Sweden," *Peer Review Discussion Paper* (Brussels: European Commission, April 2004), 6.

18. Juhani Lehto, Nina Moss, and Tine Rostgaard, "Universal Public Social Care and Health Services?" in Mikko Kautto, Matti Heikkilä, Bjørn Hvinden, Staffan

Marklund, and Niels Ploug, *Nordic Social Policy: Changing Welfare States* (London: Routledge, 1999), 116–18.

19. Sara Brachet, "Politiques familiales et assurance parentale en Suède," *CAF Dossier d'Etudes* no. 21 (June 2001).

20. Nyberg, "Parental Leave," 12–13.

21. Class sizes and the child-to-teacher ratios remain higher than they were prior to the economic crisis of the 1990s. Nyberg, "Parental Leave," 6.

22. Victor Pestoff and Peter Strandbrink, "The Politics of Swedish Childcare," report prepared for the EMES Research Network, 2002.

23. Three months of parental leave are paid at a flat rate of SEK 60 per day. Those parents who were not in paid employment before having a child can receive a flat rate of SEK 180 for thirteen months, and then the SEK 60 amount for the remaining three months of the leave. "Swedish Family Policy," Fact Sheet no. 11 (Stockholm: Swedish Ministry of Health and Social Affairs, April 2005).

24. Linda Haas and Philip Hwang, "Parental Leave in Sweden," in *Parental Leave: Progress or Pitfall?*, ed. Peter Moss and Fred Deven (Brussels: NIDI CBGS Publications, 1999), 50; "Swedish Family Policy."

25. Anita Nyberg, "From Foster Mothers to Child Care Centers: A History of Working Mothers and Child Care in Sweden," *Feminist Economics* 6, no. 1 (2000): 16.

26. A 1994 study by the International Social Survey Program (ISSP) shows that 9 percent favor mothers' full-time work when they have preschool-aged children, and 62 percent favor part-time work. By 2002, the percentage of those favoring full-time work had risen to 14.3 percent, while 66.5 percent favored part-time work. ISSP, Family and Changing Gender Roles II and III.

27. Christina Bergqvist, Jaana Kuusipalo, and Auður Styrkarsdóttir, "The Debate on Childcare Policies," in *Nordic Democracies: Gender and Politics in the Nordic Countries*, ed. Christina Bergqvist, Jaana Kuusipalo, and Auður Styrkarsdóttir (Oslo: Scandinavian University Press, 1999), 140–41.

28. Pestoff and Strandbrink, "Politics of Swedish Childcare," 37; *Babies and Bosses: Reconciling Work and Family Life*, vol. 4, *Canada, Finland, Sweden, and the United Kingdom* (Paris: OECD, 2005), 106.

29. Much private child care is run on a nonprofit basis, often by parent cooperatives, and aims to provide an alternative curriculum from that found in the public centers. Pestoff and Strandbrink, "Politics of Swedish Childcare," 11.

30. Anne-Marie Daune-Richard and Rianne Mahon, "Sweden: Models in Crisis," in *Who Cares? Women's Work, Childcare, and Welfare State Redesign*, ed. Jane Jenson and Mariette Sineau (Toronto: University of Toronto Press, 2001), 155.

31. Jonas Hinnfors, "Stability through Change: The Pervasiveness of Political Ideas," *Journal of Public Policy* 19, no. 3 (1999): 293–312.

32. Christina Bergqvist, "Family Policy and Welfare State Reconfiguration in Sweden," paper presented at the European Consortium for Political Research Conference, Marburg, Germany, September 18–21, 2003.

33. Daune-Richard and Mahon, "Models in Crisis," 162–63. Pestoff and Strandbrink note that this was true until the 1990s, when more children from moderate-income and working-class families gained access to these services. See "Politics of Swedish Childcare," 24.

34. Linda Haas, "Equal Parenthood and Social Policy: Lessons from a Study of Parental Leave in Sweden," in *Parental Leave and Child Care*, ed. Janet Shibley Hyde and Marilyn J. Essex (Philadelphia: Temple University Press, 1991), 392–94.

35. Bergqvist, "Family Policy and Welfare State Reconfiguration," 8.

36. Maud L. Eduards, "Toward a Third Way: Women's Politics and Welfare Policies in Sweden," *Social Research* 58, no. 3 (Fall 1991): 677–304.

37. Bergqvist, "Family Policy and Welfare State Reconfiguration," 8; Irene Wennemo, interview by the author, Stockholm, June 8, 2004.

38. Brachet, "Politiques familiales et assurance parentale"; Livia Oláh, "Gender Neutral and Gender Specific Categories in Swedish and Hungarian Law: The Case of Parental Leave," Stockholm University Demographic Department Internal Memorandum, November 4, 1994.

39. Not all of this leave was covered at the high rate of 90 percent of wages (up to a ceiling); in 1980, three months were still paid at a low flat rate.

40. Daune-Richard and Mahon, "Models in Crisis," 163–64.

41. Marianne Sundström, "Part-Time Work in Sweden: An Institutionalist Perspective," in *Women in Japan and Sweden: Work and Family in Two Welfare Regimes*, ed. Carl le Grand and Toshiko Tsukaguchi-le Grand (Stockholm: Almqvist and Wiksell International, 2003), 125.

42. Siv Gustafsson, "Separate Taxation and Married Women's Labor Supply: A Comparison of West Germany and Sweden," *Journal of Population Economics* 5 (1992): 61–85; Sundström, "Part-Time Work in Sweden," 8.

43. Sundström, "The Growth in Full-Time Work among Swedish Women in the 1980s," *Acta Sociologica* 36 (1993): 139–50.

44. This description is based on Bergqvist, "Family Policy and Welfare State Reconfiguration."

45. For a discussion of these changes, see Daune-Richard and Mahon, "Models in Crisis"; Pestoff and Strandbrink, "Politics of Swedish Childcare."

46. Nyberg, "Parental Leave," 3. Many are parent cooperatives, but there are private companies running these programs as well.

47. This is an important development because access to Swedish child care was often conditional on parental employment or enrollment in educational programs. The fiscal crises facing municipalities during the 1990s also led many of them to reduce the entitlement of parents who were studying, unemployed, or home on parental leave with a second or third child to have access to the child care system. Pestoff and Strandbrink, "Politics of Swedish Childcare."

48. Ulla Nordenstam, National Agency for Education, Stockholm, interview by the author, June 8, 2004.

49. Pia Edin, Ministry of Education, Stockholm, interview by the author, June 4, 2005; Hillevi Lenz Taguchi and Ingmarie Munkammar, "Consolidating Governmental Early Childhood Education and Care Services under the Ministry of Education and Science: A Swedish Case Study," *UNESCO Early Childhood and Family Policy Series*, no. 6 (Paris: April 2003).

50. Pestoff and Strandbrink, "Politics of Swedish Childcare," 37.

51. Ann-Zofie Duvander, Tommy Ferrarini, and Sara Thalberg, *Swedish Parental Leave and Gender Equality: Achievements and Reform Challenges in a European Perspective*, working paper 2005/11 (Stockholm: Institutet för Framtidsstudier, 2005), 12–13.

52. Irene Wennemo, interview by the author, Stockholm, June 8, 2004; Paula Burrau, Press Officer, Ministry of Health and Social Affairs, interview by the author, Stockholm, June 9, 2004. On the move to increase the role of fathers in child rearing, see Helena Bergman and Barbara Hobson, "Compulsory Fatherhood: The Coding of Fatherhood in the Swedish Welfare State," in *Making Men into Fathers: Men, Masculinities and the Social Politics of Fatherhood*, ed. Barbara Hobson (Cambridge: Cambridge University Press, 2002), 92–124.

53. Paula Burrau, Press Officer, Swedish Ministry of Health and Social Affairs, interview by the author, Stockholm, June 9, 2004.

54. In September 2005, a government-appointed commission called for expanding Sweden's well-paid parental leave to fifteen months and reserving five months for the mother, five months for the father, and five months for the parents to use as they wished. The proposal met with immediate praise from some, sharp criticism from others.

55. Brachet, "Politiques familiales et assurance parentale"; Duvander, Ferrarini, and Thalberg, *Swedish Parental Leave*, 19.

56. Cecelia Magnusson, parliamentarian, interview by the author, Stockholm, June 9, 2004.

57. Universalized access for children aged three and older also reflected the drop in births since the late 1970s, which opened up more places in the preschool system.

58. Alain Norvez, *De la naissance à l'école: Santé, modes de garde et préscolarité dans la France contemporaine* (Paris: Presses Universitaires de France, 1990), 427–32.

59. Bernard Eme and Laurent Fraisse, "Transformations des structures familiales et évolution des politiques sociales: Les services de la petite enfance comme services de cohésion sociale," TSFEPS Report (September 2002), 22. Around half of preschool-aged children are cared for by a parent outside of school hours, while the rest are in after-school programs, family day care, or other forms of child care. Francine Fenet, Frédérique Leprince, and Liliane Périer, *Les modes d'accueil des jeunes enfants* (Paris: Editions ASH, 2002), 43.

60. For the third child, women are entitled to twenty-six weeks. Men also are entitled to roughly two weeks of paternity leave. See Eurostat, *Development of a Methodology for the Collection of Harmonized Statistics on Childcare* (Luxembourg, 2004).

61. Jane Jenson and Mariette Sineau, "France: Reconciling Republican Equality with 'Freedom of Choice,'" in Jenson and Sineau, *Who Cares?*, 88–117; Antoine Math and Evelyne Renaudat, "Developper l'accueil des enfants ou créer de l'emploi? Une lecture de l'évolution des politiques en matière de modes de garde," *Recherches et prévisions* 49 (September 1997): 5–17; Jeanne Fagnani, "L'allocation parentale d'éducation: contraintes et limites du choix' d'une prestation," *Lien social et politiques* 36 (Autumn 1996): 111–21.

62. Conseil d'Analyse Economique, *Emplois de proximité* (Paris: La Documenta- tion Française, 1998); Marie-Thérèse Letablier, "L'activité professionnelle des femmes en France sur fond de pénurie d'emplois," *Lien social et politiques* 36 (Autumn 1996): 93–102.

63. OECD Net Social Expenditures database, 1980 to 1998.

64. Jeanne Fagnani, *Un travail et des enfants: Petits arbitrages et grands dilemmes* (Paris: Bayard Editions, 2000), 17–18.

65. Julien Damon, Patricia Croutte, and Georges Hatchuel, "Les opinions sur les modes de garde des jeunes enfants," *L'essentiel* no. 11 (Paris: CNAF, April 2003).

66. Patricia Croutte and Georges Hatchuel, "Prestations familiales et accueil de la petite enfance: Les grandes tendance de l'opinion au début 2003," *Crédoc Collection des Rapports* no. 232 (December 2003).

67. Lenoir, "Family Policy in France since 1938," in *The French Welfare State: Surviving Social and Ideological Change*, ed. John S. Ambler (New York: New York University Press, 1991), 161–62; Olivier Büttner, Marie-Thérèse Letablier, and So- phie Pennec, "L'action publique face aux transformations de la famille en France," Centre d'Etudes de l'Emploi Research Report no. 2 (February 2002), 53–54.

68. Christiane Therry, secretary general of the Fédération Nationale de Familles de France, interview by the author, Paris, April 15, 1998; Hélène Marchal, UNAF, interview by the author, Paris, April 30, 1998; Büttner, Letablier, and Pennec, "L'ac- tion publique," 36, 47.

69. Ariane Dufour, Goerges Hatchuel, and Jean-Pierre Loisel, *Accueil des jeunes enfants, conciliation vie professionnelle-vie familiale et opinions sur les prestations familiales* (Paris: Crédoc, 1998), 65–67.

70. Ibid., 41–42.

71. Jacqueline Farrache, Confédération générale du travail, interview by the author, Paris, April 22, 1998.

72. For example, UNAF cannot only lobby for benefits for parental care at home. Some of its associations strongly endorse the two-earner model, either as an ideal or simply as a reality for many families, which moderates the organization's stance. Jean- Laurent Clochard, Confédération Syndicale des Familles, interview by the author, Paris, June 11, 1998; Paul Yonnet, UNAF, interview by the author, Paris, June 9, 1998. See also Claude Martin and Patrick Hassenteufel, *La représentation des intérêts familiaux en Europe: Allemagne, Belgique, Grande-Bretagne, France, Portugal* (Report for the European Commission, General Division 5, September 1997), 82–87.

73. Parents who use the *crèches* also are the most satisfied with their form of child care. See Fagnani, *Un travail et des enfants*, 59–60.

74. Norvez, *De la naissance à l'école*, 332–33.

75. Jacques Desigaux and Amédée Thévenet, *La garde des jeunes enfants* (Paris: Presses universitaires de France, 1980), 102–12.

76. Jane Jenson and Mariette Sineau chart this in *Mitterrand et les Françaises: Un rendez-vous manqué* (Paris: Presses de la Fondation Nationale des Sciences Politiques, 1995).

77. Decentralization also contributed to variation across regions in access to public day care. See Olivier David, *L'accueil de la petite enfance* (Rennes: Presses universitaires de Rennes, 1999), chap. 7.

78. The benefit, which is open to all parents regardless of income, is for children under the age of six who are in family day care. Parents also receive tax benefits that subsidize the purchase of family day care.

79. Jeanne Fagnani, "L'allocation de garde d'enfant à domicile: profil des bénéficiaries et effet d'aubaine," *Droit social* 11 (November 1997): 944.

80. The Jospin government also tried to means-test family benefits. This produced an uproar, and the government had to seriously modify its proposal.

81. The following section is based on Jenson and Sineau, "Reconciling Republican Equality," 93–94, 98–101.

82. Initially, the government required that parents have worked for two years in the thirty months prior to taking the leave. In 1986, the new law reduced the work requirement to two years out of the last ten. Then, in 1995, the requirement was raised to two years in the last five.

83. Carole Bonnet and Morgane Labbé, "L'activité professionnelle des femmes après la naissance de leurs deux premiers enfants: l'impact de l'allocation parentale d'éducation," *Etudes et Résultats* 37 (1999).

84. Büttner, Letablier, and Pennec, "L'action publique," 35.

85. Benoît Chastenet, "L'accueil collectif en crèches familiales des enfants de moins de six ans en 2003," *Etudes et résultats* 356 (December 2004): 5.

86. Hélène Périvier, "Emploi des mères et garde des jeunes enfants: l'impossible réforme?" *Droit social* 9–10 (September–October 2003): 797, 800.

87. Ibid., 799, 801–2.

88. Fagnani, *Un travail et des enfants*, 29–30.

89. Nadine Lefaucheur, "French Policies towards Lone Parents: Social Categories and Social Policies," and Siv Gustafsson, "Single Mothers in Sweden: Why Poverty Is Less Severe," in *Poverty, Inequality and the Future of Social Policy: Western States in the New World Order*, ed. Katherine McFate, Roger Lawson and William Julius Wilson (New York: Russell Sage Foundation, 1995), 257–325; Karen Christopher, "Welfare State Regimes and Mothers' Poverty," *Social Politics* 9, no. 1 (Spring 2002): 60–86.

90. *OECD Country Note: Early Childhood Education and Care in Sweden* (Paris: OECD, 1999); Barbara Bergmann, *Saving Our Children from Poverty: What the United States Can Learn from France* (New York: Russell Sage Foundation, 1996).

91. Janet C. Gornick and Marcia K. Meyers, *Families that Work: Policies for Reconciling Parenthood and Employment* (New York: Russell Sage, 2003), 214–15.

92. Marit Rønsen and Marianne Sundström, "Family Policy and After-Birth Employment among New Mothers: A Comparison of Finland, Norway and Sweden," *European Journal of Population* 18 (2002): 121–52.

93. Cédric Afsa, "L'allocation parentale d'éducation: entre politique familiale et politique de l'emploi," *Insee première* 569 (February 1998).

94. Marie-Odile Simon, "La réinsertion professionnelle des premières bénéficiaires de l'APE au titre de leur deuxième enfant," *Recherches et prévisions* 59 (March 2000): 25–40.

95. Périvier, "Emploi des mères," 798–99.

96. French data are from *Society at a Glance: OECD Social Indicators 2005* (Paris: OECD 2005) and are from 2002; Swedish data are from *Babies and Bosses*, 72. See also Nyberg, "Parental Leave," 9.

97. *Children, Pupils and Staff—National Level* (Stockholm: National Agency for Education report no. 244, 2004), 22.

98. Pestoff and Strandbrink, "Politics of Swedish Childcare."

99. Brachet, "Politiques familiales et assurance parentale."

100. Nyberg, "Foster Mothers to Child Care," 18.

101. Céline Marc and Hélène Zajdela, "Emploi et politique familiale: Doit-on s'inspirer du 'modèle suédois'?," unpublished paper, July 2004.

102. Helga Hernes, *Welfare State and Woman Power: Essays in State Feminism* (Oslo: Norwegian University Press, 1987).

103. Jyette Klausen, "The Declining Significance of Male Workers: Trade-Union Responses to Changing Labor Markets," in *Continuity and Change in Contemporary Capitalism*, ed. Herbert Kitschelt , Peter Lange, Gary Marks, and John D. Stephens (Cambridge: Cambridge University Press, 1999), 270; Jane Jenson and Rianne Mahon, "Representing Solidarity: Class, Gender and the Crisis in Social-Democratic Sweden," *New Left Review* 201 (September–October 1993): 76–100.

104. Christina Bergqvist, Anette Borchorst, Ann-Dorte Christensen, Nina C. Raaum, Viveca Ramstedt-Silén, and Auður Styrkársdóttir, eds., *Equal Democracies? Gender and Politics in the Nordic Countries* (Oslo: Scandinavian University Press, 1999).

105. Ann Towns, "Understanding the Effect of Larger Ratios of Women in National Legislatures: Proportions and Gender Differentiation in Sweden and Norway," *Women and Politics* 25, nos. 1–2 (2003): 1–29.

106. Bergman and Hobson, "Compulsory Fatherhood."

107. R. Amy Elman, *Sexual Subordination and State Intervention: Comparing Sweden and the United States* (Providence: Berghahn Books, 1996).

108. "Les pères bénéficiaires de l'allocation parentale d'éducation," *L'essentiel* no. 17 (Paris, CNAF: September 2003).

CHAPTER FIVE

1. The only exception is in California, where a 2002 law allows workers to take six weeks of paid family leave at 55 percent of their wages (below a ceiling of $728 per week). The leave is financed through a payroll tax levied on employees.

2. Jacob S. Hacker, *The Divided Welfare State: The Battle over Public and Private Social Benefits in the United States* (Cambridge: Cambridge University Press, 2002); Jennifer Klein, *For All These Rights: Business, Labor, and the Shaping of America's Public-Private Welfare State* (Princeton, NJ: Princeton University Press, 2003).

3. David Brian Robertson, "Introduction: Loss of Confidence and Policy Change in the 1970s," *Journal of Policy History* 10, no. 1 (1998): 1–14; Paul Pierson, "From Expansion to Austerity: The New Politics of Taxing and Spending," in *Seeking the Center: Politics and Policymaking at the New Century*, ed. Martin A. Levin, Marc K. Landy, and Martin Shapiro (Washington, DC: Georgetown University Press, 2001), 54–80.

4. For discussions of these changes to American politics in the 1960s and 1970s, see James L. Sundquist, *Dynamics of the Party System: Alignment and Realignment of Political Parties in the United States*, rev. ed. (Washington, DC: Brookings, 1983), chaps. 16–18.

5. Martin Gilens, *Why Americans Hate Welfare: Race, Media, and the Politics of Antipoverty Policy* (Chicago: University of Chicago Press, 2000).

6. David O. Sears and Jack Citrin, *Tax Revolt: Something for Nothing in California* (Cambridge, MA: Harvard University Press, 1982), 207–15.

7. Howard Rosenthal, "Politics, Public Policy, and Inequality: A Look Back at the Twentieth Century," in *Social Inequality*, ed. Kathryn M. Neckerman (New York: Russell Sage, 2004), 861–92.

8. David Vogel, *Fluctuating Fortunes: The Political Power of Business in America* (New York: Basic Books, 1989); Thomas Byrne Edsall, *The New Politics of Inequality* (New York: W. W. Norton, 1984).

9. Walter B. Hixson, Jr., *Search for the American Right Wing: An Analysis of the Social Science Record* (Princeton, NJ: Princeton University Press, 1992), 177–78.

10. Rosalind Pollack Petchesky, "Antiabortion, Antifeminism, and the Right of the New Right," *Feminist Studies* 7, no. 2 (Summer 1981): 206–46.

11. See figure 3.2 in chapter 3.

12. James Davison Hunter, *American Evangelicalism: Conservative Religion and the Quandary of Modernity* (New Brunswick, NJ: Rutgers University Press, 1983).

13. Hunter is using a term developed by Martin Marty. Ibid., 47.

14. Mark A. Shibley, "Contemporary Evangelicals: Born-Again and World Affirming," *Annals of the American Academy of Political and Social Science* 588 (July 1998): 70–74.

15. Ibid., 73–74, 78–82.

16. Jeff Manza and Clem Brooks, *Social Cleavages and Political Change: Voter Alignments and U.S. Party Coalitions* (Oxford: Oxford University Press, 2003), 91–99.

17. http://www.cnn.com/ELECTION/2004/pages/results/states/US/P/oo/ epolls.o.html (accessed February 18, 2006).

18. Christina Wolbrecht, *The Politics of Women's Rights: Parties, Positions, and Change* (Princeton, NJ: Princeton University Press, 2000), 6; Jo Freeman, "Who You Know versus Who You Represent: Feminist Influence in the Democratic and Republican Parties," in *The Women's Movements of the United States and Western Europe: Feminist Consciousness, Political Opportunity and Public Policy*, Mary Katzenstein and Carol Mueller (Philadelphia: Temple University Press, 1987), 215–44.

19. Nicol C. Rae, *The Decline and Fall of Liberal Republicans* (Oxford: Oxford University Press, 1989).

20. Hixson, *Search for the American Right Wing*, 225–26; Berman, *America's Right Turn*, chap. 4.

21. Wolbrecht, *Politics of Women's Rights*, 4–5; Greg D. Adams, "Abortion: Evidence of an Issue Evolution," *American Journal of Political Science* 41 (1997): 723–25; Edward G. Carmines and James Woods, "The Role of Party Activists in the Evolution of the Abortion Issue," *Political Behavior* 24, no. 4 (December 2002): 366.

22. Pierson, "The New Politics of the Welfare State," *World Politics* 48 (January 1996): 595–628.

23. Beth Stevens, "Blurring the Boundaries: How the Federal Government Has Influenced Welfare Benefits in the Private Sector," in *The Politics of Social Policy in the United States*, ed. Margaret Weir, Ann Shola Orloff, and Theda Skocpol (Princeton, NJ: Princeton University Press, 1988), 145–47; Hacker, *Divided Welfare State*, 50–51.

24. Hacker analyzes how this and other legacies of the public-private mix in the health care sector complicated and ultimately doomed the reform. *Divided Welfare State*, 260–66.

25. Sally Cohen, *Championing Child Care* (New York: Columbia University Press, 2001), 59.

26. For example, Carter's Assistant Secretary for Health, Education and Welfare argued against federal involvement in child care as potentially supplanting familial responsibility. See Cohen, *Championing Child Care*, 59–63, and Gilbert V. Steiner, *The Futility of Family Policy* (Washington, DC: Brookings, 1981), 92–95.

27. Berman, *America's Right Turn*, 35–36.

28. John R. Nelson and Wendy E. Warring, "The Child Care Tax Deduction/Credit," in *Making Policies for Children*, Cheryl D. Haynes (Washington, DC: National Academy Press, 1982), 252.

29. Erin Kelley and Frank Dobbin, "Civil Rights Law at Work: Sex Discrimination and the Rise of Maternity Leave Policies," *American Journal of Sociology* 105, no. 2 (September 1999): 455–92.

30. Kenneth D. Wald, *Religion and Politics in the United States*, 2nd ed. (Washington, DC: Congressional Quarterly Press, 1992), 234–35.

31. Michael J. Boskin and Eytan Sheshinski, "Optimal Tax Treatment of the Family: Married Couples," *Journal of Public Economics* 20 (April 1983): 281–97.

32. Alfred J. Kahn and Sheila B. Kamerman, *Child Care: Facing the Hard Choices* (Dover, MA: Auburn House, 1987), 20–21.

33. Sandra L. Hofferth, "The 101st Congress: An Emerging Agenda for Children in Poverty," *Child Poverty and Public Policy*, ed. Judith A. Chafel (Washington, DC: Urban Institute, 1993), 208.

34. This discussion is based on John R. Nelson, "The Politics of Federal Day Care Regulation," in Edward F. Zigler and Edmund W. Gordon, *Day Care: Scientific and Social Policy Issues* (Boston: Auburn House, 1982), 267–306.

35. At the time, the maximum credit was $400 for one child and $800 for two or more (20 percent of the first $2,000 in costs for one child, and/or 20 percent of the first $4,000 for two or more children). The 1981 law increased the credit and added a sliding income scale so that for couples earning more than $10,000 (adjusted gross income), the credit was $720 (30 percent of the first $2,400 in costs), while for two or more children it was $1,440 (30 percent of the first $4,800). For each additional $2,000 in income, the credit dropped by one percentage point.

36. Deborah Rankin, "Personal Finance: When Uncle Sam Is the Baby Sitter," *New York Times*, September 13, 1981.

37. Douglas J. Besharov and Paul N. Tramontozzi, "Federal Child Care Assistance: A Growing Middle-Class Entitlement," *Journal of Policy Analysis and Management* 8, no. 2 (1989): 313–14.

38. Edward J. McCaffery, *Taxing Women* (Chicago: University of Chicago Press, 1997).

39. Separate taxation has always been an option, but the tax system is structured so that this offers no financial advantages.

40. See, for example, "Indianan Criticizes Tax Cut Act's Relief from Marriage Penalty and Estate Tax," *Tax Notes* 14 (January 18, 1982); "Solving 'Marriage Penalty' Problem Creates 'Motherhood Penalty' Problem," *Tax Notes* 15 (May 24, 1982). On the hidden welfare state, see Christopher Howard, *The Hidden Welfare State: Tax Expenditures and Social Policy in the United States* (Princeton, NJ: Princeton University Press, 1997).

41. Mark Powell, "The Pronatalist Undercurrent of the $500-per-Child Tax Credit," *Population and Environment* 20, no. 5 (May 1999): 455–66.

42. *Tax Policy: What Do Families Need?* Hearing before the Select Committee on Children, Youth and Families. House of Representatives, 99th Cong., 1st sess., April 24, 1985, pp. 103–5.

43. Steven K. Wisensale, "The White House and Congress on Child Care and Family Leave Policy: From Carter to Clinton," *Policy Studies Journal* 25, no. 1 (Spring 1997): 79.

44. Spencer Rich and Barbara Vobeda, "Reagan Urged to Strengthen US Families," *Washington Post*, November 14, 1986.

45. Ibid.; *Tax Policy: What Do Families Need?* Hearing before the Select Committee on Children, Youth and Families. House of Representatives, 99th Cong., 1st sess., April 24, 1985, pp. 103–5.

46. The proposal also called for flatter income tax rates that would, among other things, serve to reduce the marriage penalty (and the tax on the second earner). Thus, while the push by supply-siders to flatten the tax rate was not primarily motivated by concerns about women's employment, many policy makers were well aware of this implication.

47. Mary Frances Berry, *The Politics of Parenthood: Child Care, Women's Rights, and the Myth of the Good Mother* (New York: Viking, 1993), 172–73; Carol Joffe, "Why the United States Has No Child Care Policy," in *Families, Politics, and Public Policy*, ed. Irene Diamond (New York: Longman, 1983), 177–78.

48. Hofferth, "The 101st Congress," 218–19. The most comprehensive account of the ABC struggles is in Cohen, *Championing Child Care*, chap. 4.

49. See the statements of Phyllis Schlafly and Robert Rector in the *Congressional Digest* 67, no. 11 (November 1988): 271–87, as well as those of Gary Bauer and the views of the Minority Committee of the Senate Human Resources Committee, *Congressional Digest* 69, no.2 (February 1990): 43–47, 57–61.

50. See, for example, Ron Haskins and Hank Brown, "The Day-Care Reform Juggernaut," *National Review*, March 10, 1989, 40–41.

51. See the statement by Mark L. Rosenberg in *Congressional Digest* 67, no. 11 (November 1988): 267–71.

52. Elizabeth Dole, "Whose Hand Should Rock the Cradle?" *National Political Quarterly* (Winter 1990): 8.

53. "Child-Care Bill Dies amid Partisan Sniping," *CQ Almanac 1988*, 367–68.

54. Cohen, *Championing Child Care*, 116–17.

55. Denise Urias Levy and Sonya Michel, "More Can Be Less: Child Care and Welfare Reform in the United States," in *Child Care Policy at the Crossroads: Gender and Welfare State Restructuring*, ed. Sonya Michel and Rianne Mahon (New York: Routledge, 2002), 239.

56. Panel studies show that women's participation in the labor force tends to produce these views, rather than feminist-oriented women joining the workforce. Arland Thornton, Duane F. Alwin, and Donald Camburn, "Causes and Consequences of Sex-Role Attitudes and Attitude Change," *American Sociological Review* 48 (April 1983): 211–27; Evelina Panayotova and April Brayfield, "National Context and Gender Ideology: Attitudes toward Women's Employment in Hungary and the United States," *Gender and Society* 11, no. 5 (October 1997): 627–56; Kristi Andersen and Elisabeth A. Cook, "Women, Work, and Political Attitudes," *American Journal of Political Science* 29, no. 3 (August 1985): 606–25.

57. Darrel Patrick Wash and Liesel E. Brand, "Child Day Care Services: An Industry at a Crossroads," *Monthly Labor Review* 113, no. 12 (December 1990): 20.

58. Mary Tuominen, "Caring for Profit: The Social, Economic, and Political Significance of For-Profit Child Care," *Social Service Review* 65 (September 1991): 461.

59. Sonya Michel, *Children's Interests, Mothers' Rights: The Shaping of America's Child Care Policy* (New Haven: Yale University Press, 1999), 256–57.

60. Sandra L. Hofferth, "Child Care in the United States Today," *The Future of Children* 6, no. 2 (Summer–Fall 1996): 45.

61. Joseph R. Meisenheimer II, "Employer Provisions for Parental Leave," *Monthly Labor Review* 112, no. 10 (October 1989): 20–23.

62. Michel, *Children's Interests*, 275–76.

63. The *Harris Family Survey II—Child Care* surveyed parents with children aged six or younger and found that 76 percent of respondents favored Bush's plan to give families with children under four a tax credit of up to $1,000, and a refundable tax credit for child care expenses; 72 percent said they favored the Democrats' plan to give financial assistance to people earning below the state median income and provide money for quality improvements. See Harris study no. 883013, Institute for Research in Social Science, University of North Carolina at Chapel Hill, 1988.

64. Parents answering "very satisfied" or "somewhat satisfied" with their child care arrangements. *Harris Family Survey II—Child Care*.

65. Berry, *Politics of Parenthood*, 184.

66. Margaret K. Nelson, "A Critical Analysis of the Act for Better Child Care Services," *Women and Politics* 12, no. 3 (1992): 1–25.

67. Cohen, *Championing Child Care*, 158–59.

68. Levy and Michel, "Child Care and Welfare Reform," 245.

69. Anya Bernstein, *The Moderation Dilemma: Legislative Coalitions and the Politics of Family and Medical Leave* (Pittsburgh: University of Pittsburgh Press, 2001), 98–99.

70. Ibid., 99–100; Wisensale, "White House and Congress," 83.

71. Schlafly, "Parental Leave: A Windfall for Yuppies," *Phyllis Schlafly Report* 20, no. 4 (1986): section 1.

72. Bernstein, *Moderation Dilemma*, 103.

73. Ibid., 101–2.

74. Ben Wildavsky, "The Divide over Day Care," *National Journal* 30, no. 4 (January 24, 1998): 167–68.

75. Mark Murray, "An Initiative's Fading Fortunes," *National Journal* 30, no. 15 (April 11, 1998): 812.

76. Sue Kirchhoff, "Child Care Proposal Sparks Debate over Working, At-Home Mothers," *Congressional Quarterly Weekly Reports* 56, no. 3 (January 17, 1998): 129–30.

77. Ibid., 129–30.

78. Laura Meckler, "Democrats Highlight Child Care," *Associated Press*, June 10, 1998.

79. Cohen, *Championing Child Care*, 85–89.

80. Linda Giannarelli, Sarah Adelman, and Stefanie Schmidt, *Getting Help with Child Care Expenses*, Urban Institute Occasional Paper no. 62 (Washington, DC: Urban Institute 2003), 7.

81. OECD, *Babies and Bosses: Reconciling Work and Family Life*, vol. 4, *Canada, Finland, Sweden, and the United Kingdom* (Paris: OECD, 2005), 72; United States House of Representatives, Committee on Ways and Means, *2004 Green Book* (U.S. GPO, 2004), p. 9-3. Swedish data are from 2003; U.S. data are from 2002.

82. Margarita Estévez-Abe, "Gender Bias in Skills and Social Policies: The Varieties of Capitalism Perspective on Sex Segregation," *Social Politics* 12, no. 2 (Summer 2005): 203–4.

83. Philip N. Cohen and Suzanne M. Bianchi, "Marriage, Children, and Women's Employment: What Do We Know?" *Monthly Labor Review* 122, no. 12 (December 1999): 27.

84. Jane Waldfogel, "Understanding the 'Family Gap' in Pay for Women with Children," *Journal of Economic Perspectives*, 12, 1 (Winter 1998): 144.

85. Stephen J. Rose and Heidi I. Hartmann, *Still a Man's Labor Market: The Long-Term Earnings Gap* (Washington, DC: IWPR, 2004).

86. Marcy Whitebook, "Child Care Workers: High Demand, Low Wages," *Annals of the American Association of Political and Social Science* (May 1999): 153–54.

87. Suzanne W. Helburn and Barbara Bergmann, *America's Childcare Problem: The Way Out* (New York: Palgrave, 2002), 171–74.

88. Ibid., chap. 8.

89. *Worthy Work, Unlivable Wages: The National Child Care Staffing Study, 1988–1997* (Washington, DC: Center for the Child Care Workforce, 1998), 18. In the late 1980s, the for-profit chain Kinder-Care had an annual turnover rate of 100 percent. See Kenneth F. Englade, "The Bottom Line on Kinder-Care," *Across the Board* 25, no. 4 (April 1988): 46.

90. There have been efforts at the state level to improve child care workers' training and benefits. See Levy and Michel, "Child Care and Welfare Reform."

91. Whitebook, "Child Care Workers," 147–48.

92. *Families that Work: Policies for Reconciling Parenthood and Employment* (New York: Russell Sage, 2003), 228–29.

93. Whitebook, "Child Care Workers," 150.

94. Mary Tuominen, "The Hidden Organization of Labor: Gender, Race/Ethnicity and Child-Care Work in the Formal and Informal Economy." *Sociological Perspectives* 37, no. 2 (1994): 229–45.

95. *2004 Green Book*, 9–16.

96. Helburn and Bergmann, *America's Childcare Problem*, 120–22.

97. Bruce Fuller, Sharon L. Kagan, Gretchen L. Caspary, and Christiane A. Gauthier, "Welfare Reform and Child Care Options for Low-Income Families," *The Future of Children* 12, no. 1 (Winter–Spring 2002): 97–119.

CHAPTER SIX

1. Pierson, "The New Politics of the Welfare State," *World Politics* 48 (January 1996): 595–628.

2. Karl Hinrichs, "Elephants on the Move: Patterns of Public Pension Reform in OECD Countries," *European Review* 8, no. 3 (2000): 353–78.

3. Bruno Palier, "Defrosting the French Welfare State," *West European Politics* 23, no. 2 (2000): 113–26; Maurizio Ferrera and Anton Hemerijck, "Recalibrating

Europe's Welfare Regimes," in *Governing Work and Welfare in the New Economy: European and American Experiments*, ed. Jonathan Zeitlin and D. M. Trubek (Oxford: Oxford University Press, 2003).

4. Jane Lewis, "Gender and Welfare State Change," *European Societies* 4, no. 4 (2002): 331–57.

5. Gøsta Esping-Andersen, *Why We Need a New Welfare State* (Oxford: Oxford University Press, 2002), 63–66.

6. Christoffer Green-Pedersen, Kees van Kersbergen, and Anton Hemericjk, "Neo-Liberalism, the 'Third Way,' or What? Recent Social Democratic Welfare Policies in Denmark and the Netherlands," *Journal of European Public Policy* 8, no. 2 (April 2001): 307–25.

7. Ann Orloff, "Farewell to Maternalism: Welfare Reform, Liberalism, and the End of Mothers' Right to Choose between Employment and Full-Time Care," Institute for Policy Research Working Paper 00-7, Northwestern University, 2000.

8. Robert Henry Cox, "The Social Construction of an Imperative: Why Welfare Reform Happened in Denmark and the Netherlands but Not in Germany," *World Politics* 53, no. 3 (2001): 463–98.

9. Herbert Kitschelt, *The Transformation of European Social Democracy* (Cambridge: Cambridge University Press, 1994); Karl Ulrich Mayer and Steffen Hillmert, "New Ways of Life or Old Rigidities? Changes in Social Structures and Life Courses and Their Political Impact," *West European Politics* 26, no. 4 (October 2003): 79–100.

10. This is evident in recent German debates about family policy. See Martin Seeleib-Kaiser, "A Dual Transformation of the German Welfare State?" *West European Politics* 24, no. 4 (2002): 25–48.

11. *National Action Plan for Employment Policy*, submitted to the European Commission, Employment and Social Affairs (Brussels: 2004), 91.

12. Jane Lewis, "Developing Early Years Childcare in England, 1997–2002: The Choices for (Working) Mothers," *Social Policy and Administration* 37, no. 3 (June 2003): 219–38.

13. Heidi Gottfried and Jacqueline O'Reilly, "Reregulating Breadwinner Models in Socially Conservative Welfare Systems: Comparing Germany and Japan," *Social Politics* 9, no. 1 (Spring 2002): 29–59; Birgit Pfau-Effinger, "The Modernization of Family and Motherhood in Western Europe," in *Restructuring Gender Relations and Employment: The Decline of the Male Breadwinner Model*, ed. Rosemary Crompton (Oxford: Oxford University Press, 1999), 60–79.

14. Kathleen Thelen, "How Institutions Evolve: Insights from Comparative Historical Analysis," in *Comparative Historical Analysis in the Social Sciences*, ed. James Mahoney and Dietrich Rueschemeyer (Cambridge: Cambridge University Press, 2003), 208–40.

15. Lewis, "Gender and Welfare State Change."

16. Jonah D. Levy, "Vice into Virtue? Progressive Politics and Welfare Reform in Continental Europe," *Politics and Society* 27, no. 2 (June 1999): 239–273.

17. Pfau-Effinger, "Modernization of Family," 68–69; 73–75.

18. Jonathan Gershuny and Oriel Sullivan, "Time Use, Gender, and Public Policy Regimes," *Social Politics* 10, no. 2 (Summer 2003): 205–28.

19. Gershuny and Sullivan, "Time Use," 217–18.

20. Hettie A. Pott-Buter, *Facts and Fairy Tales about Female Labor, Family, and Fertility: A Seven-Country Comparison, 1850–1990* (Amsterdam: Amsterdam University Press, 1993), 21.

21. Data from the 1970s shows that only 25 percent of women who worked before having their first child continued working after the birth. Wil Portegijs, Annemarie Boelens, and Linda Olsthoorn, *Emancipatiemonitor 2004* (The Hague: Sociaal en Cultureel Planbureau, 2004), 103.

22. Jet Bussemaker, "Rationales of Care in Contemporary Welfare States: The Case of Childcare in the Netherlands," *Social Politics* 5, no. 1 (Spring 1998): 82–83.

23. Anton Hemerijck and Jelle Visser, "Change and Immobility: Three Decades of Policy Adjustment in the Netherlands and Belgium," in *Recasting European Welfare States*, ed. Maurzio Ferrera and Martin Rhodes (London: Frank Cass, 2000), 235–36.

24. Hemerijck and Visser, "Change and Immobility," 237–38; Uwe Becker, "Welfare State Development and Employment in the Netherlands in Comparative Perspective," *Journal of European Social Policy* 10, no. 3 (August 2000): 224.

25. Bussemaker, "Rationales of Care," 84–85.

26. Lily E. Clerkx and Marinus H. Van Ijzendoorn, "Child Care in a Dutch Context: On the History, Current Status, and Evaluation of Nonmaternal Child Care in the Netherlands," in *Child Care in Context: Cross-Cultural Perspectives*, ed. Michael E. Lamb, Kathleen J. Sternberg, Carl-Philip Hwang, and Anders G. Broberg (Hillsdale, NJ: Lawrence Erlbaum Associates, 1992), 67–68.

27. Marolein Morée, "A Quiet Revolution: Working Mothers in the Netherlands, 1950–1990," *Netherlands Journal of Social Sciences* 30, no. 1 (August 1994): 34–35.

28. Paul Dekker and Peter Ester, "Depillarization, Deconfessionalization, and De-Ideologization: Empirical Trends in Dutch Society, 1958–1992," *Review of Religious Research* 37, no. 4 (June 1996): 325–41.

29. Carlo van Praag and Wilfried Uitterhoeve, *Een kwart eeuw sociale verandering in Nederland: De kerngegevens uit het "Sociaal en Cultureel Rapport 1998"* (Nijmegen: Uitgeverij SUN, 1999), 9.

30. Joop Hartog and Jules Theeuwes, "The Emergence of the Working Wife in Holland," *Journal of Labor Economics* 3, no. 1, part 2 (January 1985): 235–55.

31. Jelle Visser, "The First Part-Time Economy in the World: A Model to Be Followed?" *Journal of European Social Policy* 12, no. 1 (2002): 30.

32. European Commission Childcare Network, *Childcare in the European Community* (Brussels: Commission of the EC, 1990), 26. Clerkx and Van Ijzendoorn report that there was growth in commercial day care in the mid-to-late 1980s.

33. Angela Phillips and Peter Moss, *Who Cares for Europe's Children?* (Brussels: ECSC-EEC-EAEC, 1989), 17.

34. Gøsta Esping-Andersen, *The Social Foundations of Postindustrial Economies* (Oxford: Oxford University Press, 1999), 110.

35. Thomas R. Rochon, *The Netherlands: Negotiating Sovereignty in an Interdependent World* (Boulder, CO: Westview Press, 1999), 82.

36. Hans-Martien ten Napel, "The Netherlands: Resilience against Change," in *Changing Party Systems in Western Europe*, ed. David Broughton and Mark Donovan (London: Pinter, 1999), 178; Rochon, *Netherlands*, 93.

37. Rochon, *Netherlands*, 87.

38. Robert Henry Cox, "From Safety Net to Trampoline: Labor Market Activation in the Netherlands and Denmark," *Governance* 11, no. 4 (October 1998): 397–414.

39. Bussemaker, "Rationales of Care," 86.

40. Ibid., 86–87; Cox, "From Safety Net to Trampoline," 405–9.

41. Janneke Plantenga, "Differences and Similarities: The Position of Women on the Dutch Labour Market from a European Perspective," in *Population and Family in the Low Countries, 1992*, ed. Gijs Beets, Robert Cliquet, Gilbert Dooghe, and Jenny De Jong Gierveld (Amsterdam: Swets and Zeitlinger, 1992), 117.

42. Bussemaker, "Rationales of Care," 86.

43. Marie Wierink, "La place des enfants dans la combinaison famille-emploi aux Pays-Bas," *Recherches et prévisions* 75 (March 2004): 69–70. A 2004 study of public opinion found that 21 percent of female respondents agreed that it is good for babies to go to day care two or three days a week, 24 percent were neutral on the question, and 55 percent were opposed. The views of men are not substantially different. Both are more favorable toward preschoolers going to day care two or three days a week, with 27 percent opposed to the idea and the rest either neutral or supportive. Nearly half oppose primary school children going to a child care program after school. Portegijs, Boelens, and Olsthoorn, *Emancipatiemonitor*, 112.

44. Visser, "First Part-Time Economy," 30–31.

45. Ibid., 31–32.

46. The term *Poldermodel* refers to the polder lands created by Dutch engineers through a system of dykes that keep water out of wetlands. On the role of part-time work in the model, see Janneke Plantenga, "Combining Work and Care in the Polder Model: An Assessment of the Dutch Part-Time Strategy," *Critical Social Policy* 22, no. 1 (2002): 53–71.

47. Wierink, "La place des enfants."

48. Trudie Knijn, "Care Work: Innovations in the Netherlands," in *Care Work: The Quest for Security*, ed. Mary Daly (Geneva: ILO, 2001), 164.

49. Details on these changes can be found in "International Conference on Population and Development 1994: National Report Submitted by the Netherlands' Government," in *Population and Family in the Low Countries, 1994*, ed. Hans van den Brekel and Fred Deven (Dordrecht: Kluwer Academic, 1995), 275–76.

50. This was labeled a purple coalition because the traditional color of the Social Democrats is red and the Liberals' color is blue.

51. Knijn, "Innovations in the Netherlands," 163–64.

52. Plantenga, "Combining Work and Care," 56–59.

53. Currently, employers can deduct 30 percent of the costs of child care. Willem Adema, *Babies and Bosses: Reconciling Work and Family Life*, vol. 1 (Paris: OECD, 2002), 94–95.

54. Ibid..

55. Portegijs, Boelens, and Olsthoorn, *Emancipatiemonitor*, 108.

56. Ibid., 103.

57. Trudie Knijn, "Challenges and Risks to Individualisation in the Netherlands," *Social Policy and Society* 3, no. 1 (2003): 57–65.

58. Knijn, "Challenges and Risks," 62–63.

59. Ibid., 165.

60. Portegijs, Boelens, and Olsthoorn, *Emancipatiemonitor*, 69.

61. Defined as persons working fewer than 30 hours per week. OECD, *Employment Outlook 2004* (Paris: OECD, 2004), 310.

62. Plantenga and Siegel, "*Childcare in a Changing World*," 1-35.

63. Ibid., 72.

64. Ibid., 71.

65. Antonio Corral and Iñigo Isusi, *Part-Time Work in Europe* (Dublin: European Foundation for the Improvement of Living and Working Conditions, 2003), 5.

66. Colette Fagan, *Working-Time Preferences and Work-Life Balance in the EU: Some Policy Considerations for Enhancing the Quality of Life* (Dublin: European Foundation for the Improvement of Living and Working Conditions, 2003).

67. Wierink, "La place des enfants."

68. Jet Bussemaker, member of Parliament (PvdA), interview by the author, Amsterdam, August 16, 2002.

69. In general, the party calls for preserving parental "choice" in matters of child care. Margreeth Smilde, member of Parliament (CDA), personal communication, July 1, 2004.

70. Wierink, "La place des enfants," 63.

71. Knijn, "Care Work," 169–70.

72. Ibid., 172–73.

73. Serv Vinders, former director of the Uitbreiding Kinderopvang Netwerkbureau, interview by the author, The Hague, July 2, 2004; Elisabeth Singer, "Family Policy and Preschool Programs in the Netherlands," in *International Handbook of Early Childhood Education*, ed. Gary A. Woodill, Judith Bernhard, Lawrence Prochner (New York: Garland, 1992): 364–65.

74. Monique Kremer, "The Illusion of Free Choice: Ideals of Care and Child Care Policy in the Flemish and Dutch Welfare States," in *Child Care Policy at the*

Crossroads: Gender and Welfare State Restructuring, ed. Sonya Michel and Rianne Mahon (London: Routledge Press 2002): 127–28.

75. Joke Kikstra, Ministerie van Sociale Zaken en Werkgelegenheid, Arbeidsver-houdingen, Kinderopvang, interview by the author, The Hague, July 2, 2004.

76. Gornick and Meyers show that in the mid-1990s, the Swedish government spent $4,950 per child on early childhood education and care, the French spent $3,161, the Dutch spent $1,369, and the United States spent $548. *Families that Work: Policies for Reconciling Parenthood and Employment* (New York: Russell Sage, 2003), 217.

77. *Babies and Bosses,* 89–90, 102–3.

78. Wierink, "La place des enfants," 72.

CONCLUSION

1. There are only a few recent, but important, books on Christian Democratic parties in Europe. See Stathis N. Kalyvas, *The Rise of Christian Democracy in Europe* (Ithaca, NY: Cornell University Press, 1996); Carolyn M. Warner, *Confessions of an Interest Group: The Catholic Church and Political Parties in Europe* (Princeton, NJ: Princeton University Press, 2000).

2. Birgit Fix, "The Institutionalization of Family Welfare: Division of Labour in the Field of Child Care in Austria and Germany," Working paper no. 24 (Mannheim Center for European Social Research, 1998); Philip Manow, "The Good, the Bad, and the Ugly: Esping-Andersen's Regime Typology and the Religious Roots of the Western Welfare State," unpublished manuscript, Max Planck Institute for the Study of Societies, 2004; Kees van Kersbergen, *Social Capitalism: A Study of Christian Democracy and the Welfare State* (London: Routledge, 1995).

3. Göran Gustafsson, "Religious Change in the Five Scandinavian Countries, 1930–1980," *Comparative Social Research* 10 (1987).

4. Although religious parties did not have much success during the formation of party systems in these countries, small parties would form later in the twentieth century around moral and religious questions. Scandinavia would never have the powerful Christian Democratic parties found on the European continent, however. John T. S. Madeley, "Scandinavian Christian Democracy: Throwback or Portent?" *European Journal of Political Research* 5 (1977): 267–86.

5. David Bradley, "Family Laws and Welfare States," in *The Nordic Model of Marriage and the Welfare State,* ed. Kari Melby, Anu Pylkkänen, Bente Rosenbeck, and Christina Carlsson Wetterberg (Copenhagen: Nordic Council of Ministers, 2000), 39–48; Göran Therborn, "The Politics of Childhood: The Rights of Children in Modern Times," in *Families of Nations: Patterns of Public Policy in Western Democracies,* ed. Francis Castles (Aldershot: Darmouth, 1993), 241–91.

6. Finland does have a tradition of high rates of women's full-time participation in the workforce. For a discussion of the differences between the Nordic countries,

see Arnlaug Leira, *Working Parents and the Welfare State: Family Change and Policy Reform in Scandinavia* (Cambridge: Cambridge University Press, 2002).

7. Jorma Sipilä and Johanna Korpinen, "Cash versus Child Care Services in Finland," *Social Policy and Administration* 32, no. 3 (September 1998): 263–77.

8. Jens Alber, "A Framework for the Comparative Study of Social Services," *Journal of European Social Policy* 5, no. 2 (1995): 131–49; Josef Schmid, "Verbändewohlfahrt im modernen Wohlfahrtsstaat: Strukturbildende Effekte des Staat-Kirche-Konflicts," *Historical Social Research* 20, no. 2 (1995): 88–118.

9. Van Kersbergen, *Social Capitalism*.

10. Franca Bimbi and Vincent Della Sala, "Italy: Policy without Participation," in *Who Cares? Women's Work, Childcare, and Welfare State Redesign*, ed. Jane Jenson and Mariette Sineau (Toronto: University of Toronto Press, 2001), 118–45; Wiebke Kolbe, "Gender and Parenthood in West German Family Policies from the 1960s to the 1980s," in *State Policy and Gender System in the Two German States and Sweden, 1945–1989*, ed. Rolf Torstendahl (Uppsala, Sweden: Department of History, 1999), 155–65; Gerda Ruth Neyer, "Gender and the Austrian Fraternal Welfare State after 1945," in *Connecting Spheres: European Women in a Globalizing World, 1500 to the present*, ed. Marilyn J. Boxer and Jean H. Quataert (New York: Oxford University Press, 2000), 306–13.

11. Italy also experienced similar clerical-anticlerical conflicts over education and developed an extensive preschool system earlier than most other European countries. See Kimberly J. Morgan, "Forging the Frontiers between State, Church, and Family: Religious Cleavages and the Origins of Early Childhood Care and Education Policies in France, Sweden, and Germany," *Politics and Society* 30, no. 1 (March 2002): 113–48.

12. Claude Martin and Patrick Hassenteufel, "La représentation des intérêts familiaux en Europe: Allemagne, Belgique, Grande-Bretagne, France, Portugal," unpublished manuscript, September 1997; Bérengère Marques-Pereira and Olivier Paye, "Belgium: The Vices and Virtues of Pragmatism," in Jenson and Sineau, *Women, Work, and Childcare*, 56–87.

13. Marques-Pereira and Paye, "Belgium," 61–70.

14. E. R. Norman, *The Conscience of the State in North America* (Cambridge: Cambridge University Press, 1968); Hans Mol, "Australia," in *Western Religion: A Country by Country Sociological Inquiry*, ed. Hans Mol (The Hague: Mouton, 1972), 27–29.

15. Sheila B. Kamerman and Alfred J. Kahn, introduction to *Family Change and Family Policies in Great Britain, Canada, New Zealand, and the United States*, ed. Sheila B. Kamerman and Alfred J. Kahn (Oxford: Clarendon Press, 1997), 3–28.

16. The New Right in both Australia and Canada contained this dimension. See Katherine Teghtsoonian, "Promises, Promises: 'Choices for Women' in Canadian and American Child Care Policy Debates," *Feminist Studies* 22, no. 1 (Spring 1996): 123; Andrew Moore, *The Right Road? A History of Right-Wing Politics in Australia* (Melbourne: Oxford University Press, 1995), chaps. 7, 9.

17. Deborah Brennan, "Australia: Child Care and State-Centered Feminism in a Liberal Welfare Regime," in *Child Care Policy at the Crossroads: Gender and Welfare State Restructuring*, Sonya Michel and Rianne Mahon (London: Routledge, 2002), 95–112. At least some parts of Canada also could be moving away from the liberal welfare regime model on child care. Rianne Mahon, "Politics of Need, Politics of Scale: Childcare Politics in Toronto/Ontario/Canada," paper presented at the annual meeting of the APSA, Washington, DC, September 1–4, 2005.

18. Joya Misra and Frances Akins, "The Welfare State and Women: Structure, Agency, and Diversity," *Social Politics* 5, no. 3 (Fall 1998): 259–85.

19. Julia O'Connor, Ann Shola Orloff, and Sheila Shaver, *States, Markets, Families. Gender, Liberalism and Social Policy in Australia, Canada, Great Britain, and the United States* (Cambridge: Cambridge University Press, 1999); R. Amy Elman, "Debunking the Social Democrats and the Myth of Equality," *Women's Studies International Forum* 16, no. 5 (September–October 1993): 513–22.

20. Some important work is being done on this now by Sarah Wiliarty, "The Christian Democratic Union and (Not) Working Mothers: A Corporatist Catch-All Party Tackles Family Leave," paper presented at the Annual Meeting of the American Political Science Association, San Francisco, August 30, 2001. Another interesting approach examines the role of state feminists in government agencies in promoting gender equality issues. See Amy G. Mazur, ed., *State Feminism, Women's Movements, and Job Training: Making Democracies Work in the Global Economy* (New York: Routledge, 2001).

21. Kathleen Thelen, "How Institutions Evolve: Insights from Comparative-Historical Analysis," in *Comparative Historical Analysis in the Social Sciences*, ed. James Mahoney and Dietrich Rueschemeyer (New York: Cambridge University Press, 2002): 208–40.

22. Nancy Fraser, "After the Family Wage: Gender Equity and the Welfare State," *Political Theory* 22, no. 4 (November 1994): 591–618.

23. Sabrina Regent, "The Open Method of Coordination: A New Supranational Form of Governance?" *European Law Journal* 9, no. 2 (April 2003): 190–214.

24. Nicole Richardt, "Europeanization of Childcare Policy: Divergent Paths towards a Common Goal?," paper presented at the annual meeting of the American Political Science Association, Washington, DC, September 1–4, 2005.

25. Rianne Mahon, "Child Care: Toward What Kind of 'Social Europe'?" *Social Politics* 9, no. 3 (Fall 2002): 343–79; Maria Stratigaki, "The Cooptation of Gender Concepts in EU Policies: The Case of 'Reconciliation of Work and Family,'" *Social Politics* 11, no. 1 (Spring 2004): 30–56.

26. *Babies and Bosses: Reconciling Work and Family Life, Canada, Finland, Sweden, and the United Kingdom*, vol. 4 (Paris: OECD, 2005), 21; Rianne Mahon, "The OECD and the Reconciliation Agenda: Competing Blueprints," in *Children in Context: Changing Families and Welfare States*, ed. Jane Lewis (Edward Elgar, forthcoming).

27. *OECD Country Note: Early Childhood Education and Care Policy in Norway* (Paris: OECD, 1999).

28. Birgit Pfau-Effinger, "The Modernization of Family and Motherhood in Western Europe," in *Restructuring Gender Relations and Employment: The Decline of the Male Breadwinner Model*, ed. Rosemary Crompton (Oxford: Oxford University Press, 1999), 60–79; Eva Nebenführ, "Austria: Heading towards Gender Equality, and New Forms of Solidarity," in *Population, Family and Welfare: A Comparative Survey of European Attitudes*, ed. Hein Moors and Rossella Palomba (Oxford: Clarendon Press, 1995), 74.

29. There continue to be campaigns at the state level to develop a paid parental leave, and California has already adopted just such a policy. Some of the options are discussed in Edward F. Zigler, Matia Finn-Stevenson, and Nancy W. Hall, *The First Three Years and Beyond* (New Haven: Yale University Press, 2002), 60–62.

30. Sheila B. Kamerman and Alfred J. Kahn have spent decades trying to educate policy makers about child care, parental leave, and flexible working time policies elsewhere in the world. A recent book that attempts to do the same is Janet C. Gornick and Marcia K. Meyers, *Families That Work* (New York: Russell Sage, 2003).

31. Theda Skocpol makes a similar plea for policies that help middle-class families in her book *The Missing Middle: Working Families and the Future of American Social Policy* (New York: W. W. Norton, 2000).

32. One proposal that makes use of schools to address child care needs is in Matia Finn-Stevenson and Edward Zigler, *Schools of the 21st Century: Linking Child Care and Education* (Boulder, CO: Westview, 1999).

Index

Page references in italic refer to tables and figures.